THE DOMINO DIARIES

THE

DOMINO

DIARIES

MY DECADE BOXING WITH OLYMPIC CHAMPIONS AND CHASING HEMINGWAY'S GHOST IN THE LAST DAYS OF CASTRO'S CUBA

BRIN-JONATHAN BUTLER

PICADOR

NEW YORK

www.picadorusa.com
www.twitter.com/picadorusa • www.facebook.com/picadorusa
picadorbookroom.tumblr.com

Picador® is a U.S. registered trademark and is used by St. Martin's Press under license from Pan Books Limited.

For book club information, please visit www.facebook.com/picadorbookclub or e-mail marketing@picadorusa.com.

Designed by Steven Seighman

The Library of Congress Cataloging-in-Publication Data is available upon request.

ISBN 978-1-250-04370-2 (hardcover)
ISBN 978-1-250-04371-9 (e-book)

Picador books may be purchased for educational, business, or promotional use. For information on bulk purchases, please contact the Macmillan Corporate and Premium Sales Department at 1-800-221-7945, extension 5442, or write to special markets@macmillan.com.

First Edition: June 2015

10 9 8 7 6 5 4 3 2 1

For Leidys and Amanda

I am Cuba.

My sugar was carried away in ships.

But my tears were left behind.

Sugar is a strange thing, Mr. Columbus.

So many tears go into it,

And still it's sweet.

—"Soy Cuba"

(from the 1964 film *Soy Cuba*)

With cities, it is as with dreams: everything imaginable can be dreamed, but even the most unexpected dream is a rebus that conceals a desire or, its reverse, a fear. Cities, like dreams, are made of desires and fears, even if the thread of their discourse is secret, their rules are absurd, their perspectives deceitful, and everything conceals something else.

—Italo Calvino, *Invisible Cities*

HOW DID THIS WHITE MOTHERFUCKER GET INSIDE MY HOUSE?

MAYBE THE REAL SUBJECT of every interview is how you really can't learn much about anyone from an interview.

Back at his gym in Los Angeles, the only instruction Freddie Roach, the world's most famous boxing trainer, gave after offering Mike Tyson's phone number was a warning: "*Don't* blindside him. It doesn't matter if *I* sent you. If you see Mike and you blindside him, he's capable of attacking you."

"I'm not looking to blindside anyone here," I lied.

"Be careful, son."

And then a couple months later, on Easter Sunday of 2010, I entered the front door of Tyson's Vegas home into a thick cloud of marijuana smoke while he descended the stairs toward me with just one question:

"So how did this white motherfucker get inside my house?"

On June 27, 1988, a twenty-one-year-old Mike Tyson made in ex-
cess of twenty-one million dollars for ninety-one seconds of work.
That's how much the world wanted him. To put that into per-
spective, it took him just over fourteen seconds to pull in more
money than Michael Jordan, in his prime, made for an entire *season* of work that year. But maybe you never cared much about
sports or athletes and prefer art instead. So you might accept Andy
Warhol's dictum that you can measure the worth of an artwork
by what you can *get* for it. At Tyson's pay rate that night, after another round or so (227 seconds, to be exact), the work of art he
created in the ring would've earned as much as Vincent van Gogh's
efforts on a canvas—*Irises* had become the most expensive work
of art in the world just several months before Tyson's fight, selling for 53.9 million dollars.

For most people, Tyson's legacy was staked on two equally
shocking extremes. On November 22, 1986, at the age of twenty,
he had become the youngest heavyweight champion in boxing history. And only three years later, he was on the losing end of the
biggest upset in sports history when he was beaten by Buster Doug-
las. At his peak, critics used to laugh and tell you Mike Tyson never
had a style, he just fought everyone as if they *stole* something from
him. "All things truly *wicked*," Ernest Hemingway once wrote,
"start from innocence."

Long before I ever had a chance to blindside him, Mike Tyson
had blindsided me.

Even though we'd never met, seeing a reprinted photo booth

picture of Tyson as a little boy saved my life. Mike Tyson's identity as a destination didn't mean anything to me until I'd gone
back and packed some of his luggage to understand the journey
he made. But I guess "Kid Dynamite," like most boxers, was like
any other powder keg made out of commonly found household
items.

Start off with where the center of his universe is located:
Brownsville, Brooklyn, one of the bleakest dungeons of poverty
and violence America could dish out. Install an abusive pimp for
a father and have him abandon the alcoholic mother before Tyson's third birthday. Make sure the mother sleeps with everyone
in the neighborhood so the household and its inhabitants gain a
glowing reputation from well-wishers in the community. Contam-
inate his soul with a sense of how worthless a human life can be
as people he recognizes overdose or get robbed or raped or murdered. Make him an even more attractive target with no friends
or any hope of protection in the neighborhood. Don't let him walk
in any direction without it feeling like a plank. Never allow him
to turn a corner without fearing for his life. And when anything
catches up with him, make him too timid and sensitive to ever
fight back. Hang cowardice as another millstone around his neck.
And after you've torn his heart out, why not fan the scent? Best
of all, when he begs for help, make sure his voice is so high and
delicate he'll be afraid to scream no matter how much he wants
to. And if the pathetic little faggot everybody has always insisted
he is ever caves, why not give him a lisp as well. As far as he knows,
he'll be dead and forgotten before he blows out the candles for his
thirteenth birthday.

But before you finish him off, give him one place to hide. Offer him a hideaway where he can take refuge from the world. Let

him stumble onto the rooftops of those abandoned tenements of Brownsville and fall in love with the pigeons up there. Watch him spend every dime he can scrape together for feed so he can reward the pigeons from his coop for doing what he can't: fly away. Make the relief of this refuge something that marks him forever and leaves a trail that others can find and hunt down.

Soon, some rapacious, observant predator in the neighborhood can observe the change in Tyson and follow him up there. He can trespass undetected into Tyson's most private world and savor the pillage to come. Let him find Tyson fully exposed, feeding and caring for his birds, and allow him to at once grasp the whole story behind it, the whole pawnshop of broken dreams in Tyson's heart. Let him hatch a plan to finish off another boy's life that's better than just pulling a trigger or pushing him off the roof. That way, when Tyson returns the next day to the rooftop and discovers one of his pigeons being choked inside the fist of this sadistic fuck he'll beg him not to hurt it. Tyson can helplessly watch as the bully takes his time soaking up Tyson's entreaties and savoring the spectacle of a shattered human being unraveling before twisting off the head of the pigeon and laughing at the heartbreakingly predictable outcome.

But instead, for the first time in his life, Tyson stood up for himself and summoned everything that once made him weak to unleash the first bars of his own Ninth Symphony with his fists. "Fighting to me is what theory was to Einstein," Tyson later explained, "or words were to Hemingway or notes were to Beethoven."

I used to wonder how long after that moment, when the world first heard that melody, it took Tyson to realize what *real* problems were in store for him. I used to wonder how long it took Tyson to get a whiff of *us*, and how, as Norman Mailer once said of

George Foreman, a previously nightmarish boxer America had a fetish for, "Anyone is supposed to prepare to defend himself against the thoughts of everyone alive."

At a certain point Mike Tyson and I reacted to violence a little differently. After my first fight, I was afraid to leave my house for three years, while Tyson became the heavyweight champion of the world. But, at first, our cowardice and trauma defined us both.

In the summer before tenth grade, back in 1994, I wrote a letter to inmate 922335, inside the Indiana Youth Center in Plainfield, Indiana. I'd never mailed a letter to anyone before. Up to that point the only letter I'd ever written had been a suicide note.

The week before, totally by accident, my mother had seen an interview with Tyson broadcast from prison, and at the end of it she was crying. I only caught the last few minutes. My mother was terrified of Mike Tyson for the same reasons everybody was terrified of Mike Tyson—yet, by the end of the interview, she loved him. I could see in her face the battle raging between her head and her heart. All I'd heard him talk about in the interview was reading books in the hole and how badly he'd been bullied in childhood. She filled me in on the rest.

I was writing a convicted rapist a thank-you letter. It's true that I didn't know whether or not Mike Tyson was guilty of raping an eighteen-year-old beauty contestant in Indiana, a crime for which he'd been convicted. But I did know without a doubt that he was responsible for sending me two places I'd never been on my own before: a boxing gym and a library. And, more important, I knew as clearly then as I do now, those places saved me.

And, later on, those places led me to Cuba, a place infamous around the world for resisting the most powerful nation on earth: the United States.

Mike Tyson had visited the island in 2002 while I was there training as an amateur boxer. Ostensibly that was why Freddie Roach had agreed to give me Tyson's phone number in the first place. At that time, Roach was training Guillermo Rigondeaux, the most notorious Cuban boxing defector in history. For Cuban boxers, America and Cuba had been distilled to the choice of fighting for Don King or Fidel Castro. Rigondeaux had already filled me in on what it was like fighting for Fidel; I wanted to hear Tyson shed some light on King.

So, once Mike Tyson got down the stairs, I answered his question about how this white motherfucker got inside his house. "*You* brought me here."

After I'd explained to him how I'd come full circle and ended up in his living room, we both sat down opposite each other and he shook his huge head and smiled before asking:

"Is that all true?"

"What do you think?"

"So I'm guessing you being here, in my home, sitting across from me right now—I'm guessing this is pretty intense for you right now, huh?"

On Easter of 2010, the day I interviewed him, Mike Tyson's boxing career had been over for nearly five years. At this point, Tyson was more famous as a national punch line for biting off someone's ear than for any career achievement or even squandered potential. Besides that, a country sixteen trillion in debt mocked and remained endlessly fascinated by the question of how someone like Tyson could possibly have pissed away his entire fortune.

The last picture I'd seen of him, taken a couple months before, showed a man who had ballooned to well over three hundred pounds. Though he had miraculously dropped most of it since then, he looked deflated from his championship days. Tyson lived in a gated community just outside Las Vegas in the town of Henderson, Nevada.

When he was only eighteen, Tyson's managers would market him with posters reminding you that if your grandfather had missed Joe Louis, or your father Muhammad Ali, you didn't want to miss Tyson. But what they didn't mention was that Joe Louis and Muhammad Ali were a boy's *dream* of a fighter. Before long Tyson understood his customers a little better and modified the sales pitch. Tyson figured out, in his era, that America really craved a nightmare.

Tyson's first trainer, Teddy Atlas, had said this of his star pupil and America's addiction to him: "People are full of shit. They want to see something dark. People want to feel close to it and in on it, but, of course, only from the distance of their suburban homes. They want to have the benefit of comfort, security, safety, respect, and at the same time the privilege of watching something out of control—even promote it being out of control—as long as we can be secure that we're not accountable for it. . . . We wanted to believe that Mike Tyson was an American story: the kid who grows up in the horrible ghetto and then converts that dark power into a good cause. But then the story takes a turn. The dark side overwhelms him. He's cynical, he's out of control. And now the story is even better."

"Okay." Tyson glared, leaning forward in his chair across from me. A Sandra Bullock rom-com was muted on the flat-screen TV beside us; some of his children's toys were scattered by my feet. "You said I was your hero growing up. I wanna know who your other heroes are then."

"They're all suicides."

"Is that a prerequisite or something?" he smiled.

"For a while there, to be honest, I never thought you'd ever live long enough for me to have a chance to meet or say thank you."

"Me neither," Tyson said under his breath, looking over at his wife in the kitchen. "I was sure I'd be dead by now, too."

"On the way over here I drove through Las Vegas for the first time. I've never had a desire to see Las Vegas. I hate everything about it. Joe Louis was a hero of mine. And even more depressing than a whole city built up by all the loss and suffering of ruined lives, it's the idea of someone like Louis, after all he did for this country, ending up broke and strung out on drugs working as a greeter at Caesar's Palace that—"

"You," Tyson said, pointing his finger at me. "You know what your problem is? You're too sensitive. You probably don't think you had enough pain in your own life so you take on the pain of other people to make up for it. Taking on the pain of my life or Joe Louis's life doesn't help us. It doesn't help you, either."

Tyson scratched the tattoo of famed African American tennis champion Arthur Ashe on his shoulder while his mother-in-law scurried into the kitchen with Tyson's baby in her arms.

"What was the next book you read after all those biographies on me?" Tyson asked.

"*Days of Grace* by Arthur Ashe." I shrugged.

"Didn't anyone warn you that it's dangerous meeting your heroes?"

"You're not a very easy person to have as a hero, Mike."

"That's true." He smiled. "But how am I doing so far today?"

I smiled back at him.

"That Jewish proverb is true, man. 'The brighter the light, the darker the shadow that's cast.' Whatever people think of me, most countries in the world that I visit, it's kings or presidents that want to greet me. I've been the most famous face on the planet. Why do you think that is? I've met anyone you can meet. And we're all part of the same club. The feeling of worthlessness is what drove us to greatness. Content people don't strive for anything. They don't *have* to. I never walked out to the ring without having dreamed the night before of losing."

"When I mentioned to Freddie Roach that you were one of the most knowledgeable boxing historians in the world he interrupted me. He said, 'Not *one of*, Mike Tyson is *the greatest boxing historian who ever lived*.'"

"So what's the connection with you and Cuba? That's what my assistant mentioned you wanted to talk to me about."

"I know you were in Cuba back in 2002."

"How the fuck do you know that?"

"I was in Havana when you arrived."

"Okay," Tyson conceded. "I was there."

"What were you doing there?"

"I wanted to meet Teófilo Stevenson, the Cuban Muhammad Ali."

"Did you have a chance?"

Tyson shook his head. "I got in some trouble and had to go."

"If you had to choose between Fidel Castro or Don King, who do you think would be worse fighting for?"

"Cubans aren't fighting for money. They're fighting for glory.

They're saying they're better than money by turning it down. They're better than us as human beings. All that stuff."

"If you were born there and could only make money by leaving your family . . . If that was the choice you had to make. Could you do it?"

"Where I'm at now? No. I couldn't leave my family. But I was born here. They'll put me in the ground here. Those Cubans like Stevenson or Savón represent all that insane stuff over there, I represent all *our* insane stuff. You have to think that boxing is just narrative. Stories. Why was everyone willing to put more money in the cash register for mine than anyone else? Was I the best? Maybe. But I had the story they cared about most. They saw themselves the most in me, whether they admit it or not."

"I heard you answer that question once by saying it was because you were angelic and scum. Is that America, too?"

"Who knows."

"I saw an interview with you once where you were crying. You were young. You weren't champ yet. But you were upset because you said how much you missed fighting when it wasn't just about the money."

"Listen, man. I can't really believe this because I still can't figure out how you got in my house today. And I can't believe I'm going to talk about this to a stranger, but listen. You said the first book you ever read was about my life. Whatever. At least then you probably know what human being brought me more pain than anyone. And that woman, my mother, she was dead before I was sixteen. I'm the son of a pimp and an alcoholic. But if I ever brought anything home of value into my mother's house, she knew I'd stolen it. I never saw her proud of me in my entire life. Not once. And somewhere, somewhere I always had that in my mind. I was

fighting to make this woman who caused me more pain than anyone in my life—" Tyson cleared his throat and wiped his face a
couple times. "Deep down, I was always fighting to make that
woman . . . I wanted to make that woman proud of me. That's
what I was always fighting for."

Right then a clock next to us tolled, then once more for two
o'clock. Tyson cradled his face in his hand and cleared his throat
again. The moment was gone and the assistant entered the room
and told Mike Tyson they had appointments to meet.

"You like F. Scott Fitzgerald, man?" Tyson asked.

"Yep."

"He said something like, 'There are no second acts in American lives.' Some shit like that. Maybe I'll prove him wrong."

2

THE ONE-EYED KING

In the Soviet Union, capitalism triumphed over communism. In this country, capitalism triumphed over democracy.
—Fran Lebowitz

What is the robbing of a bank compared to the founding of a bank?
—Bertolt Brecht

I'VE SUFFERED FROM A TERRIBLE sense of direction all my life. My internal compass must be broken. I'm always lost. Yet almost every friend I've ever made I met asking for directions. I take a lot of care in choosing the strangers I approach.

Not long ago I was walking under the construction of the World Trade Center with a stranger. He was a former amateur fighter I'd just met for an interview named Eric Kelly. For a child growing up in the ghetto, a boxing gym was a lifeline to avoid a life working on a street corner. Gyms like that were now largely extinct across New York, traded in for more profitable gentrified white-collar gyms. Kelly had risen from the streets to become a four-time national amateur champion. Then, just before embarking on a professional career, he lost everything. His dream evaporated after he mouthed off to the wrong person in a pool hall and had a pool cue smashed over his eye. Multiple surgeries weren't able to fix the damage to the nerve endings and muscles over Kelly's eyelid.

Only recently Kelly had gotten famous around the country after a video went viral of him training various masters of the universe—mostly Wall Street bankers in the Financial District—to fight, and gleefully deriding them all as "softer than baby shit." In a country where four hundred people controlled as much wealth as the bottom 150 million, Eric Kelly paid no attention to the bank statements of his clients and instead explored their *worth*.

I interviewed one of Kelly's boxing clients from J.P. Morgan who explained, "Maybe, deep down, we just miss that whole Occupy Wall Street movement a little bit. Maybe some of us are a little nostalgic for that hatred they had for us, and Eric Kelly picks up the slack."

Another trader chimed in, "Maybe it's the stress of being full of shit as soon as you leave your front door every morning. Being full of shit at work. Where *don't* you have to be full of shit in this city? But you don't have to be *here*. I love Kelly. I signed up for a full year in advance after my first day with him. He doesn't care where you come from or how much you make. He's constitutionally incapable of being dishonest."

I'd never heard of anyone from the 99 percent sought by the 1 percent—outside of dominatrices and day laborers—with Kelly's job description before. But then Trey Parker, America's answer to Jonathan Swift, once bemoaned *South Park*'s impotence to satirize America given the nation's incapacity to feel shame about *anything.* Since I'd moved to Manhattan, Kelly's gym was the most interesting intersection of race and class I'd heard of in upstairs-downstairs New York society. America ate it up as CNN, *Fox News*, and *Bloomberg Businessweek* all covered the story. The William Morris agency signed Kelly within the month. After the uproar not only was Kelly not fired, but more Wall Street clients than ever lined up at his gym in the Financial District to have Eric Kelly do little more than tell them the truth. I'd seen Kelly's clients stare at themselves in the mirror, shadowboxing, searching for something they still weren't able to find. "Ain't you heard, motherfuckers?" Kelly would shout over. "You can look as hard as you want in the mirror, but vampires ain't *got* no reflection. But look away from the mirror and at me, and I'll see what I can do for you."

"So what do you think being able to fight says about somebody?" I asked Kelly. "In that video and your gym, when you're making fun of these Wall Street guys for not being able to fight, what are you trying to say?"

"*You* ever been in a fight?" Kelly asked.

I nodded, feeling Kelly's damaged gaze unriddle me.

"You out looking for it or did it find you?" he followed up.

"The one that really counted—the *first* one—found me."

I was eleven, lured out to a field in front of half my school, waiting like everyone else to watch a fight that was supposed to happen. I'd never seen any of the fights kids had organized before. I was small and terrified of violence. I kept looking around waiting for it to start until I was pushed from behind onto the ground and everyone swarmed in. For the few agonizing minutes it took me to escape, the kids not close enough to stomp or kick took turns clearing their throats to spit. The worst day of my life didn't just happen in front of everyone I knew, rather they had all *joined in.* Eventually, physically at least, I managed to get away, but it took me years to outrun the humiliation and cowardice all those people exposed in me that day. And even though New York was 2,500 miles and twenty-two years away from cowering into a ball under that mob's collective heel, it was pretty obvious to Kelly, as I explained the incident to him, that that day had marked my life as much as Kelly's in a pool hall.

"It's the only fight I've ever had outside a ring," I told him.

"So tell me something—" Kelly paused, performing an ultrasound with his stare. "Did you learn something about yourself you never learned before from that experience?"

"Getting beat up changed my life forever," I confessed.

"At least you admit it." Kelly smiled. In my insecurity it took me his entire pause to let down my guard and find the sympathy in it. "It changes anybody's life forever, kid. You were hurt pretty bad?"

"I was humiliated."

"All fighters are more afraid of being humiliated than getting hurt." Kelly smiled again. "But that need to get to the bottom of who the fuck we are takes over. Stuff happens in life. You get tested. You gotta be ready to step up to the plate. Life ain't like them bankers fuckin' up the economy, gettin' bailed out when you fuck up. Out here you gotta live with the consequences of the choices you make. Look at my fuckin' eye, man. You think those guys I train could have lasted a minute in the world I came from?"

3

THE AUDITION

Boxing is an unnatural act. Everything in boxing is back-
wards to life.... Instead of running from pain, which is
the natural thing in life, in boxing you step to it.

—F. X. Toole

MY FIRST VISIT to a boxing gym was less about gaining accep-
tance in the ring than it was about auditioning for the rest of my
life.

All boxers are liars. Con men. The better the liar, the better
the fighter. If you knew what was in a fighter's heart, if you knew
what he was thinking, he'd be easier to find. And if you could
find him, he'd be easier to hit. And if you could hit him, you never
know, you might expose him. You might expose every person they
never stood up to and every person they never stood up for. Sometimes even a single blow can unveil the watermark of a man's soul
in a way nothing else ever could. And like all compulsive cheats,
boxers are addicted to decoding truth. It's not an accident that, for
security, banks hire ex–bank robbers and casinos hire ex-cheats.

Honesty doesn't necessarily require *any* understanding of the truth, but for a liar, it's vital.

I stepped into my first boxing gym in Vancouver when I was fifteen, summoning everything I had in order to hide the fact I'd never stood up for myself physically outside of a gym. After puberty provided my first growth spurt, I stood five-foot-two and 115 pounds. I'd used up most of my courage that night just *approaching* the neighborhood where the gym was located. Skid row in Vancouver was my hometown's dirty little secret. None of my friends went anywhere near it. But the best boxing gyms in the world tend to be located in the most dangerous, wounded neighborhoods their cities can dish out. Like lighthouses, they operate almost as a kind of protest against the darkness. They're there to remind the people searching them out that they're the safest place on earth for a simple reason: because everybody who lives there, wherever and whatever they came from, were just as scared as you the first time they came. But you only find that stuff out if you return. Everybody stepping into a boxing gym feels like the uncrowned, pound-for-pound champion of cowardice—I know I did.

I was scared for a lot of reasons. Boxers are the only artists who damage their instrument each time they use them. The great artists of boxing paint their canvases in blood, and at any moment they risk losing everything they have forever. What could possibly entice people to risk their core like that? But then a lot of people I knew with real opportunities in life were dead set on chasing careers they knew would leave them miserable. The more options their parents had left them with, the more afraid they were of making the wrong choices in life. Nobody wants the success of what they chase after to look more depressing than the failure of others to attain their aims.

That first boxing gym was situated in the basement of the Astoria Hotel, located in the festering heart of Vancouver's Downtown Eastside. It was only a few miles from where I grew up, but it was another hellish world away. It wasn't like ghettos I saw on TV or in the movies. It was never known as a particularly violent area. There weren't tenements or drive-by shootings or action that people who didn't live there would get a voyeuristic thrill peeping on. It was a different angle on the darkness of human nature. Instead of sudden death in a flash, it offered slow death in a ghoulish fade. It had the highest rates of HIV and intravenous drug use in North America, and this was all publicly on display as thousands of lives were left to rot. Any time I'd driven through it I would observe the procession of imploding lives starved for a fix. My father's child protection law firm, which had a good portion of the area's at-risk kids as its charge, wasn't far away, though the firm was about as useful as throwing matches into the wind. The situation further deteriorated once the city shut down the mental health hospitals and thousands of former patients flooded the area, their sickness treated as a criminal rather than as a health issue. In no time, with even greater expense to taxpayers, the prisons filled up with the same mentally ill addicts who were once looked after in hospitals.

That first rainy night, I turned the corner at Main Street's bustling open drug market, as frantic at all hours as a kicked-over anthill, and walked alone along Hastings. Half a block away police lights splashed against boarded-up stores and stained a few by-the-hour hotels. I hurried up just as a couple of tormented souls in handcuffs were dragged screaming and thrown against the hoods of a police cruiser. I watched crumpled bills stuffed into palms for Baggies and vials. Strangers limped past me smoking crack from hollowed-out Bic pens or pipes. Strung-out prostitutes touched up their makeup on street corners while homeless junkies shot up behind Dumpsters down the alleys. And later on I found out that at the same time I was commuting to my gym in the mid-1990s, Canada's most notorious serial killer, a pig farmer by the name of Willie Pickton, was combing the area for runaway and drug-addicted hookers that would, over the years, eventually add up to, according to Pickton's later boasts, forty-nine girls. While the shelters reported dozens of these girls missing, for years the city ignored them and allowed Pickton to carry on with his own demented version of population control in the area. Nobody charged with the responsibility of protecting people even bothered to muster an effort to slow him down.

I took a deep breath and climbed down the Astoria's dark, rickety stairs toward the stench of stale beer and mildew in the basement. There was an ice machine humming down there beside stacks of empty beer cans and bottles loaded onto a conveyor belt that climbed up toward the hotel pub. As I descended the creaking steps a timer somewhere below chimed in the distance. Even before my nose could register the salty sting of sweat, a clammy moisture rose over me. A few steps more and I spotted the entrance and behind it heard the muffled percussion of speed bags over the slap of skipping ropes. I opened the door and although nobody turned around, it was clear they all knew fresh meat had arrived.

I stood in the entrance just as a short, shirtless Asian man elbowed past me, dropped his gym bag on my foot, and spread out his arms.

"Can someone in the fuck tell me how I'm supposed to train right now after the best blow job I ever had in my life?"

The gym in unison: "Shut the fuck up, Loi!"

Some years later I read that this same man, Loi Chow, a former jockey, would accept the tidy sum of $1,500 to become the first ever man to fight—and decisively lose—a three-round professional bout against a woman billed as a "Battle of the Sexes."

My initiation at the Astoria gym, by design, was baptism by fire. They tossed every new kid who arrived into the ring to have their heads taken off in front of everybody, cowboys and Indians style. Before I even knew how to wipe my nose in boxing, that's how it went for me. They say the worst blows in boxing are the ones you don't see coming. But when you're a beginner you see plenty of them coming; the problem is you can't do anything about it. You don't know how.

If you're out of shape or new, the ring is one of the loneliest places in the world. The worst blow, for my money, is that first big one that *hasn't* hit you yet, it's just hanging there *on the way* to hitting you. I'd say you have roughly the same idea what it's going to feel like as you do the first time you put your dick inside a girl. The notable difference is that you can't *learn* to take a punch. Whether you have a glass chin or you don't, the only way of finding out is having it land. And when this punch happens in a gym, the news is going public in a hurry.

They threw me in there with a Golden Gloves champion, and before long I took a couple of right hands flush on the jaw—ones that I saw coming a mile away and had no clue how to avoid—and it was lights out. I was still on my feet, but I'd checked out. The impact was a surprisingly euphoric sensation. Somewhere in the darkness a ribbon of color smeared across my sight line. As I came to, glassy-eyed and goofy, I was still on my feet with a blurry figure I'd never seen before dancing in front of me, dipping one shoulder in preparation for a left hook to finish me off. The moment I remembered where I was and what was going on, I hugged him and wouldn't let go. He drove me back into a corner.

"Leggo, you fuckin' faggot!" he yelled in my ear.

But I didn't. I couldn't. He'd given me a lot to think about.

My head still wasn't clear, but I feebly attempted to consider his appraisal. At fifteen I hadn't kissed a girl yet. I'd never been attracted to a man but, then, maybe what my opponent was suggesting was that I simply hadn't met the *right* man. He was right insofar as I couldn't *entirely* rule it out. While it seemed fairly unlikely, it was indeed possible. How could you know? Maybe it explained all my problems. . . .

The bell rang and the bald trainer stepped into the ring and removed my headgear and gloves. By this time, the euphoric sensation of being knocked out had shifted into a throbbing dizziness and I couldn't breathe properly.

"Take it easy, kid." The trainer smiled. "Take it easy. So we'll see you same time tomorrow?"

It was his tone that conveyed what he really meant: I didn't belong.

I later found out that the trainer at that time was a municipal judge who channeled as many troubled kids as he could through that boxing gym instead of sending them to juvenile prison. My father had educated many of the social workers who represented the kids who entered this man's courtroom.

All I knew or cared about after he laughed and called for two more kids to get in the ring was that I never wanted to see him or anyone else from his gym for the rest of my life.

I rode home on the bus with a swollen cheek pressed up against the window, trying to soak up as much of the outside chill as I could. It wasn't hard to envision them still laughing at me back at the gym. I imagined that that sadistic trainer was probably egging them on. My jaw was too sore to enunciate the words, but I swore a thousand times on that ride that I'd never go back.

The next day I was more pissed off at him than sorry for myself, so I decided I would go back.

Of course it was only after I went back that they started to look after me. It took me a while to wise up enough to understand that maybe this was the point. They'd really been looking after me the whole time. If you don't come back after that first beating in front of all the strangers at the gym, you would be wasting your own time with boxing as much as theirs.

4

DIRTY SECRETS

I've learned that people will forget what you said, people will forget what you did, but people will never forget how you made them feel.   —Maya Angelou

YOU LEARN PRETTY FAST that fighters who need to look around for inspiration rarely amount to much. Maybe it's the same thing for writers. If you're waiting around for a breeze to fill your sails you probably have no business sailing upstream against anything in the first place. Besides, all the greatest boxers had a lot of holes in their sails.

In his book *Why We Can't Wait*, Dr. Martin Luther King Jr. wrote:

> *More than twenty-five years ago, one of the southern states adopted a new method of capital punishment. Poison gas supplanted the gallows. In its earliest stages, a microphone was placed inside the sealed death chamber so that scientific observers might hear the words of the dying prisoner to judge how*

*the human reacted in this novel situation. The first victim was
a young Negro. As the pellet dropped into the container, and
the gas curled upward, through the microphone came these
words: "Save me, Joe Louis. Save me, Joe Louis. Save me, Joe
Louis. . . ."*

Would you believe me if I told you that Joe Louis only became
Joe Louis because his mother hated boxing? She tried to get him
interested in playing an instrument, so he hid his gloves from her
in his violin case. When it came time for his first amateur fight,
Joe Louis Barrow omitted the "Barrow" when he signed the register to keep his boxing a secret from his mother. The name stuck.
Louis lost his first fight. But he hung around in boxing anyway.

It's a sneaky thing, revealing some of the most intimate aspects
of your life and having your opponent know less about you afterward. You never know what kind of chemistry you'll have with a
stranger. I met a fighter once who told me his style was based on
Mona Lisa's smile: "I always keep 'em guessing." There is an over-
whelmingly strange, naked sensation when your life comes together with another human being that you've never met before, a
person who has done no harm to you or anyone you know, and
for a handful of rounds you're expected to find the motivation to
shatter his will. If possible, you're obliged to steal every ounce of
hope, hijack any instinct for self-preservation, and take hostage
all determination he has to remain standing in front of you. Then
there's the fact your opponent is working himself up to do just
the same against *you*. You've made an enemy of a stranger simply
by your proximity in a shared, enclosed space.

It might be true that boxing is one of the only places where
people with prison records and otherwise rotten resumes don't start

at the bottom, but then again, nobody's a more dangerous fighter than a *happy* fighter. Did *Ali* ever look like he was having a bad time when the odds were stacked against him? Deep down you feel a bit like that *Voyager* probe they launched into space with that Golden Record tossed in as the best argument earth could make that we're worth preserving. The *Voyager* probe has Beethoven's Fifth; you have to find your own best excuse justifying why you belong.

A year after I started, boxing for me was a dirty secret. I had filled out and improved enough in the gym to handle Golden Glove champions and provincial champions for a few rounds. People started treating me differently. But then one day my run ended before it really had a chance to start. I always knew that one day a punch was around the corner that would expose me as a tourist to the sport. I just never expected it would be a punch *I* landed.

I never did manage to pull together a boxing *career*, or a memorable fight in front of a big crowd, or even to lace up a glove for a round as a professional. All my big moments happened in the gym, like an unsent letter I'll keep tucked away. I think this was because, early on, I *did* land a great punch against a great fighter. His name was Ronnie Wilson. I was sixteen. It had only been a year since I first started boxing, but I was making up for lost time. I landed that punch on Ronnie's jaw the first day we met and he ended up in my corner.

Ronnie was born outside Vancouver a few months after my dad in 1949. At eighteen he moved to California and turned professional. In those days, if they were excited enough, the crowd could double what a fighter earned on his contract. Ronnie had crumpled bills and change tossed into the ring after his victories. And back then if someone got sick or was otherwise unable to fight, you could offer to fight again in their place the same night. This happened many times to Ronnie. Ronnie Wilson fought so often in those first five years of his career that by the time he was twenty-three, he had competed in *seventy-eight* professional fights. He must have been one of the busiest prizefighters in the world during the 1970s. Before too long Ronnie got married and his wife gave birth to a daughter. I don't remember anymore if he was the one who mentioned the child, but I knew from a few people she was out there somewhere.

At his peak, Ronnie was in *Ring* magazine as a top-rated light heavyweight. But I never found that out from him. He never mentioned—let alone *bragged* about—anything to do with his accomplishments. After I hounded him to see the magazine in question, he reluctantly brought it in, though he insisted on not being in the same room with me while I looked at it.

A few times he came within a fight of challenging for a world title, but it never came through for him. Pretty early on in his life drinking followed by drugs became another struggle Ronnie was up against. His career ended in San Diego, on January 25, 1983, after a tomato can named Marcos Geraldo knocked him out in the third round. His final record stood at seventy wins, thirty-five defeats, and seven draws. He spent just shy of a thousand rounds in the ring. That's three thousand minutes. Fifty hours. Ronnie fought the equivalent of just over two solid *days* in the ring. I don't think there was anywhere else on earth he felt safer.

Physically, Ronnie eerily resembled Jack Dempsey: tall, with the same boyish haircut close-cropped on the sides and a little bushy upstairs, and they shared the same battered yet beautiful face. Ronnie weighed the same at forty-six as he had at eighteen, right at the light heavyweight limit of 178 pounds. There was always a bounce in Ronnie's step and if he stopped to ask anyone something, he rocked his weight back and forth on his toes. When he sparred he wore an ancient pair of purple Everlast trunks over long johns. Ronnie's ensembles were straight out of black-and-white photographs from boxing history books. I copied the look immediately.

Ronnie was never a talker, but his voice sounded a lot like an old blender chugging away. Hard liquor and a lot of leather thrown his way created a kind of rockslide effect with the features of Ronnie's face. Whenever he smiled it was like he was taking dynamite to all that rubble. Everybody tried to make Ronnie smile or laugh however we could because he was the sweetest presence any of us knew.

Every snapshot I have of him in my mind includes his generosity. Whatever situation you brought to that gym, you had this supportive man, with all his bias, in your corner to stand up for you. For a lot of us kids who knew him he was sympathetic to us when a lot of people who were supposed to be in our lives weren't. Really, that was his signature quality. And I suppose he must have been punch drunk after all those wars in the ring because he was always too dumb to ask for anything back.

The first time I ever saw Ronnie at the gym he'd already spotted me. He was watching me out of the corner of his eye while he was sparring with some other people. Ronnie routinely sparred ten rounds or more, rotating in a new, fresh face every couple rounds. He'd fight anybody. Nobody who saw him at forty-six, let alone fought him, ever considered for a moment he was past his prime. He had boundless energy that only increased if he was pushed to the edge. He loved fighters who could push him out there. For better or worse, that ledge was his soul's permanent address.

He had finished seven or eight rounds by the time I got to the gym that day, and was looking over at me from the corner. The whole time I knew him, I never saw Ronnie *glare* at anyone. But then, he never had to. Ronnie was one of those rare people out there who'd been hurt by almost everyone he'd deeply cared about, yet he never wanted to take it out on anyone, aside from himself. But I didn't know that up front. I was too busy shitting my pants with his eyes on me. All I saw meeting his glance was someone who had probably seen a lot more with his eyes than I'd ever be able to handle. Far and away the scariest fighters out there are the ones who never have to try to act tough. It never even occurs to them.

As I was on my way to the changing room, I heard Ronnie ask the gym owner, jerking his head in my direction, "Who's the kid?" The owner said my name and Ronnie repeated it before the bell rang. "Say, get *Brinny* in here before I'm done."

Only the closest people to me ever used that nickname. Only a handful of people my entire life had thought to call me that. The owner of the gym surely never used it. My heart sunk when I heard Ronnie casually use a term so intimate for me. I knew I was going to get hurt, and any time you got hurt there was a chance you could spend the rest of your life picking up the pieces.

A few minutes later I was skipping in front of the mirror watching Ronnie fight a young professional fighter he was taking it easy on. Around them were a lot of posters with adages about not giving up, posters of proud champions posing or in battle. Jimmy, a close friend at the gym, came over because he'd already heard I'd be sparring with Ronnie in a few minutes. Jimmy was a featherweight originally from Fiji with lightning feet and hands. He also had an incapacitated, incontinent, career drunk of a father at home whom he regularly had to bathe since his dad had attempted suicide by swallowing battery acid a few years before. We both had alcoholic fathers, but my dad had a much more forgiving environment than Jimmy's father did. My dad smoked three packs a day but refused to use a lighter. *Smokers* use lighters. He drank every day (though I never saw my father order a drink in public in my life), but he never missed a day of work, or visibly suffered, or inflicted any of the terrible things they warned us in school alcoholics did. His drinking felt much more like an ominous game for which he created the rules but refused to reveal them to anyone else. It left our home feeling vaguely haunted, empty and claustrophobic at the same time, something like a knockoff Overlook Hotel. *The Shining* was a film my father and I watched together so many times after my parents separated that the ribbon snapped on the video cassette we owned. Everybody at school joked how much my father looked like Jack Nicholson and it wasn't stated entirely as a compliment. But I loved how uneasy my father's presence was for people.

Jimmy and I were both sixteen and had showed up at this gym at more or less the same time. The owner had twenty-five kids who wanted to get involved in amateur boxing, so he set us all up to spar round robins continuously for two hours a night. After a month, twenty-five kids bled down to just Jimmy and me. While I was a lot bigger, I could never catch up to him.

"You'll do fine." Jimmy smiled. "Keep your hands up. He'll come at you hard but you can catch him. Wait for an opening and rip his head off. Don't even think about it."

The buzzer rang.

A French Canadian trainer came over with his familiar words of encouragement. "*Tabarnak,* what are we waiting around for? Get the fuck in there. Ronnie's waiting."

I tried to lean in and whisper into his ear, "Can we do it another day? I'm really not feeling well today."

"Speak up, *tabarnak*."

I pointed at my stomach and shook my head.

"Listen, *tabarnak*, after three rounds I'll buy you a lollipop. Go on, cutie pie."

So you take a deep breath and climb the stairs and hold the middle rope open for the last fighter to exit, and keep holding it up so you can enter. The apron is under your toes and you dance around trying to get loose, snapping out some punches.

Someone turned the music down in the gym and several people broke away from hitting the bags or skipping and took a round off to get cozy next to the ring and watch.

I was shorter and Ronnie had a lot of reach over me, but by then I'd built myself up into Ronnie's weight class. I was a little more muscular than Ronnie and I had heavier hands, too. Ronnie wasn't built like a puncher. He was a grinder who loved getting in wars regardless of whether that made any sense for him strategically.

Ronnie took out his mouth guard for a second and grinned at me. "You *look* a bit like Tyson, but can you fight like him, too? I guess we'll find out."

Tyson's identity was my sanctuary and foxhole. At that time there weren't a lot of white kids with shaved heads who weren't undergoing chemotherapy or regularly attending white supremacist meetings. But either interpretation served to keep people away from me and pushed me further down the path I was traveling on my own. I ran every morning at four thirty for five miles and shadowboxed round after round, studying his style in fights and his life and manner in documentaries on VHS I borrowed from the library. Tyson had invented his own menacing legend as a construct of the fighters he most identified with and admired. As a kid competing in the amateurs he even lied that he was Sonny Liston's nephew.

When the bell rang and we raised our gloves to each other Ronnie circled me for a while, waiting to see what I'd do. We were both tentative for the first couple minutes. Finally Ronnie settled down and threw a straight right hand poised to break my nose. In a flash I'd slipped it and his fist mopped some sweat off my shoulder before sailing over. He was off-balance with the miss and I was already low and coiled. A split second before Ronnie had his glove safely protecting his cheek, I took his head off with a left hook that landed flush against his jaw. The impact of that punch echoed across the gym and stopped everything that was going on. Ronnie's feet came off the ground, and when they touched down he had spaghetti legs for a second. From the corner of my eye I saw that French Canadian trainer yank a rope, torn between being excited for me and scared Ronnie was hurt. "Ronnie, you good?" he hollered up. Ronnie was dazed and slack-jawed, but he held up his glove. Just as I was going to try to finish Ronnie off I held up to let him clear his head. Ronnie just smiled over at me, and a few seconds later the bell rang and he gave me a hug.

"So you wanna be a *fighter*," he growled, massaging his jaw.

The truth was, not after that. And even less so once a couple of shady people in the gym who had watched us spar offered to stake me a couple thousand dollars a month as managers if I turned pro. I didn't have any other prospects, but that punch drove home loud and clear I didn't belong in the sport as a boxer. The dirty secret I kept after landing that punch was that I wanted to learn how to protect people like Ronnie a lot more than I wanted to learn how to hurt them. I didn't give up fighting at that point, but I never dreamed of being a *fighter* after that.

But Ronnie still desperately wanted to be a fighter. He had his last pro fight four years later on his fiftieth birthday. He was beaten so badly and bleeding from his face so profusely the referee stopped the fight in the first round. I wasn't there. Nobody from our gym was. We didn't know he was fighting. He never told anyone. His age aside, Ronnie was in no condition to fight. He'd started drinking again.

Before that last fight happened, just after I started my amateur boxing career with Ronnie working my corner as an assistant trainer, he went AWOL from the gym. He disappeared for a few days. We filed a missing person report with the police and finally another trainer found him strung out on Hastings surrounded by other junkies and drunks slumped over park benches in Pigeon Park. My gym's owner helped him get into rehab, but Ronnie couldn't stick it out. The owner tried a couple more times getting him back into rehab, but it just never worked.

Once it became clear that Ronnie wasn't coming back, I wasn't sure what to do next with boxing, let alone my life. I stumbled across Ronnie just before he fought his last fight, a few weeks before I flew to Havana for the first time to look for a new trainer. I heard later he contracted HIV and a lot of other viruses on the street. He'd ended up in the hospital a few times after being beaten pretty badly by kids looking to thump someone defenseless. Ronnie was always so hard on himself, I wonder if he even bothered to fight back. Maybe he felt like he deserved it.

When I saw him he'd grown out a beard and his toes poked out of his shoes and he looked broken and lost. I barely recognized him. He barely recognized me. Some part of me kept hoping it was all just wardrobe and makeup for a movie part he'd gotten. As we stood looking at one another, I could almost feel him absorb the sadness between us like some mournful breeze rattling a wind chime.

I didn't know what to say and wasn't sure what to do, either. I'd tried with him as I'd tried to help my own father to quit harming himself with alcohol, but in both cases nothing worked. You have to get past the pain of knowing who someone isn't to accept loving them for who they are.

Finally he did recognize me, without remembering my name.

"Heya, look at this, hey kid?" he said, exposing some lost teeth. "Look where I ended up, huh? Can you believe it? Look where I ended up. Ah, Jesus. *Look* at me."

"Are you okay, Ronnie?"

"Look where I ended up. Can you believe it?"

"Are you okay?"

"I'm real sorry, 'cause I know I know you. I do. But I can't for the life of me remember your name. My head ain't too good. It would really help me out if you could spare anything. I swear I won't buy any dope."

I gave him what was in my pocket and he kept repeating the same thing over and over: "Look at me." Then, instead of saying good-bye, he just moaned with his voice breaking, "Guess I'm all washed up, ain't I?"

5

HURRICANES AND BREEZES

*In a sense, we are all crashing to our death from the top
story of our birth to the flat stones of the churchyard and
wondering with an immortal Alice in Wonderland at the
patterns on the passing wall.*   —Vladimir Nabokov

MY HOMETOWN HAD BREEZES it treated like hurricanes; Havana
had hurricanes it treated like breezes.

In 1492, Columbus first described looking upon Cuba as "the
most beautiful land that eyes ever beheld." On the way over, Columbus was the first man from the Old World to record an encounter with a hurricane. The very word "hurricane" was invented
by the native Taino population of Cuba as the name of a deity they
feared and sought to soothe, Hurakan. Soon enough Columbus
and the Spanish were convinced the worsening hurricanes they
endured in Cuba were their Christian God's curse for their overwhelming cruelty against the island's inhabitants.

After all those Tyson biographies, *The Old Man and the Sea*
was the first novel I ever read. It introduced me to Cuba. I was

fifteen and the first keyholes I peeked through toward the island were Ernest Hemingway's novelization of his twenty years there, the enigma of Cuban boxers who casually rejected offers of vast fortunes from American promoters, and Cuba's courage to stand up to the most powerful nation on earth (Fidel was actually carrying Hemingway's *For Whom the Bell Tolls* looking for pointers on guerrilla warfare while he was up in the Sierra Maestra mountains during the revolution). These entry points to Cuba were like the Pyramids, but what loomed like the sphinx was the character of the people themselves.

Why had Hemingway—one of America's most beloved writers—spent the last third of his life on the island and declared himself a Cuban? Why, in 1976, when America offered Cuba's greatest boxer, Teófilo Stevenson, five million dollars to leave Cuba and fight Muhammad Ali, had Stevenson turned the tables and instead asked of the offer itself, "What is one million dollars compared to the love of eight million Cubans?" And why would anyone *want* to resist America, let alone wish to assume the role of David against a Goliath only ninety miles away?

Before I ever set foot on Cuban shores, I wondered what Shakespeare might have done with Fidel Castro and his cursed treasure chest of an island Columbus had tried to plunder, along with all the other intruders ever since. And then an hour later after my first visit in 2000, when I was only twenty, it became clear that the better question was what *Fidel Castro and Cuba* would have done with Shakespeare. Everywhere I looked, I was confronted with the same question: Who would believe this society ever existed in the first place, let alone for this long?

During my first week in Havana, I took a gypsy cab over to Cojimar and tracked down Gregorio Fuentes, the still living

103-year-old model for Hemingway's *The Old Man and the Sea.* I asked him, "If Hemingway wrote about every *other* war he'd chased after around the world, why not the revolution going on in his backyard?" Gregorio shrugged and took a puff from his cigar. "He liked boxing. Maybe Hemingway's knowledge of boxing taught him enough to know to punch your weight." He smiled. As for a hero like Teófilo Stevenson turning down all that money to leave, on my final trip to Cuba, eleven years after my first visit, Stevenson reluctantly granted me the last filmed interview of his life before his sudden death a year later, in 2012. When the *Miami Herald* ran a front-page feature about that interview, in which Stevenson asking me for a hundred dollars in return for our session somehow overshadowed all the millions he'd turned down during his career, it cost me my ability to ever return to an island I love and greatly admire. I'd handed ammunition to a lot of enemies of the Cuban government by exposing one of its idols. And over half a century after Fidel Castro seemed to be taking a joyride on the *Titanic,* dedicating his life to opposing America, with the latest banking collapse, suddenly our *unsinkable* ship of capitalism was taking on water with a limited supply of lifeboats to go around. Maybe with *The Old Man and the Sea,* a lovingly told story embracing the haunting beauty found in certain failed journeys, Hemingway spoke with equal truth to both sides of the ninety miles separating his adoptive home and his native country.

The first thing that happens when you arrive in Havana is you feel your heart's watch resisting your mind's clock about what time it is. The Cuban poet Dulce María Loynaz once described the shape of her island as "like the drawn bow an invisible archer raises in the shadows, aimed at our hearts." I was warned like all visitors that books were banned in Cuba. This had the unintended consequence, at least for me, of redoubling my desire to go to a place where books were still that *powerful*. No matter what was written in a book in most places in the modern world, who would think to waste their time banning it? It was hard enough getting people unplugged for long enough to *read*, let alone care enough to rally against one. When the revolution triumphed, four out of five soldiers who marched into Havana with Fidel were illiterate. Forty years later, when I arrived in 2000, the city boasted one of the highest literacy rates in the world.

Havana is a city of bright lights and dark corners I explored as much as I could, on and off, for twelve years. It's very difficult to see anything clearly for long. It never seems to finish what it has to say, and part of its essential mystery and beauty is how you always come away missing something.

6

HUNGARIAN JOKES

The formula "two and two make five" is not without its
attractions.   —Fyodor Dostoyevsky

My INTRODUCTION TO CUBA came in the form of the punch line
of a Hungarian joke my grandfather left behind for me after his
death. We'd never talked much, but in the last decade before his
death we hadn't spoken at all. I lost someone I never really had.
Then, after my mother gave me some photographs from his youth
and an old cigarette tin from his mandatory service in the Hungarian army, my feelings for him started to change. My mother
saved the biggest surprise for the breakfast table not long after he
died. She wanted to use what little money he had left her to send
me to Cuba.

As far as I can tell, most Hungarian jokes have two central ob-
jectives: making you laugh to avoid crying or crying your way into
laughter. Alcoholism and suicide rates among Hungarians are
some of the highest in the world (and my own family did their

part to chip in on both fronts), so perhaps this is to be expected. My deepest connection to my grandfather is through the Hungarian minor chord in music. The composers Béla Bartók and Erik Satie favored the Hungarian minor chord in some of their compositions, whereas most composers avoided it, because too many listeners found the unresolved nature of the melody simply too haunting. Any untrained ear can decipher whether most melodies are happy or sad, but the Hungarian minor chord conjures an ambiguity that leaves you off-balance and unsettled, much like a Hungarian joke.

My grandfather escaped Hungary in 1956 as a refugee while Russian tanks were rolling down the streets outside his family's apartment. One of my mother's first childhood memories was seeing the tanks outside her window. While in Canada, he sent back whatever money he could to support his family and saved in order to bring his family over with him. It was always his intention to reunite with his wife and two children. It didn't work out that way. The distance was too much and finally both my grandparents moved on with their lives and divorced six years after his escape. My grandmother met the love of her life while my grandfather never truly recovered.

My uncle was caught trying to escape Hungary and was sent back, but my mother succeeded ten years after my grandfather's escape and followed him to Canada. At sixteen she reunited with my grandfather but he was a changed man, a drinker, hardened and abusive. She tried to take off three times before she finally got away. That same year she became pregnant with my brother, and married the father. Almost as soon as she gave birth, she was pregnant again. Seven months after giving birth to her second child, he died from crib death. Things kind of spiraled out of control for her after that, until she found God. My grandfather never reached out with any help during that time. She had another child from an affair two years later that ended her first marriage. From then on my mother and brothers lived in the projects while she supported her family on welfare and odd jobs she could get cleaning houses or working with the elderly.

My grandfather, at least while I knew him, was a grumbling, unhappy, standoffish man fastened to the portable whipping post of regret. He shared my mother's enormous pale blue eyes but lacked the kindness and generosity that kept hers lit up. My favorite story my mother told about him centered on a wedding he attended after he divorced my grandmother. He'd fallen in love with a woman already engaged to someone else. After failing to persuade her against the marriage, he showed up at the wedding and hanged himself in revenge during the ceremony. In the banquet hall, my grandfather swayed for two minutes from the noose before anyone was able to cut him down. He spent the next fifty-six days in a coma.

In his old age, my grandfather expected his family to reach out to him, but I could never find much about him to justify bothering. After about the age of ten, we stopped communicating altogether and the last time I ever saw him was when I visited him in the hospital a few days before his death, not long after his eightieth and my twentieth birthday. He'd had a stroke and could no longer communicate verbally. I couldn't get past the doorway to his room as he lay there staring at me.

During the last year of his life, the only times I heard his voice were when he would sing Hungarian and Gypsy folk songs on my mother's answering machine. It was such an uncharacteristically sweet, warm act that I wasn't even sure how to approach asking my mother why he'd begun regularly doing it. My mother visited him at the hospital as often as she could in the last days of his life. There were silly, petty issues with his will where the obvious desire he'd had to look after his two children was complicated by fears of being exploited. He didn't have much money in the first place, yet his wish to offer something to my mother was botched at the end, and she never complained despite always having financial constraints herself. She laughed about how typical it was of him.

She invited me for a *palacsinta* (Hungarian crepes) breakfast a few months after he died.

"*Darrrrling*," she began in her Count Chocula accent, as I braced myself.

Our breakfast table had always been a dangerous place for me. When I was eight, after having watched her light a candle on the anniversary of my dead brother's birthday, I asked over *palacsinta* how anyone could possibly get over the death of a child.

"Well, *darrrrling*," she smiled, "your mother lost the will to live."

I stopped scraping jam over the pancake.

"I couldn't feel *anyt'ing*. The only place I could feel anything was tw'oo sex. Not making love. Just sex. Sex was the only t'ing that made me feel like a human being."

"Sex?"

"Sex was the only t'ing, Bwinny."

The week before we'd clarified that sex, making love, and fucking were three *entirely* different things. But it would be another year before I'd seek clarification on which of the distinctly different, obviously designated holes one was supposed to use when seeking to lose one's virginity. Was it insulting to ask for the "fuck hole" or "sex hole" with a girl? Did *all* women expect their first time to be through the "making love hole"? If you lost your virginity to someone who'd already lost theirs, was it insulting to ask for the "making love hole"?

"Sex?" I repeated.

"You asked me so I'm telling you."

"You were still with the husband before daddy?"

"No." She smiled. "T'ank God I was free of dat."

"So you were with daddy?"

"No. Dis is *before* I met your fadder."

"*Okay.*"

"Let me have some of your jam if you're not using it."

Little was functioning inside me as I contemplated what she was telling me.

"*Sex* was the only thing that helped you to feel alive?"

"Yes," she said, fiendishly jamming her knife into the jar of strawberry jam. "Sex was the only t'ing. So every weekend I went to discos and I watched very carefully for the best dancer and I went over to dance. Then after, I would go home with them and we would have sex. On Saturday and Sunday, every week, for an entire year this is what your mother had to do to find any reason to live."

Multiplication was part of the curriculum that year and, while not having memorized the times tables, I felt confident I had easily gleaned enough to comfortably handle this one. Fifty-two weeks, times two of the best dancers in these clubs every week, equals . . .

"You slept with *two thousand* men in one *year?*"

"Around a hundred, I would say. But then I got much better just before I met your fadder."

Four years later, at the same table, pancakes steaming on the plate, she brought up the sexual education pamphlet I'd brought home from school the day before.

"Bwinny, I read what you brought home. We have always been open with each other, right?"

"Yep."

"Have you ever woken up with the sheets moist? I don't mean pee."

"I don't think so."

"You have never had an *or-gasm*? You know what dat is, right?"

"I don't think I have."

"It might happen soon. All I vant to say, it's very, very *normal*."

"How old were you when you had your first one?" I asked her.

"I was eleven. In Budapest they have a beautiful park called Margaret Island. Very beautiful place in the summer. I was dere one summer afternoon and saw an old man feeding birds on zee park bench. All the birds were so happy and some flew into his hand to eat the birdseed. So I sat down across from him and asked for some birdseed."

"Mom," I interrupted. "What the hell does this have to do with your first orgasm?"

"I tell you. Zee old man was very kind and asked me to cup my hands and reach over so he could give me some seed. I did and he gave me some and then I started to feed zee birds. But zen zee old man did an interesting t'ing. First he put down the bird-seed. Then he came over close to me on zee bench. Then as I kept feeding the happy little birds he reached down and put his hand slowly up my dress and he was touching me."

"Mom."

"Let me finish the story. You asked, so I am telling you this story."

"I don't want to hear this story."

"He was touching me there right on the bench and I had never felt deez sensation in my life. I wasn't scared or hurt, I was confused. But I didn't say anything or do anything. I just felt this new sensation building and building until, finally, an amazing thing happened. And at that *exact* moment, this very old man took his hand away, grabbed his birdseed, and walked off."

"Your first orgasm was from being molested by an old man on a park bench?"

"It's true."

"Something like this would scar a woman for life, wouldn't it?"

"Why? He gave me pleasure and I was never hurt. I t'ink it's interesting. Someone else can have it mean somet'ing else. I won't argue with them, they shouldn't waste time arguing with me."

When I mentioned this story to my father, he ventured that my mother had been denied the kind of love she needed in her childhood. And maybe that desperation was why she was willing to take such risks in finding it, even from this stranger's touch. My father always nursed a grudge against my mother's dad that I adopted very early on. It ended one day after I was back at the breakfast table after my grandfather's death.

"My father and you never had much closeness. I'm sorry for dat. For both of you. He was better than I think you realize."

"I don't know." I shrugged.

"I have a silly question." My mother smiled. "If you could go anywhere in the world. Where do you think you would go?"

I'd just finished reading *The Old Man and the Sea* and a teacher at school had told me that Hemingway's captain and friend from the story was still alive and kicking at 103 years old in Cojimar, the same town as in the story.

"Cuba," I told her.

"Why Cuba?"

"To find a boxing trainer and to meet the guy from *The Old Man and the Sea*."

"Okay, then today your grandfather is sending you to Cuba. He didn't leave much, but there's enough to buy you a ticket. I think he would enjoy giving you this present. So you will have to look up many of my friends in Havana."

"You have friends in Cuba?"

"Don't be ridiculous. Of course I do."

"I've never heard you mention knowing *anybody* in Cuba."

"That's because I haven't met them yet. But *they're there*. You'll see, darling."

7

VALET PARKING

It is well known that curious men go prying into all sorts of places (where they have no business) and come out of them with all sorts of spoil. This story [Heart of Darkness]*, and one other . . . are all the spoil I brought out from Africa, where, really, I had no sort of business.*

—Joseph Conrad

A WOMAN SITTING next to me on my first plane ride to Havana was underlining an entire passage from a story she was reading, *La causa que refresca (A Cause for All Seasons)* by José Miguel Sánchez. The story was about a Cuban male prostitute waiting at the airport for a tourist he would spend the next six weeks with. After reading just the first few sentences over this woman's shoulder, I asked if I could copy it into my notebook:

I'm only a guide, but I'm like a priest in a way. . . . I absolve you, but I leave you with just enough guilt so that you will come back soon to this Cuba, which lies behind the pic-

*ture postcards, to this game of masks that we play, and you play,
too. . . . I absolve you and rekindle in your heart your faith in
the cause, a cause for six weeks of the year of Latin love and
forbidden fruits, of sex and idealism. A safe and cozy cause.
Easy to carry around. A cause for all seasons.*

The philosopher Slavoj Žižek once said that fantasy is for those
who can't cope with reality, while reality is for those who can't
cope with their fantasies. I've gone back and forth my entire life
about which, between the two, really triggers the more lasting
damage. Some people are homesick the moment they leave their
front door, others are homesick from birth for a place they can
never find. Some girls enjoy the walk to a new boy's house more
than they will ever enjoy the boy himself.

My first trip to Havana was in February of 2000, right in the
middle of the Elián González fiasco. As with everything about
Cuba, nobody could agree on anything. And now, what the press
referred to as "political kiddie porn" had entered into a Cuban civil
war fought across ninety miles of ocean. What was portrayed as
a custody case by some (and a kidnapping by others) became an
existential crisis for millions of Cubans on both sides of the issue.
With Elián's story, millions of Cubans saw their own family's
breakup writ large.

At the age of five, Elián González and his mother, along with
twelve other passengers, had fled Cuba on a small aluminum boat.
The boat's faulty engine gave out after they encountered a storm
while attempting to cross the Straits of Florida. Only Elián and
two other passengers managed to survive the journey. Elián's
mother died—*heroically,* some in America said—trying to save
her son from the horrors of a life in Cuba. To allow any child to

live under Castro's rule in Cuba was tantamount to child abuse, is what seemed to be implied. The survivors were discovered floating at sea by two fishermen. The fishermen handed the survivors over to the U.S. Coast Guard and all hell broke loose in Miami and Cuba. It turned out Elián's mother had taken Elián from the boy's father in Cuba, without his knowledge, let alone permission. After some negotiation at the highest levels of government in the United States and Cuba, Elián would be sent back. The young boy became yet another feather in the cap for Fidel against the United States.

For my own research, I was reading *Pitching Around Fidel: A Journey into the Heart of Cuban Sports* by S. L. Price. Price's book was the most current, in-depth breakdown of Cuba's enigmatic powerhouse sports machine. I wanted to learn how to locate boxers and how to properly approach them to see if any would be willing to teach me. I had no idea how to handle negotiation in Cuba or what the risks involved were. But I'd read that the black market economy in Cuba eclipsed its official economy. In the book, Price details how each elite athlete he profiled encountered the same hopelessly impossible decision to stay or leave as every other Cuban on the island, only with a lot more money at stake if they managed to escape. Whereas Teófilo Stevenson had rejected five million dollars in the 1970s to fight Muhammad Ali, the going rate offered to Félix Savón, Cuba's latest heavyweight destroyer, was in the neighborhood of twenty million, to defect to America and fight Mike Tyson. Even the act of writing a book exploring the ambiguity of the choice involved had caused Price to be banned from ever returning to Cuba. "You have penetrated an impenetrable system," he was told by security agents. The bombshell of the book was a Cuban boxer, Héctor Vinent, a two-time Olympic champion, confessing to Price his desire to escape. No Cuban athlete, *in* Cuba, had ever confessed such a thing on the record before. Yet Vinent never managed to escape. He was punished before he'd ever had a chance to try. Vinent only wished to leave Cuba after the government had banned him from boxing for the rest of his life. Price's book didn't say what became of Vinent, whether he remained in Havana or had returned to be with his family in Santiago de Cuba in the east of the island. If Vinent was living in Havana as I flew over, he was twenty-eight, and my guess was he could probably use some extra money training me at a local gym. It was as good a place as any to learn about his island, too.

My mother's prediction about friends I hadn't met yet came true before the plane ride was over. Across the aisle from me a middle-aged Latino, wearing reading glasses that kept falling off his nose, was devouring pages from *For Whom the Bell Tolls* nearly as fast as the rum and Cokes he was ordering. I noticed his hands were getting steadier with each sip of alcohol. There was a casual sense of doom about him that intrigued me. He was ordering rounds for the three people sitting next to him as if they were his friends, and then drinking them all himself. I've always spooked pretty easily around heavy drinkers. They tend to hold up a mirror that I have difficulty turning away from. And this guy was getting *steadier* the more he drank, not sloppier. In his novel *Under the Volcano*, Malcolm Lowry describes this sensation as "the shakes of too little and the abyss of too much." As I looked across the aisle and tried not to think about the stranger who epitomized this, he smiled at me.

"You don't even seem drunk," I said.

"Drunk?" He held up his empty glass. "Why would I be drunk? *This* isn't drinking. I'm in *training*." He reached up and pushed the button for the flight attendant again. When she arrived he ordered another round. "My name is Alfonso."

"I'm Brin. You're Cuban?"

"No *Brinicito*, I'm Guatemalan, but I've divided my time evenly between Havana and Toronto for many years now. I need to get off this fucking plane and get something to drink."

Alfonso wasn't kidding. His cirrhosis, I'd find out later, was pretty far along already and his drinking on the plane was small potatoes compared to after we'd landed. After the flight attendant cut him off he asked me to start ordering drinks and pass them over to him.

"What are you looking for in Havana?" he asked me. "A girl?"

"I'd like to meet some of their best boxers and see if I can get some training and maybe meet the guy from *The Old Man and the Sea*. I heard he's still alive over there."

"Gregorio Fuentes! I'm reading Hemingway now. I love that America's favorite writer is even more popular in his adoptive 'state sponsor of terror' home in Cuba. I mean the moment he had to go back to America he blew his brains out! But Gregorio is still there. Gregorio is a national treasure. You'll love him. And you have the best boxers in the world to see over there and get to know. Cuba is a wet dream as much as it's a nightmare. That's why America has always been so obsessed with it."

"Can you hire any of these Olympic boxers to train you? Is that done?"

"That's easy. With a little money and perseverance anything is available to you in Havana if you know the right people. Heroes are for sale everywhere, but in Havana heroes make twenty dollars a month. You know anyone for that?"

"I don't know a soul over there."

"Order me two more drinks and I can help you. I know athletes over there. Not in boxing, but they all know each other. They all wear their Olympic Cuban tracksuits like uniforms on the street. Stick with me when we get off the plane. I can help you there. But they will hold me at immigration after the flight. They always do. They treat me like a criminal every time I arrive and leave. It's just a routine thing for me over there. They are afraid I'm stealing treasures over there for peanuts and selling them back home for millions. They treat me trafficking books like I'm smuggling Cuban heroes off the island myself."

"What do you buy?"

"Rare books. Cuba may be famous for old cars and sports, but they have collectibles in many other rare things, too. People are making fortunes off of baseball cards right now. But I love books. That's the extraordinarily beautiful thing about a country that makes certain books illegal to read; it reminds you that books still *mean* something. If you enjoy gray, the paradoxes over there are like nowhere else on earth."

"I don't have a place to stay in Havana. I was just going to find something when I arrived."

"That's a bad idea. *Jineteros*—those are the hustlers and prostitutes, latterly 'jockeys'—love people like you to ride. They will hiss at you all over the tourist areas. Let me take care of everything. Just wait for me after the police questioning and this drunk stranger you just met can give you some keys to open some interesting doors. Havana is my favorite city in the world. Whenever you return to Havana you will always find me here and have a friend. And all my friends will be your friends."

When we got off the plane, just as he'd predicted, Alfonso was taken in for questioning in a private room and held for three hours by the police. Before we'd gotten off the plane Alfonso had given me some money to buy him a twelve-year-old bottle of Havana Club and a carton of Popular cigarettes from the little airport shop to resuscitate him. I waited for him in airport arrivals until midnight, when they finally released him. Alfonso trudged out of the holding room soaked in sweat, his face blanched, lugging two huge articles of luggage that I ran over to help him carry.

"Brinicito, don't worry about my luggage. Where's my fucking medicine?"

I gave him the bottle and cigarettes as he stumbled over to a chair in the arrivals section of the airport and collapsed on his stomach, moaning. His hands were trembling.

"Do we need a taxi or a fucking ambulance?" I asked him.

"Neither." Alfonso rolled over and tried unsuccessfully to unscrew the bottle. "Can you do this for me, please? My hands shake too badly. Hurry, please."

I took the bottle and unscrewed the cap and handed it to him. He slumped down over two chairs and held it over his head with one hand while tearing open the carton of cigarettes.

"I don't need an ambulance or a driver. I have an eighteen-year-old nurse waiting for me where we're going. And our driver has been waiting for us all this time in the parking lot. Just give me some time to recover from that ordeal. Maybe get me some Bucanero beer from the little shop. A twelve-pack, please."

When I came back with the beer I saw he'd consumed half the bottle while chain-smoking his way through a twisted mass of cigarettes resting under his chair. He was upright now, with the color having returned to his face, eyes alert, hands steady. Miraculously, Alfonso looked almost energized.

"My friend, I'm sorry for how long you've had to wait before meeting this beautiful city. But now you'll always remember your first meeting with Havana at night. That will put a spell in your heart always. Meeting a city for the first time at night is like making love to a woman before you've even spoken with her. I'm very envious of you tonight."

I stepped outside into Havana's muggy, tropical embrace. Before my eyes could adjust to see anything beyond palm trees swaying in the moonlight, the intensity of Cuba's perfume entered my bloodstream and I dropped Alfonso's bags on the ground. All at once the swirl of belched diesel fumes and cigar smoke, highlighted with the stale sting of oxidized alcohol, hit me before the stench of some nearby forever-unflushed toilet almost knocked me over.

"Even the *smell* of Cuba has the intensity of a priest giving in to sex." Alfonso smiled, lighting another cigarette. "Don't talk anymore until we're inside the car. Let's go, our ride is waiting for us."

We walked out into the moonlight toward a mostly empty parking lot when something violently hissed at us. Alfonso laughed and an engine turned on a car about twenty yards off. A lanky, nervous Bill Cosby lookalike in a Cuban tracksuit quickly approached us and grabbed the handles of Alfonso's luggage from me.

"Do I let him take them?"

"Of course. Montalvo is family."

After we loaded the trunk of his small Lada with our belongings, I got in the backseat while Alfonso threw his arm around the driver. As soon as the car lurched forward it promptly stalled.

"*¡Cubaneo!*" Montalvo slapped the steering wheel. This

expression, I later found, was used to describe the particular strain of bad luck indigenous to Cuba.

"*¡Hermano!*" Alfonso laughed, taking another slug from the bottle. "My brother, it is always so good to see you. But always so serious! Brinicito, this is Montalvo. Montalvo was a silver medalist in the hundred-meter dash from the Pan Am games. He's an even better person than he was a runner. Forgive us, but I have some things to discuss with my friend in Spanish, so we can sort out where you will stay and all that."

We were out on the highway now and it struck me that I had no idea who the two men in the front seat of the car were or where we were going. The Cuban night felt less like reality and more like the dreamscape of Fidel and his people. The Cuban highway was anarchy, with American cars manufactured in the 1950s, Russian-made Ladas, and military trucks with soldiers sitting in the back raging over the broken-down pavement while horse-drawn carriages and bikes drifted along the road shoulder. In addition to the nightmarish jumble of the scene, the highway lacked streetlights or any highway signs, and the only updates about our progress toward Havana were the occasional ghostly billboards that were illuminated in our flickering headlights, featuring political exhortations I couldn't understand.

As we got closer to Havana I thought of Alfonso's description of meeting a city at night for the first time. The silhouettes of palm trees whisked past us, and after a while I could see the dim copper glow of Havana spread out like broken glass shattered across the hulking darkness of the city's skyline. We turned off the highway and entered a narrow, pothole-laden side street winding into a neighborhood like a hand reaching into a dark cupboard. Finally there were a few streetlamps and I could read some of the billboards on the side of the road. A painting of Castro's beaming face was situated beside the words *¡VAMOS BIEN!*

"What is that referring to?" I asked Alfonso.

"That everything is going well. It's *always* going well."

Alfonso translated what he'd said to me to Montalvo and Montalvo moaned in response, "*Sí, sí. 'Vamos bien.' Cuarenta y un años y siempre ¡vamos bien! Dios mío.*"

"There is a joke about the revolution, which says that literacy, health care, and sports are its great achievements. And its failures are breakfast, lunch, and dinner. When I first started coming here during the worst of the Special Period in the early 1990s, parents would name their pets Breakfast, Lunch, or Dinner to protect the children from attachment before they ate them."

We passed another sign on the side of the road with a Che Guevara mural next to an illegibly scrawled sentence.

"What does that mean?" I asked.

" 'Be like Che!' You'll find out how it is. Much is a lie here just as it is in America." Alfonso laughed. "I think Cubans believe the bullshit less than you. Cuban advertising tries to help individuals get over human weakness, while American advertising encourages you to give in to it."

"Does Montalvo have a place for me to stay?"

"We're taking you to somewhere that should be available near the Plaza de la Revolución, the huge square where you will be able to see Castro give a speech while you are here. Seven-hour speeches sometimes!"

"Seven fucking hours?"

"This is what Americans always say. But in Lincoln's time he did the same thing. The population was informed and had an attention span. Remember what Gore Vidal said about genius in America?"

"What did he say?"

"That if students year after year insist American history is the most boring subject, you need look no further than American history teachers to find geniuses at work. Look out your window, *that's* the Plaza. We're close to where you're staying."

The Plaza itself looked like one enormous vacuum of an empty parking lot surrounded by distant, stale government structures, and then I saw Che's face glowing, six stories high, stenciled against the side of a building.

Cuba's secular saint was once declared by America's CIA as the most dangerous man in the world before they gave the order in 1967 to execute him in Bolivia. The man who pulled the trigger still proudly wore Che's watch in Miami as a souvenir he claimed from the execution. This country's adoptive hero was America's terrorist distilled now into a mouse pad, T-shirt, the flotsam of kitsch. Out the other car window a three-hundred-foot-high marble tower, seemingly donated by the Klingon Empire's most distinguished architect, loomed as a monument to the poet José Martí. Shadowy buzzards circled over the tower. In all of the darkness the junglescape felt like a nightmare predator ready to spring into action and blindside you.

That first night, watching the scenery slide by outside my window, every inch of the island I saw was accompanied by the reminder that this population had rallied behind a leader who had been instrumental in bringing the world closer to oblivion than at any point in human history. Castro had closed every casino and outlawed all gambling, yet this was a man who was willing to risk destroying the world itself rather than cave an inch against the American way of life.

"The monuments here mean nothing." Alfonso laughed. "Fidel doesn't have a statue or a plaque anywhere. There's no cult of personality. It's these fucking people themselves and their culture that are bigger than any pyramid or Empire State Building. If Cuba contributed the eighth wonder of the world it would be the Cuban people themselves. You'll see. My friend lives close to here and you'll be staying with him at the house of Jesús. Tomorrow I'll send a friend over to get you who can be your tour guide, and I'll sort out getting you in contact with the boxers."

Montalvo turned off the Plaza and drove around a bend surrounded by groomed hills that merged with the jungle. Even in the shadows it was evident the area was heavily guarded by bereted soldiers either patrolling or staring out from treehouse-like towers. Motorbikes and a fleet of bicycles loaded down with girls passed by on the shoulder of the road as we turned down a quiet side street that Montalvo carefully navigated to avoid potholes and stray cats skittering across the pavement. I could see children playing stickball on the next street under a flickering streetlamp. As we neared, the streetlamp cut out and Montalvo stopped the car, his headlights the only illumination left for their game.

At night in a broken, new place it's easy to lose your thoughts and find them drifting toward people you care about who are holding bad cards. Sometimes they have their own deck and sometimes they've invited someone else's into their lives. You think about faces you've loved getting older. I was warned Havana was a heavy place on a lot of people. Many lives worn out searching for things they can't find.

"You see the small man pitching to his son?" Alfonso asked.

"Both are wearing the Industriales baseball caps. Industriales are the New York Yankees of Cuba. That's Jesús and Jesusito. They'll look after you. Jesús has a little apartment attached to their home."

I got out of the car with my bags just as Jesús lofted his pitch well over his son toward me. "¡*OYE!*" Jesus hollered, as the kids laughed. "Think fast, gringo!"

8

PUNCHING YOUR WEIGHT

Cannery Row in Monterey in California is a poem, a
stink, a grating noise, a quality of light, a tone, a habit, a
nostalgia, a dream. . . . Its inhabitants are, as the man once
said, "whores, pimps, gamblers, and sons of bitches," by
which he meant Everybody. Had the man looked through
another peephole he might have said, "Saints and angels
and martyrs and holy men," and he would have meant the
same thing. —John Steinbeck

JUST BEFORE DAWN MY APARTMENT was caught in the crossfire of roosters on the rooftops scattered across the block declaring morning. There was a knock on the door; completely disoriented, I opened it to find Jesús still wearing his Industriales baseball cap from the night before, holding a tray of sliced fruit while his son handed me a thermos of coffee. Jesusito was wearing the same cap as his dad and might have been eleven, but they were nearly the same height at around five feet. They shared the same kind face and intelligent eyes.

"My friend, breakfast is early at our house. My English no goo'. No baa', but no goo'. I have to go work soon."

"Where do you work?"

"I am an engineer. First I wanted to introduce you to your *barrio*. Finish breakfast and we go meet our neighborhood before your friend come to show you Kid Chocolate and boxing in Habana Vieja."

"Do you guys sleep with those Industriales hats on?" I asked them.

His son looked up at his father for clarity.

"Industriales is our team, my friend. Cubans love boxing, but baseball is life and death in my country. The stadium is five minutes from here. We go. You understand everything. Last night there was a riot in the sixth inning. The government sent the military over to Latinoamericano stadium. Today when you go into Habana Vieja, you ask your friend to take you to Esquina Caliente where they discuss the *béisbol*."

"How far are we from Old Havana?"

"An hour walk. But your friend will explain and show you how taxis work here in Havana. Much easier. The Ladas are for tourists and expensive. Ex-lawyers and doctors drive them and pimp *jineteras*—prostitutes—for tourists. The Cuban taxis are cheap, but you need Cuban pesos and some more Spanish. If *policía* stop a Cuban taxi with a tourist, they can lose their car. Be careful. Any Cuban on the street who walks with you can be stopped by the police and taken in for questioning. If he does not carry an ID card to show the *policía* he can be taken to the police station for the night."

"Are you serious?" I asked Jesús.

"*Claro*," Jesús said gravely, but cracked a smile almost as quickly.

"But we Cubans say that life itself is a joke to be taken very seriously. You'll see how the game is played. Eat and we meet my family and the rest of the block."

"Everybody is already awake?"

"Of course. This neighborhood is your home now while you stay with us."

My mother has lived in the same house for the last thirty-two years (we moved there when I was three) and we hardly ever knew our neighbors, let alone anyone on our block. When FOR SALE signs went up and new people moved in around the neighborhood, nobody ever welcomed them. I have a close friend that I've known since I was five. He lived two blocks from me during our childhood and I visited his family home hundreds of times and was never invited for dinner. A lot of homes I visited as a child sounded a kind of silent alarm when you stepped through the door that seemed to say, "Welcome! *When exactly are you leaving again?*" And here was my first taste of Havana, where you were supposed to be trespassing safely into the tragedy of Cuban lives caught beneath the wreckage of a broken system. Maybe Cuba was frozen in time, but this first glimpse into the human cost I was warned about instead mirrored the breakdown of families and neighbors and support systems where I came from.

As dawn broke, Jesús, holding his son's hand, their small family sausage dog in pursuit, escorted me to each front door on the quiet, leafy street. From every home I could hear radios or televisions talking about Elián González and returning the boy home to his country and family. More marches were planned. More speeches. From what I could gather, Castro had found yet another winning angle, by making his adversaries in Florida look like fanatics defending a kidnapping. The best argument made against sending the boy back to his father and country was that doing so amounted to child abuse. How could any child wish to live in such a society inflicting so much harm? And this protest against child cruelty offered from the wealthiest nation on earth that also permits one child in five to grow up below the poverty line.

We knocked on the front door of the home across the street belonging to Cucho, a Ricardo Montalbán lookalike eighty-one-year-old who had received his house from a state-run lottery many decades before. Cucho was the patriarch of the twelve family members residing in his home. We were invited in for coffee served in shot glasses as I was introduced to his family, each female leaning over to give and receive a kiss on the cheek. Cucho had worked at the Hotel Nacional in the 1940s, when it was run by gangsters like Lucky Luciano, and moved over to the Havana Hilton at the end of the '50s, right up until Fidel Castro rolled in and set up his government headquarters in the top two floors at the newly named Habana Libre. Cucho was also the neighborhood CDR (Committee for the Defense of the Revolution), a neighborhood watch program that escalated in darker times into spy operations that reported to the government on fellow citizens.

Cucho's neighbor was a frail young doctor with a failing heart named Jorge, married to a Penelope Cruz–sumptuous wife named Nancy. Ernesto lived in the next home, 250 pounds of seething bitterness as he stared down a government-required year's wait to join his wife, Blanquita, who had just left to join some of her family in Spain. Cuba's answer to Doogie Howser, Manolo, a surgeon in his forties who looked like a teenager, lived by himself after a divorce. As we had another *cafecito* with Manolo, there were three separate deliveries of produce, freshly butchered chickens, and cement brought over in a little dragged wagon. "Have you heard the word *palanca* before?" he asked in perfect English.

I shook my head.

"*Palanca* is slang for offering a helping hand. Since you literally cannot survive in this country without breaking the law, corruption is institutional. The black market economy is larger than the traditional economy. We all offer something to someone in exchange for something. So don't be surprised to see deliveries at all hours of the day of things that may seem very strange to you."

There was a knock at Manolo's door and Jesús got up to answer it. He returned to the dining room with a linebacker-sized dark-skinned Cuban, not much older than me, dressed in matching canary-yellow dress shirt and pants. He stared at me with such warm anticipation I felt like I was meeting a pen pal I'd been corresponding with for years.

"Hello, my friend! I'm Lesvanne." I was quickly discovering that every Cuban deserved his own eponymous sitcom. "You must be the writer boxer I have heard so much about. Obviously Hemingway helped bring you here, I take it? Of course he did. Montalvo and Alfonso asked me to show you around and help you with finding your way in our city. Today I take you to Rafael Trejo gym to find a trainer, too, no?"

"I would love that," I said.

"Also transportation." Jesús grabbed my shoulder. "Walk around until he has more of a tan and then show him our taxis and get him some Cuban pesos."

"Of course." Lesvanne smiled.

"Where did you get these clothes?" Manolo teased him, pinching a sleeve. "These are not from Calle Obispo."

"What's Obispo?" I asked.

"Obispo is a street for tourists," Lesvanne explained casually. "I was just in Miami and brought back some clothes. Only three weeks in Miami visiting some family."

For both Jesús and Manolo this was a bombshell they endured in silent shock. I was fairly confused by how matter-of-fact Lesvanne was about a journey such a high percentage of his countrymen had died trying to make. His tone suggested that of a man taking a whirl on the Staten Island ferry. Who exactly was this person that Alfonso had lined up as my guide? Who exactly was Alfonso?

Suddenly Lesvanne's face twisted in agony. "*¡MariCÓN!* I gave my ass a paper cut this morning. Cuba*neo*. The first luxury I miss from Miami and Gringolandia is the availability of toilet paper. A page from José Martí's poetry slit me open this morning and I am still bleeding."

Lesvanne put his hand on my shoulder and turned his wide, conspiratorial smile toward me. "Obispo is the Hemingway tourist street. The El Floridita bar where Hemingway would have drank himself to death, if not for the suicide. La Bodeguita del Medio for the mojitos is five minutes, but every Cuban knows he never drank mojitos there and the owners just made it up. There are no better capitalists than communists. And the Ambos Mundos hotel where he wrote *For Whom the Bell Tolls* is near the bottom of Obispo. Fidel carried that book with him in the mountains to help learn guerrilla warfare. At Obispo there is much shopping, too, if you have tourist dollars to spend. The high-end *jineteras* work Obispo for the lonely tourists who wish to pretend they can seduce all the pretty Cuban girls."

Jesús laughed. "Should we arrange a girl for him tonight?"

"He doesn't need a pimp." Manolo smiled. "I'm sure you can find the right girl on your own. You come back and tell us everything or we'll report you to Cucho."

As soon as we left our block, Lesvanne informed me he needed a couple glasses of *guarapo* for energy and led us zigzagging down a few streets to find some. "A girlfriend from Texas leaves tomorrow so I must have energy for her so she is faithful back home. I'm so madly in love with this woman. If you heard her accent calling my name! And she's big as a Texas woman should be. I love that. She's forty. So beautiful."

He pointed out the direction of some peso fruit markets and another supermarket for American dollars that had a security guard out front. "The tourist apartheid is everywhere. I can't walk with you into a hotel or a nice bar. It used to be illegal for us to carry even one American dollar." Lesvanne shook his head. "During the awful Special Period, one market existed that had actual supplies and good food while everything else had nothing. People were starving. We called this market with everything 'God's Market' at that time. Things are better now since that period, but still very difficult." Finally we arrived at an open garage that was surrounded by sweaty construction workers huddled in the shade wiping the foam from their lips and patiently holding out glass cups waiting for refills.

"This is a *guarapotería. Guarapo* was what the African slaves who first came to Cuba drank. Good for energy to work or to fuck really good if you meet the right girl. We love it. It's very good and fresh. You can find them all over Havana and have a glass for only a Cuban peso. There are twenty Cuban pesos to each converted peso for tourists. These two currencies are very important to be aware of because you will be cheated if you are not careful.

So be careful to get your change and to keep it when you first use the converted peso. Until you write a bestseller or win the heavyweight championship, Cuban pesos are good to have to use for transportation or food that tourists are not allowed to use. I'll show you how our taxis work soon."

I watched as a dwarf woman jammed huge stalks of sugar cane into a massive metal grinder that she worked over with a crank when the stalks were inserted deeply enough. She had the sneer of a male porn star as she worked. The dwarf's coworker was a woman who looked like she was born a hundred years before when the Platt Amendment was signed. She collected the juice from a pail and dumped it into carafes full of ice. Once the carafe was full with the milky-yellow juice she refilled the cups of the eager construction workers on their break. We waited our turn for a glass and I watched Lesvanne wipe the chilled foam off his lips before my glass arrived.

"You just came back from Miami?" I asked.

"Yes." He grinned shyly. "My first time."

"Your first time?"

"The first time I have traveled *anywhere* in my life outside of this . . . *place*. Miami is paradise. For a nonbeliever, it is the closest thing I have ever seen to heaven on earth."

"We're going to have a strange day together, aren't we?" I asked.

"What is a *normal* day in a place like this, which no one will ever believe existed two weeks after it's gone? Pick up a newspaper this morning in Miami, and things have never been worse here. Pick up *our* newspaper and things have never been better. That is the reality we live with every day of our lives. This is *normal* to us."

He was right: the only place where *normal* seemed halfway as slippery as here was in America. Guidebooks spoke of Havana as frozen in time like wreckage, but that was only true if you looked everywhere *but* at the people. When Napoleon first encountered the Sphinx he measured every inch of it. I didn't know how to do that here. I didn't have the right equipment. For the Cubans I saw, time had slowed in an entirely different way than I'd been told it would, along the edge of a blade. Life at the extremes is always slowed down, magnified, surreal. It was as if, all around me, forty-one years' worth of Cuban society was in the backseat of a car Fidel had used to run through one of the world's most profound red lights, and instead of finding oblivion as its consequence, it created a different kind of tragedy by just keeping going and going. It wasn't long before that Fidel was nominated for a Nobel Peace Prize *and* was having charges brought against him in Spain as a war criminal at the same time. Communism had petered out everywhere else and given way to the real revolutionary force with legs that swept the planet: capitalism. But here everyone was popping a tire on communism's last bend of memory lane.

Still, I wasn't sure how to approach the obvious question: *Why hadn't Lesvanne stayed in Miami?* How had he gotten out? Why wasn't Cuba's answer to Sophie's Choice something that devastated Lesvanne the way it seemed to everyone else?

Just then Lesvanne's name was hollered from down the block. We looked over and saw a large woman smiling as she held the hands of four little girls wearing red scarves and school uniforms at her sides. As I finished another glass of *guarapo*, Lesvanne patted my shoulder and headed in their direction to say hello. "I come right back. This is a close friend of my mother. I *love* this woman." The construction workers and I watched him kiss the cheek of each member of the group and offer a bear hug to the woman that lifted her off the ground until she squealed and playfully flailed her arms to be put down. The girls all reached over to take Lesvanne's hands as they walked back up the street toward me. Lesvanne introduced the group and each child stared up until I bent down to say hello and offered a cheek for them to kiss. I kissed the cheek of Lesvanne's mother's friend and she apologized before insisting the children were late for school and they had to leave. The construction workers around us waved at the children and the children smiled and waved back.

"Is everyone here so comfortable with strangers?" I asked.

"But you're not a stranger, you're a *visitor* to our home."

"One of the first things I was taught as a kid was not to talk to strangers. Stranger equals danger."

"But this is not protection. This is just instilling fear. This is just propaganda. Of course there is a risk to trusting your environment. There are bad people and accidents in life, some are avoidable and some are not. But if you don't trust there is a guarantee you will lose all things available to you only through trust. To sacrifice that for a false sense of security is *protecting* children?"

I shrugged.

"Well." Lesvanne shrugged back. "If you have something to lose, that is very logical. In Miami I saw many walls protecting houses. Here all the walls are falling down. The nice cars in Miami all had alarms. Here almost nobody can afford a car. There the division is very important in their society and the fear of the poor trespassing on the rich is on everyone's mind. Look at all the guns there people feel they need to defend themselves from their own neighbors. Miami has both extremes. Of course here we are nearly all poor. What is there to steal? Even the most moral believers in the values of the revolution must steal from the govern-

ment with corruption to support their families, but there is little
to steal from each other."

"If there was something to steal, *would* people steal here?" I
asked.

"With this much difficulty and how much we rely on others
to survive—I don't think so. Even if you could escape responsibility, you could not escape seeing the damage. There are no strangers for us in Havana."

"And in Miami?"

"In Miami everyone is your stranger. You would not know who
lives next door. Look at the mansions protected from everyone.
But I miss many things I saw in Miami tremendously. It is impossible to have anything I saw there here. That is why, when I'm
ready, I will make Miami my home. When I am ready. And I
could never leave without my wife. Let's go to Centro Habana and
I can show you my photos from Gringolandia."

I offered to pay for a taxi, but Lesvanne insisted we hitchhike.
We walked over to a busy street and he flagged down a motorcycle with a sidecar in minutes. He sat behind the driver and
pointed for me to take the adjoining seat. Our engine snarled at
stray cats darting across the traffic as we headed back to the Plaza
and Che's monument.

We took a smoother road into the city with the Havana Libre's penthouse peeking over the palmy skyline as buzzards
swerved above us in the early morning cool before the real heat
of day arrived. Elián González's face was on signs and T-shirts
all throughout the city. Lesvanne pointed toward lone musicians
serenading the jungle with trumpets. We drove past a bus station overwhelmed with lines snaking around the block. Hitch-
hikers were everywhere waiting for rides into work, students to

the university, families trying to get home. After a bumpy climb skirting the border of a columned monument worthy of a Roman emperor, Lesvanne mentioned the university was around the corner. The Napoleon museum was just behind it, he shouted. He leaned close to the driver's ear and mentioned Coppelia as our destination. The driver nodded and accelerated toward a red light at an intersection like a kamikaze and picked up speed as we swung past the grandeur of the front steps of the university until we screeched to a stop under the towering shadow of the Habana Libre, just across the street from a ballerina's crossed slippers on Coppelia ice cream stand's famous sign. Under the sign hoards were already lined up to grab a bowl.

"It's a short walk from here to Calle Neptuno, where we can catch a ride into Habana Vieja. You can hail your first Cuban taxi. Hold out two fingers to the first old American car and if the driver has room and stops, you tell him 'Capitolio.' Say nothing else. I need some more *guarapo* for tonight. After the photos."

"What's tonight?" I asked.

"After we find you a trainer . . . This woman who stole my heart last year just arrived on the island again from Oklahoma. This girl is amazing. I can't disappoint this girl. You must see the letter she wrote me."

"Aren't you married?"

"Of course. To the love of my life. I will show you photos of my wife with the photos of Miami. This area is Vedado, the edge of Vedado and Centro. Centro is very poor. My mother is in a bad part of Centro near the Malecón where many buildings are falling down. Many have no running water and blackouts happen with frequency. But it's very beautiful there, too."

As we walked toward the ocean and his mother's house, Les-

vanne explained how he supported his family. He slept with
wealthy American tourists—preferably middle-aged, large, divorced, and with children back home—for gifts provided they
weren't from California. The women of California were to be
avoided at all costs no matter how attractive they were. Lesvanne
was a man of principle. Californian women never returned his love
letters.

"You like this more mature type of woman because they are
the most generous with you?" I asked.

"Never." He laughed. "Because I find this type of woman to
be the most desirable! They are real women in their full expression of femininity! And with an American accent, too, that is the
ultimate turn-on for me."

But Lesvanne's biggest problem as a *jinetero* with these female
tourists was that he couldn't stop falling in love with his prey. He
fell madly in love with all of them and spent most of his life lick-
ing his wounds from the heartbreak of them not writing him once
they returned home.

"You want them to marry you so you can leave?"

"Never. I'm married already to the love of my life. They should
move here until I'm ready to leave for Miami with my wife."

Lesvanne led us away from the leafy open squares and private
homes of Vedado into the cramped, dusty streets of Centro Habana. Chinese bicycles jerked down the street over potholes as stray
dogs and cats combed for scraps. Children played stickball with
rocks. As we moved deeper into the neighborhood more and more
eyes looked out at us behind the bars guarding front doors and
windows. A hundred radios blared from apartments. Pedestrians
stopped on the sidewalks and hollered "*¡Oye!,*" only to have bas-
kets lowered from balconies with a string offering a wrench or a

battery or an article of clothing. The neighborhood gave every indication of being a slum yet the mood was entirely unlike any·of
the Western ghettos I'd visited in my life. Men hissed at women
from all corners, yet the women would just smile coyly and laugh.
Nobody appeared to fear anyone else. I'd never seen women walk
with such self-possession and pride. But then, of course, there
weren't magazine stands anywhere to remind them of how ugly
they were.

At Lesvanne's mother's apartment he introduced me to his
mother, who had a cold and remained in her rocking chair without getting up. A framed portrait of her at fifteen was behind her,
facing me, above a cupboard. The two versions of the same woman's face smiled at me before she turned back to the television. She
was intently watching a roundtable discussion on Elián González.
They showed images of the boy's father and then cut to a million
people gathered to listen to Fidel giving a speech about him.

"What do you make of this Elián González thing?" I asked
Lesvanne.

"There's a joke about when the Pope came to Havana a couple
of years ago. Fidel rode with him in the pope mobile on the
Malecón. It was such a nice day they opened the roof and the Pope's
hat flew off from the sea breeze and blew into the ocean. Fidel
jumped out and hopped into the ocean without getting wet. He
walked on the water to grab the Pope's hat floating on the waves.
After Fidel returned the hat to the Pope the next day's headlines
about the event came in from *Granma*, our newspaper: 'Fidel proves
he is a god. He walks on water.' And then the Vatican newspaper: 'Pope performs miracle allowing Fidel to walk on water.' And
in the Miami newspapers: 'Fidel can't swim.'"

Lesvanne grabbed a scratched, beat-up digital camera, fetched some batteries from a drawer, and kissed his mother good-bye as we left her home.

As we made our way back to Calle Neptuno with him still searching through the camera to find his Miami photos, he was stopped in the street dozens of times. People hollered out from their homes and invited us in for coffee. Kids egged him on to kick a soccer ball around or play *béisbol*. Storekeepers left their shops to reach out and shake his hand and give him a hug. Old women selling sweets and flowers asked about his mother. He kept embracing people over and over with affection and warmth. Every time he tried to show me a photograph people came over to look and ask questions about his trip to Miami. Twice a policeman guarding a corner saw us walking together and asked Lesvanne to produce his identity card. They asked me in broken English if he was following me and if I wanted him to leave me alone.

A few paces away from the police officer Lesvanne gently shook his head. "You see how shamefully we treat our own citizens here?" He returned to his camera and showed me a few photos of his common-law wife and a few hundred photos of the American tourist female "friends" he'd made since he was fifteen. "I love all of these beautiful women. I miss all of them." Finally he located Miami inside his camera. Nearly all of the photos were an inventory of the materialistic orgy he had partaken of in Miami Beach. There were hardly any people in his photos, just things. They were things Lesvanne saw that he was determined to own once he moved to America and got busy making a success of himself: Hummers, houses, pools, jewelry, plastic-breasted women on posters at gift shops, bars, boats, condos. Lesvanne's favorite outfit, which he bought in Miami, was what he wore nearly every day since his return, and he washed it every night until it was blindingly bright.

I asked him if his American "friends" presented any kind of problem with his "wife" and he asked why it should.

"Would you like to see a video of my wife?" he asked.

I nodded.

All I could make out from the camera monitor were blurs of undulating color.

"What am I looking at here?"

"That's her gallbladder. Isn't she *beautiful*?"

"Come again?"

"Isn't she beautiful?"

"I still don't know what I'm looking at," I said.

"You're looking inside my wife. This is from an operation I filmed."

Later, when I could breathe again, I asked him why he would film his wife on the operating table having her gallbladder removed.

"Because I love *all* of her, man. Inside and out. I want to know all of her."

I didn't say anything until he'd finished showing all the pictures.

I'd lost count of how many people he'd kissed and hugged hello on our walk. It threw me because after ending my first long-term relationship I went months before I realized that I was having no human physical contact. How did that happen?

"So you want all this shit once you're settled in Miami?" I asked him.

"Of course I do. I've never had *anything* here. I'd like to work for these things."

"Okay. You get all that shit—Hummer, house, pool, hot wife, jewelry, yacht. That whole photo album of other people's stuff becomes *your* stuff. You're loaded. Then you're happier than here?"

"Why not? I could bring the things I love here over there and have the stuff to enjoy also."

"Okay, so you're loaded but maybe you're also afraid of losing everything all the time. You're afraid your wife is going to take you for half if she divorces you. You have to live in a gated community because you're afraid of everyone. You have no sense of community or even give a fuck about your neighbor. Your kids don't respect you and just want money to buy shit to distract themselves from being bored all the time. All the old people you know are in old folks' homes because nobody wants to deal with them. You can't be friends with any kids because everyone will think you're a pedophile. You can't hug any guys because they're afraid you're gay or *they're* gay or *everyone* is gay. You can't really touch *anybody* without second-guessing it."

"If I couldn't touch anyone I'd *die*, man. I'd die. This country is a fucking cage. My island is a zoo. Without this contact life would be unlivable."

Once we crossed the invisible border of Paseo del Prado into Old Havana, Lesvanne led us south, away from the elegant entrance to the Prado promenade guarded by lion statues and past the Hotel Inglaterra, Graham Greene's old stomping grounds. A group of musicians were covering kitschy Buena Vista Social Club hits for sunburned European tourists smoking cigars and sipping mojitos outside the hotel, waited on by locals. Some older bachelors had young local girls at their sides fawning over them.

"This is the new Cuba greeting visitors with open legs," Lesvanne remarked. "Even if we had the money, ordinary Cubans are forbidden inside these hotels. Before the revolution, blacks could not visit hotels, some beaches, or even enter parks. Fidel changed that. Blacks became proud of being Cuban, too. But now this *new* tourist apartheid has begun to replace the money we have lost from Russia after their collapse. We call this *resolver.*"

Lesvanne pointed across the street to Havana's Parque Central and the Esquina Caliente (Hot Corner), a group gathered near a giant statue of José Martí pointing accusingly in the direction of the United States. Esquina Caliente was a forum where the Cuban government had designated a small mob of fanatical *béisbol* fans "professional fans," charged with engaging in screaming matches of almost homicidal intensity about the merits of current players, teams, and other unresolvable historical debates. Several debates were going on at once inside the crowd of perhaps seventy-five men, their women and children seated nearby on benches relaxing under the shade and snickering at choice sound bites delivered by the men.

"This is for *baseball*?" I asked.

"They look like they're all ready to commit murder." Lesvanne smiled and shook his head. "But in all the years I have watched them, I have never even seen them come to blows. This is one of the only places in my country where you can debate everything in the code of baseball. Even defections can be discussed if done carefully."

Beyond the men, Lesvanne pointed, was Obispo and tourist alley. We walked to the edge of Central Park and crossed the boulevard so Lesvanne could buy a peso ice cream from a vendor. I noticed more policemen on the corners glaring at Lesvanne, who now walked a little less freely under their surveillance. "Do the police look at you like that because I'm with you?" I asked Lesvanne. He nodded before lifting his chin toward the Capitolio, Cuba's bizarro replica of Washington's Capitol Building that was built in 1926 by a U.S. construction firm. Dollar portrait photographers were setting up their hundred-year-old cameras just below the fifty-five great front steps leading up to the entrance of the Capitolio while a couple shriveled, dolled-up "authentic" old Cuban women with unlit baseball bat–sized cigars between their teeth waited to pose with some tourists.

A friend stopped Lesvanne in the street and asked him about seeing some boxing at Kid Chocolate the following day. A regional tournament was about to start.

"How close are we to Kid Chocolate?" I asked both of them.

"It's right beside us! Twenty steps."

Lesvanne started drifting up the sidewalk with his ice-cream cone as I followed. He pointed his melting cone toward the chipped mural of Kid Chocolate's face smiling teasingly behind an ancient, rusting fence locked with chains that looked as if they'd been recovered from the bottom of the ocean.

They had named the auditorium after one of Cuba's greatest champions. Eligio Sardiñas Montalvo was a boy who used to fight in the Old Havana streets for change back in the 1920s before he earned the nickname Kid Chocolate. As Jack Johnson had done before him in the United States, Chocolate learned to fight where the money was most available, mostly in battles royal paid for and attended by whites. A handful of blindfolded men, sometimes as many as ten, would fight until the last man standing could claim victory and the prize money. Before he'd left his teens, Kid Chocolate won every one of his 162 fights. In 1931, at the age of twenty-one, he became Cuba's first professional world champion. Chocolate was so popular with women he'd defended his title dozens of times while suffering from untreated syphilis. He was such a confident champion he was often found in bars with a woman under each arm, freely drinking and smoking in the days leading up to his title defenses. After victories in America, where he had a house in Harlem, Chocolate would return to the streets of Old Havana in a new car and shower the fans who swarmed him with flowers and coins. He'd died an alcoholic in grueling poverty in 1988, long after most of the world had believed he'd already died.

"Brinicito." Lesvanne laughed. "We have bad luck about seeing boxing here. Today there is none. But I think we have good luck with the man you're looking to train you."

"What?"

"Look in the grocery store beside us. You see the man in the Cuba tracksuit with his back to us? You see the man with the newspaper under his arm? Héctor's always reading. That's him."

The grocery store across from the entrance to Kid Chocolate had a giant security guard working the front door. I couldn't see anyone past his bulk. Someone finished paying at the counter and as he left the store I saw the sleeve of a red jersey filled out with a broad shoulder and a flash of a shaved head. After another person was finished at the register, I watched this man reach into his back pocket and produce several plastic bags for the checkout girl to place the items he'd purchased. His face was sullen yet his body language was confident. He pointed eagerly through the glass counter at chewing gum and a small bar of chocolate. The checkout girl teased him, reaching over to tap his tummy. Millimeters before contact he snatched her hand—savored her startled shudder for a split second—only to squeeze it gently with affection. She nodded and they kissed each other on the cheek good-bye.

"You see?" Lesvanne reached into his own back pocket and held a fistful of his own plastic bags. "A two-time Olympic boxing champion like Héctor is just like any other Cuban who wants to go grocery shopping. He could have left and made millions anywhere else on earth, but here he has to wait in line and bring his own bags. We *all* carry those bags because none of our stores have them."

"*That's* Héctor Vinent?"

"*Claro qué sí.* Maybe a little heavier than his fighting days, but that's Héctor Vinent Charón. Watch—*¡HÉCTOR! ¡CAMPEÓN! ¡OYE!*"

Héctor looked out the window at us without smiling and reflexively held up a fist and winked.

"Jesus fucking Christ," I gasped. "It is him."

"He doesn't live any better than someone selling peanuts in the street."

As I looked on I couldn't help trying to imagine stumbling upon Joe DiMaggio at a supermarket or Jack Nicholson waiting in line to catch the bus. Maybe it was more like unearthing a Cézanne while rummaging through piles of used Ikea prints at a garage sale. This was a human being who represented a deliberately uncashed winning sweepstakes ticket. Like any of the elite Cuban athletes, Héctor Vinent, in the bloom of his career, encompassed the most expensive human cargo left on earth. There were over twenty thousand boxers officially employed by Cuba. If a fraction of them along with the cream of the *béisbol* crop washed onto American shores tomorrow, they would be worth billions on the marketplace.

When I first saw him, Héctor was twenty-eight, maybe thirty pounds over his fighting weight, and he was banned from competing for his country for the last four years by the most powerful political forces in Cuba. It happened after two of his teammates defected at the Atlanta Olympics in 1996, leaving him to live out the rest of his life as a kind of living double-exposed photograph of the future he gave up in America versus the one awaiting the rest of his life in Cuba. Maybe his headline was a completely different cautionary tale depending on which side of the Florida Straits you told the story on, but staring at him, the fine print was completely illegible to me.

Héctor shook the hand of the security guard who held the door open and glared at me with a mixture of curiosity and wariness.

"Héctor?"

"*Campeón,*" he grunted, offering his hand. "*¿Boxeador?*"

I nodded.

Héctor turned to Lesvanne, who turned to me. "I'll ask him if he'll train you. How much are you willing to pay?"

"Whatever he thinks is fair."

Héctor proposed to train me at Rafael Trejo the following week for six dollars a day, nearly half his monthly wage for training children there. We could train as often as I liked, but there was also a daily surcharge of two dollars for the women who looked after the gym for the state. Palms had to be greased. Lesvanne shrugged and said it all sounded reasonable to him.

"What's the going rate for private lessons from two-time Olympic champions where you come from?" asked Lesvanne.

"*¿Está bien?*" Héctor asked me.

"*Sí,*" I answered. "Lesvanne, I don't know the word but please tell him it's an honor to meet him and I'm grateful for this."

Before Lesvanne could translate, a beautiful girl in a red dress passed behind Héctor, and he caught me following her movements. He laughed and quickly turned to look at her before crying out, "*¡Oye! ¡Mi amor! Mi amiga. ¡Yaima!*" The girl stopped, recognized Héctor, and they embraced. Héctor introduced Lesvanne and me to Yaima, who delicately leaned in to be kissed on the cheek by each of us. After I kissed her she leaned back and assessed me with a slowly curling smile. Héctor took a step toward Lesvanne and his gruff voice whispered gently into Lesvanne's ear.

"He says you look a little lonely and if you'd like to have Yaima visit your apartment tonight or be your girlfriend while you stay in Havana, none of that would be a problem."

9

LA LUCHA

Don't try to understand me too quickly.

—André Gide

A MONTH GOES BY and the best I can do to explain anything to myself is to admit how many things don't work here, but they don't seem to work the other way, either. In Old Havana, the names of the streets before the revolution provided a glimpse into the city's state of mind. You might have known someone who lived on the corner of Soul and Bitterness, Solitude and Hope, or Light and Avocado. After the revolution, they changed the names and put up new signs, but if you asked directions from a local today you'd get the old names. They all meant something personal to the people who lived on those streets. That *avocado* grew in the garden of a convent. That *hope* was for a door in the city wall before it was torn down. That *soul* refers to the loneliness of the street's position in the city. Sometimes these streets lead you to dead ends and other times you stumble onto cathedrals, structures built with the intention of creating music from stone. The sore heart Havana offers never makes you choose between the kind of beauty that gives rather than the kind that takes something from you: it does both simultaneously.

While guidebooks might tell you that time collapsed here, another theory says that in Latin America, all of history coexists at once. Just before the triumph of the revolution, progress took shape in ambitious proposals made by American architects to erect grand skyscrapers all along the Malecón seawall offering a fine view and convenient access to a newly constructed multicasino island built in the bay. To accommodate the gamblers, vast areas of Old Havana were to be demolished and leveled for parking access. In 1958, Graham Greene wrote, "To live in Havana was to live in a factory that turned out human beauty on a conveyor belt." Yet this beauty the people of Cuba unquestionably possess walks hand in hand with their pain. Whoever you might encounter in this place lacking the ability to walk or even to stand for whatever reason will inevitably remain convinced they can dance. When Castro was put on trial in 1953 by Batista's government and asked who was intellectually responsible for his first attempt at insurrection, he dropped the name of the poet José Martí. From the little I'd learned of it, the revolution's hold on Cubans resembled not so much poetry as the chess term *zugzwang*: you're forced to move, but the only moves you can make will put you in a worse position. Cuba had become an entire population of eleven million people with every iron in the fire doubling as a finger in a dike.

I hitched a ride in a gypsy cab most of the way to the boxing gym with a black Cuban who gave me the dime tour of the greatest potholes in Havana. He was literally serenading the potholes before we could even see them. Out my window there were lineups and police icily keeping their eyes peeled. "¿*Último?*" someone shouted as they joined the line, followed by another "¡*Último!*" confirming who was the last person in the line. This was how people found their place in queues all over the city. The driver told me what was clearly an old joke: stop anywhere in Havana for five seconds and you'll start your *own* lineup.

I looked up at clotheslines strung between columns, women in curlers leaning against the railings of their balconies. I saw tourists snapping photos of the architecture of a building where Lesvanne took me to visit a friend. We had coffee while his family complained incessantly about the broken stairwell and leaky roof. Finally the harbor came into view with the waters that in the early twentieth century were banned to fishermen because of all the bodies being thrown from the Morro Castle by government thugs. Trumpet players on the Malecón blew at sea puddles on the pavement. A policeman checked a man's identification while staring at a cruise ship coming in on the horizon. We drove a little farther and the whole colonial theme park faded in the distance.

The driver lit a cigarette and reached back to press play on a little broken-down ghetto blaster in the backseat, and Nat King Cole's voice came overenunciating in Spanish through the speakers. The driver imitated it and grinned wide: "*Pen-sannn-doh.* I luuuv it. He recorded it in Havana. My father saw him in a nightclub perform before the revolution.

"My friend, did you know they needed three tries to find Havana before they got it right?" he asked me.

I looked at his face and asked him for one of his cigarettes.

"Did you know that originally Cuba was named 'Juana' after Juana La Loca, the insane daughter of Ferdinand and Isabella? They were Columbus's patrons. All of that little girl's relatives have been screwing with our lives ever since. We can stop for·a beer and I could tell you more."

"I'm training at the gym very soon."

"But you're smoking."

"I'm a very complicated man."

We shared an uneasy silence for a moment or two.

"I could pick you up after your training. My friend, I know some great girls I could introduce you to. Any color you like. I have a business card."

He conducted a frantic search of the vehicle before he produced the business card, but he was clearly quite proud of it once he straightened out the wrinkles with the side of his hand against the dash.

"Thank you."

"My friend, I like to drink Hatuey beer. I once drank a beer with Ernest Hemingway in San Francisco de Paula when I was a boy. Do you like our beer?"

"I don't drink."

"My father was an alcoholic, too." He winked. "But you get over it eventually. Let me tell you a story about my favorite beer. When the Spanish first came here an Indian chief named Hatuey sailed from Hispaniola to warn the people. The resistance was brave but it wasn't much. Hatuey was burned at the stake. Just before they burned him they offered him a last-minute conversion so he could enter heaven. Hatuey asked whether there were any Christians in heaven. After they assured him that there certainly were, he told them he'd rather go to hell than anywhere where there were people as cruel as the Spaniards. In Gringolandia Pocahontas was a little friendlier when John Smith arrived. Maybe all there is in this world is underdogs and whores."

"They named your *beer* after this person?"

"Can you imagine a greater honor to bestow?"

The silence went by a little smoother this time.

"My friend, I can introduce you to some very nice, clean girls."

"My schedule is a little booked. I have a backlog of about 4,500 'very nice, clean girls' I already have to meet."

"You haven't seen *my* girls. You have my business card."

My boxing gym, Rafael Trejo, was located in what was once the cheapest red light district in the city, only a few minutes' walk from José Martí's childhood home, now converted into a museum. One of the largest funeral processions in Cuban history was for the notorious pimp Yarini Ponce de León, who was shot in a duel in the area.

These days most of the prostitution in the city is run, curiously, by cab drivers. Right after the revolution they reformed most of the prostitutes into cab drivers. Job reorientation. Now cab drivers are mostly composed of lawyers and doctors looking to scrounge enough tourist dollars to cover the basic needs of their family that their wages as professionals can't accomplish.

About the only thing you can trust in this neighborhood is that nothing is trustworthy to an outsider. I had my boxing gloves hanging off my bag and some of the small kids joyously raised their fists at me while their older siblings eyed my belongings. The neighborhood was a maze of narrow streets closely monitored by thieves. I figured if I was going to be passing through on a daily basis for appointments at the gym, I might as well just accept being robbed soon enough and probably with the use of a blade of some kind. All I brought with me was the money I owed Héctor and my gloves and skipping rope, as I didn't want to enter this place with suspicion or even caution. I elected to give into whatever toll the neighborhood expected from me and just said hello to anyone who looked me in the eyes no matter who they were. While, as anyone, I've never enjoyed being played for a sucker, I also can't remember experiencing anything worthwhile without trust regardless of how little trust was warranted. Trusting the world is a risk, while not trusting it is a *guarantee* you'll be left with nothing.

Trejo is one of the oldest boxing gyms in Cuba; it's outdoor, and every great champion the country has produced has passed through and was forged in the open air. Different sets of the same mildly sinister women who look like the Macbeth witches guard the entrance from tourists and procure a toll for entry, snapshots, or stories. The witches rest their chairs against a wall of photographs under portraits of great world or Olympic champions who spent time staining Trejo's lone ring with their blood and sweat.

Cuba's answer to Muhammad Ali, Teófilo Stevenson, was featured among the portraits, along with Félix Savón, who turned down even more millions than Stevenson to leave Cuba, but this time to fight Mike Tyson. Also José "Mantequilla" Nápoles, Kid Chocolate, and some other names I didn't recognize, and finally there was Héctor, attached by scotch tape in his Olympic heyday with his arm raised in victory. I paid the witches to tell me the stories behind the faces and in their words, always, more than any achievements in the ring, these boxers' greatest legacy was the money they refused to betray the revolution. It was strange to see the gleam of pride in their eyes as they envisioned the kinds of lives these men had forgone in favor of embracing their role as symbols of a cause greater than any individual. These men stood for the highest literacy rate in the world, universal health care, free education, better lives for their children and all Cubans. I listened and absorbed the reports of their virtues, but I knew full well that most Cuban champions were so desperate for money that many had sold off all their Olympic medals and even uniforms to the highest tourist bidder. That part of the Cuban sports legacy was omitted from their tales. So were the defections of boxers starting in 1967, five years after Fidel Castro banned all professional sports from the island. All those who had tried to leave, successful or not, had essentially committed social suicide: they ceased to exist in their native land.

Cuban eyes often look close to tears. Tears never seem far away because both their pain and their joy are always so close to the surface. There's an open wound that defines the national character and the tide of emotions is always raw and overwhelming. Kid Chocolate was my gateway drug into those emotions. They didn't have enough money for a bell to clang to announce the fights or declare the beginnings or ends of rounds, so they used an emptied fire extinguisher and a rusty wrench instead. My high school gym had more money sunk into it than the most famous arena residing in Cuba's capital city. Did that detract from the atmosphere or impact? Donald Trump named everything after himself while nothing in Havana, not even a plaque, had Fidel's name attached. Who would history remember? Nobody fighting there was paid to fight any more than anyone watching had paid to attend. Cigar and cigarette smoke curled into the rafters as bottles of rum were passed around and swigged in the audience. The place was packed and at first I assumed everyone was forced to attend these matches the same way seven-hour Fidel speeches invariably had hundreds of thousands of bored, nodding-off citizens in attendance at the Plaza de la Revolución. But it wasn't the case. All the faces still carried the same strain from what was going wrong outside Kid Chocolate, but they also knew they were watching sports in a way that the rest of the world could only dream about. That's why what I was looking at, at first, didn't even register as Cuban; it was an *American* wet dream of sport. At least while the fights lasted, it was pure.

No interviews. No cameras. No advertising. No commercial breaks. No merchandise. No concession stand. No thanking of sponsors. No luxury boxes. No Tecate or Corona ring girls. No autographs. No VIP seating. No scalpers outside. No venue named after a corporation or corporately owned anything, *anywhere*. No air conditioning or even fans to mitigate how fucking hot it was in there. No amenities of any kind, but instead you had a full auditorium of intensely proud people who didn't require cues to cheer or applaud. Without the incentive of money, I watched people fight harder in the ring than anywhere else I'd ever seen. And they fought this way before an audience who cheered louder than anywhere I'd ever heard. And nothing separated them. The best of the boxers might have lived on the same block as anyone in the stands. Sport wasn't an opium for these people; their culture was an opium for sport. Who walked into a museum anymore without asking how much the masterpieces had sold at auction for? If van Gogh captured the world's imagination in part for never being able to sell some of the most treasured works of human expression ever put to canvas, he was certainly *trying* to sell them. This society's experiment went further and they knew it: heroes weren't for sale. But how long could that last? How long could *anyone* resist not cashing in? And if no price was acceptable to sell out, what was the cost of that stance?

During the last fight of the evening, a hometown Havana kid was beating another boy from Sancti Spíritus terribly. So badly, in fact, that someone in the crowd raced down from the rafters and threw his bunched-up towel into the ring since the Sancti Spíritus coaches had refused to throw in *their* towel.

He'd cupped his hands to scream at the referee, "Alright then you son of a bitch, I'll spend the night in jail for *your* crime, you motherfucker!"

The crowd ignited as they watched that towel leave the man's hand in a sweaty clump and sail unfurling under the lights toward the ring, with the referee conspicuously unaware of the attempt on his life.

Héctor had arranged for me to sit ringside next to one of the trainers named Alberto Brea, along with the rest of the Havana team, and all of us betrayed our team's fighter in the ring to cheer on the heckler. When the towel found its target and compressed like an accordion against the referee's ear and we heard every last sweaty drop behind the wet slap of its impact, Brea nudged me: "This man is a noble martyr for Sancti Spíritus. If I was his father I would be proud."

Another coach turned to Brea: "What makes you think you *aren't* his father?"

Brea was delighted by this possibility—along with every other child on the team who heard it and doubled over laughing—but conceded, "He didn't get an arm like that from me. *Béisbol* was never my game."

As the protester stood on the stairs glaring at the referee and screaming obscenities, with both hands high over his head gesticulating wildly, the referee calmly halted the fight to pick up the towel and contemplate it in his hands for a moment before attempting to locate the heckler. Even the judges at ringside were having trouble keeping a straight face.

The rest of us in Kid Chocolate watched as the uniformed *policía* stormed down the steps to arrest the protester. He didn't flinch when the four cops grabbed his arms, shirt, and pants and began hauling him toward the exit. He kept his eyes on the referee in the ring and kept talking to him as though he were microphoned.

The referee patiently held on to his new towel while the commotion was dealt with.

But then something magical happened, after which *nobody* in the arena had a harder time holding their composure together than the referee.

Another towel entered the ring and lightly—almost *obediently*— touched down on the canvas near the referee's feet. Sancti Spíritus had finally had a chance to inspect the damage on their fighter and quit on his behalf.

There was agonized panic to get this point across to our arrested towel thrower before it was too late. The protester was in the doorway of the exit when he broke loose of the police grip long enough to look back over his shoulder and grasp the full meaning of the moment. Everyone collectively forgot to breathe as we all waited to see what he'd do next. Suddenly his hands shot up as he wailed with vindication, and even the police laughed as everybody got to their feet to whistle and cheer his achievement.

The referee gazed toward the arrested man, shook his head, and smiled as he waved the fight off.

When the revolution triumphed, one of the strange and beautiful sights across Havana was the destruction, by the thousands, of any and all parking meters. The mafia had collected all the money from those parking meters and much of it had been pilfered, along with hundreds of millions from the Cuban national treasury, by Batista and taken with him into exile in Spain.

I went outside into the parking meter–less night and walked over to the corner of the block and bought a peso ice cream from a pretty light-skinned Cuban girl reading a weathered and wrinkled-up celebrity magazine from the 1980s. She held the cone under the spout and pulled the arm of the machine, all the while hypnotized by a photograph of Madonna. She handed me the cone and reached up and took her hair in a fist trying out the hairstyle. I watched her for a bit trying other styles until the security guard from the little dollar grocery store next door began flirting with her. When she gave him a smile he turned with satisfaction in my direction.

The grocery store he was supposed to be guarding had dozens of people lined up outside the entrance, peeking through the windows into the glass display cases of chocolate, makeup, gum, toothpaste, soap, suntan lotion, American cigarettes, and other "luxury" items.

It was worse a few blocks down the street at the Adidas store on Calle Neptuno. You'd see kids buying sneakers at American prices—the equivalent of eight months' salary for a Cuban neurosurgeon—acting casual about the transaction. Phony designer T-shirts were available on the *mercado negro*. You could spot the occasional busted-up, discarded tourist cell phone carried like

a talisman in the hand of a teenager. Every now and again you'd
see useless, tossed-away cell phones carried around in the hands
of Cubans as a status symbol, their best attempt at conspicuous
consumption.

The designated tourist Lada taxis were waiting across the street
in front of the steps at the Capitolio and the drivers were all leaning over the hoods of their cars chatting and smoking with a few
of the drivers of horse-drawn carriages. The cabbies were some
of the best-connected men in Havana: girls, drugs, whatever you
need for your stay. "You don't like the food? Don't you know the
best meals are all cooked at secret locations? Would you like to
visit the private home that cooked for Steven Spielberg? Come,
my friend, let me show you. . . . Have you tried our cocaine yet?
Have you seen how we smoke joints through our nostrils? You
need a girl who will treat you right, not like the stuck-up ones you
have back home. I have an uncle who has several boxes of Trini-
dad Cigars stolen from Castro's personal collection for diplomats.
Don't worry, my friend."

Nothing alerts me to the fact that I'm out of my depth like pre-
emptive assurances of my safety. All the hustlers worked this area
of town day and night looking for tourists to ride. Which was fair,
because a hefty cross-section of tourists pretty much only fre-
quented the areas of Havana where they could give young Cuban
girls a ride.

Police were everywhere but lots of product—cigars, merchandise, even drugs—was being moved in secret stashes all over town.
Everybody had a friend or a relative who could get it for you.
Another herd of tourists arrived fresh off a cruise ship or from a
bus visiting from Varadero, where locals were no longer able to
vacation with their families. The government had forbidden them.

I watched them march through Parque Central headed for Calle Obispo and some Hemingway daiquiris at El Floridita, where the first daiquiri was invented and poured.

Past the entrance to Rafael Trejo, the sun blazed down and there were rows and rows of bleachers surrounding a ring, barely covered by a roof. For warm-ups, students raced up and down the bleachers and their footfalls were as loud as a New York express subway train until the coaches whistled them on to the next task. Car tires were set against an iron railing for boys to practice their combinations, snapping their punches. In place of bags, sacks were hung next to the tires. A tractor tire lay in the shade under the far-side bleachers, where an instructor swung a sledgehammer over one shoulder and then the other, plunging the hammer down and showing a kid the proper technique of incorporating the entire body with each swing and the mechanics of the weight transfer involved. The ring was the centerpiece of the gym, its canvas blood-and sweat-stained, with a little neighborhood mud smeared here and there. There was a lucky child who lived next door, on the second floor of his building, who spied with his friends on the action below from his window.

Héctor walks into Rafael Trejo in jeans and an undersized Cuban national volleyball team shirt that accentuates a growing paunch. I'm shadowboxing in the ring with half a dozen other students, all several years younger than me. Héctor has a book and a folded newspaper in one hand and one of the other coaches quickly hands him a bundled-up shoelace necklace with a whistle hanging off. Héctor lays the book and newspaper over the equipment table and drapes the necklace over his bowed head. It's a daily ritual with a ghostly nod to the elephant in our roasting, open-air gym. I can't help but try to imagine how he copes with the two Olympic gold medals that were placed around his neck in Barcelona and Atlanta, this future barely earning enough in a month to afford the cost of a movie ticket as his reward.

Héctor puts his hands on his waist and watches me expressionlessly.

"*¡Oye, Brinicito!* Three more rounds of shadowboxing, then we'll work."

I nod and look back at the ground and throw more combinations in the air, spilling more sweat over my shadow. The old ring creaks and moans under the collective feet finding their rhythm and transferring weight to give force to our blows at imaginary opponents.

I've taken Héctor to dinner a few times after our lessons but he's not interested in the conversation veering toward defection stories or even boxing, really. He's more interested in the fact that both of us are the only people at Trejo who bring in novels to read. He loves Hemingway and *Don Quixote*. He's desperate for more books the government won't permit locals to read. He enjoys the work of Gabriel García Márquez so deeply he asks if I could bring him Márquez in English when I come back to the island. He thinks it would be the best way to learn the language. Mostly Héc-.tor just seems grateful to enjoy a full meal without having to worry about the looming fight that in the past he'd have had to make weight for.

Héctor yells for another kid to imagine squishing a cigarette under his back toe when he throws his right hand. He's not turning it properly. *Where's your ass in that punch? How do you expect the weight between your shoulders to snap without the full extension of your punch? Where's your balance?* Héctor gestures to steal the cigarette from an onlooker's mouth and flick it into the ring to help the education along.

Three more rounds of the art of shadowboxing for me, a lifetime of battling against their shadow selves over in America for Héctor and any other Cuban boxer that remained on the island.

"Our athletes are and always will be an example for all" are words painted over a sign hanging in the entrance to Rafael Trejo. The same sign hangs over most boxing gyms across the country, I was told by the Macbeth witches for a tourist dollar. "Men's sacred values are beyond gold and money," Fidel once explained. "It's impossible to understand this, when you live in a world where everything is bought and sold and gotten through gold." Professional boxing had been banned for thirty-eight years at that time, since 1962, and, in part to vindicate Fidel's explanation, only a fraction of fighters from then until now had left. This was rarely if ever a story outside reporters gave much credence to, let alone bothered to explore. Tough to find a peg on which to hang that story.

But as I peeked up from my shadow at Héctor, unfurling his newspaper to read a few paragraphs of the state news, I wondered what was the example Héctor was meant to convey to the next generation of Cuban children by his choices? Or perhaps the better question was, what could be made of the powerful revolutionary figures taking Héctor's choice away before he ever had a chance to betray their ideals? In Cuba you could be convicted of crimes you were only *suspected* of committing, all under the Orwellian umbrella term of "dangerousness." Fidel hogged the credit for any athlete that stayed as proof of the revolution's triumph, but by the same logic, when boxers defected how much of a referendum was it about why all Cubans might be torn about remaining?

Héctor hadn't spoken freely to me much since I'd first met him, but I'd done some homework on him. Héctor Vinent Charón was born in Santiago de Cuba, an eastern province where the bulk of the best boxers are found. Many in that region, like Héctor, come from large families who suffered the worst before the revolution and were some of the biggest beneficiaries of the revolution's reforms. Massive literacy drives, eradicating obscene rates of death by curable diseases, lowering infant mortality rates below nearly all first-world countries, agrarian land reform, access to education, an emphasis on social justice that made a tangible impact across the country, an end to racial discrimination—a massive overhaul of a whole society conspiring to help the weakest and end widespread corruption and exploitation. The upper crust in Cuba got the shaft and most fled. While the ideals of the revolution resonated deeply with almost every Cuban I encountered, the results in so many areas, especially over the last ten years, had driven home just how untenable this regime in power truly was. But the United States and the embargo had rarely missed an opportunity to antagonize matters and essentially let the government off the hook in the eyes of many. Fidel's bogeyman was just as stubborn as he was.

Then again, Héctor was almost thirty and already the father of five children he was clearly struggling to support. He was only eight when the Mariel boatlift took place in 1980, during which ten thousand Cubans attempted to gain asylum at a Peruvian embassy. An exodus of 125,000 Cubans fled the country. "Fidel has just flushed his toilet on us," Maurice Ferré, the Miami mayor at that time, famously remarked. Héctor had won his first Olympic medal in 1992, just as Cuba entered its Special Period, after the collapse of the Soviet Union ended the Soviets' massive subsidies to the island. "We're in a Special Period," Fidel spoke before a crowd at that time. "Why? Because we're alone confronting an empire. . . . Only a weak, cowardly people surrenders and goes back to slavery."

Héctor won his second medal in Atlanta, as the Special Period's hardships reached their peak with widespread blackouts, fuel shortages, and starvation. The choice to remain for any Cuban, let alone an elite athlete, had never been more difficult. And Héctor was part of a continuum of Fidel's champions, meant to reject any offer to leave and be a proxy for Fidel and the revolution's values, displaying they were still strong enough to dominate those of Americans stepping into the ring and challenge America itself.

Héctor was a chubby young boy when he began training as a boxer, stepping into a broken-down gym called Los Songos to throw his first punches. It didn't take him long to get noticed and selected for entry into La Finca, the special elite school in Havana for boxers. The Cuban sports machine might have been the most effective apparatus on earth for uncovering and developing athletic talent and Héctor was exactly the kind of world-class athlete they were looking for. Héctor's talent was never inconspicuous. Barely into his teens, he left his family behind in Santiago and took the train across the country, and before long he became a national champion. He won the nationals six times in all. He won a junior world championship in Lima at age eighteen. By twenty, when the Barcelona Olympics rolled around, he cruised to a gold medal with a combined score of 85 points to his opponent's 11. The Cubans trounced the Americans at the Olympics that year, winning seven gold medals to the United States' one. Héctor had also proven, pound-for-pound, he was one of the greatest living fighters in the world. What made him even more enticing to foreign promoters was his professional style: he was a tenacious, brutal puncher who savored finishing off opponents and electrifying crowds.

I'd heard one of his eyes was damaged from a detached retina after the accumulation of punishment he endured over his hundreds of amateur fights and sparring. He'd given some interviews to foreign journalists using the injury as the reason his boxing career was finished. But in truth, after the 1996 Olympics, when his teammates Ramón Garbey and his best friend Joel Casamayor defected—Casamayor being the first Olympic champion ever to do so—Héctor took the brunt of the consequences back home for their actions. Héctor's fate was sealed when he was only twenty-four years old.

"*¡Oye!*" Héctor hollered and blew his whistle. "Come outside the ring. Today we spar a little."

"With whom?" I asked, climbing out of the ring.

"*Me.*" Héctor grinned and offered two thumbs he happily tugged back at himself. He put his arm over my shoulder and let loose a deep, growly laugh. "The Olympic Games are in Sydney soon. Maybe they'll let me make a comeback. I need some sparring just in case."

"Who is the best boxer Cuba is sending to Sydney?" I asked.

"Guillermo Rigondeaux," Héctor answered immediately. "*El mejor.*"

"No question?"

"*Por favor.* Nobody close. He's magnificent. But what a sad face he has! We both came from Santiago de Cuba. He came from a coffee plantation. He is only 118 pounds, but we've never seen anything like him. Most people like the big guys, but they are very limited in terms of skill. To be small you must have *everything*. Rigondeaux might be the most beautiful boxer I've ever seen. He is a little Stradivarius of a boxer. I'm friends with Félix Savón, the captain of the national team. A very simple but good man." (A running joke in the gym and across the island was Savón's Yogi Berra–like quote, "Technique is technique because without technique there's no technique.") "Savón has told me he will hand over his captaincy to Guillermo after these games. Only one gold medalist has defected, never someone that high profile. Who knows, Rigondeaux will turn twenty the day he wins his gold medal. He could easily be the first man in history to win four. Certain things in my country make his choices different than when I was twenty and won my first medal."

"The offers followed you everywhere you fought?"

"Everywhere." He laughed. "Suitcases of money popped open from ringside. Crumpled-up paper thrown into the ring with dollar figures just to talk. Just to *talk* more money than I would see in ten years living here."

"You like Dickens?" I asked Héctor.

"Yes, I like him."

"Aren't you Rigondeaux's ghost of Christmas Past?"

"A Christmas Carol was not so popular here." Héctor smiled. "Christmas was banned in Cuba for many years until the Pope visited our island and Fidel reinstated it. He did not reinstate El Duque, and so he escaped to the Yankees."

"But not you."

"Not me." Héctor shook his head, and when he looked away I wasn't sure if he was looking into his past or Rigondeaux's future.

10

THE OLD MAN AND THE SEA

Kilimanjaro is a snow-covered mountain 19,710 feet high,
and is said to be the highest mountain in Africa. Its west-
ern summit is called [by] the Masai "Ngàje Ngài," the
House of God. Close to the western summit there is the
dried and frozen carcass of a leopard. No one has explained
what the leopard was seeking at that altitude.

—Ernest Hemingway, *The Snows of Kilimanjaro*

It's HARD TO WALK in any direction here without bumping into politics. What King Midas was to gold, Fidel might be even more to politics. Sports took you there. Hemingway did, too. Like his metaphorical leopard, I'd wondered for a long time what America's most famous writer was seeking from Cuba for the last twenty years of his life. How could someone like him support Fidel? I'd heard the captain of his beloved *Pilar* had even gained his permission to carry explosives for the revolutionaries. How could America give Hemingway such a pass for this?

Hemingway and Castro only met once, in 1960. Very few

photographs of the meeting exist and the one movie camera filming their union lasts about as long as the Zapruder film. They met right after Fidel entered—and *won*—Hemingway's annual fishing tournament. Fidel was asked why he was so eager to meet Hemingway and casually explained that he'd always envied his adventures. Hemingway had lived in Cuba for twenty years leading up to and during the revolution. While Tolstoy had, in Hemingway's terminology, "gotten in the ring" with Napoleon, Hemingway—after taking on World War I, the Spanish Civil War, and World War II, with the Cuban revolution taking place in his own backyard—never went near Castro or what he was up against in print. To me, that was a far more compelling mystery than whatever that leopard was sniffing around for.

After training one day, I took the long way home along the sea, turning off the Prado promenade, with the Morro fortress and the lighthouse behind me. While I was training with Héctor, one of his students tapped me on the shoulder and warned me about not missing him fighting on HBO when I got home. "You'll see." His eyes sparkled. "Don't be surprised when you see me." Of course this was a kid who had zero access to HBO or any other American television that wasn't pirated and sold on the street. If he had been growing up in the 1990s he could have been thrown in jail for having so much as an American dollar on him.

It gnawed at me as a fisherman along the Malecón waved hello. An old fisherman with a mustache cast a hunk of bread just over the crest of the last wave that broke against the wall. A fish bit quickly and he reeled it in and removed his shoe in order to clunk the fish on the head and drop it wriggling into the pail nestled between his ankles. He rigged another hook and relit his peso "torpedo" cigar. Beyond the fisherman's line were some cruise ships headed for the harbor. Beyond them were warships. The fisherman wasn't paying attention to either. He stared at his line while the death rattle of the fish in the bucket petered out.

The day before, the staff had let me inside the Finca Vigía, Hemingway's house on a hill in the nearby town of San Francisco de Paula, about seven miles away from Havana. Five minutes outside of Havana by car and you're in a different world all over again. Modern technology assumes an even lower profile. I'd gone alone. A gypsy cab agreed to drive me there and back for five tourist dollars. Letting me inside the home was against the rules—too much to steal and no security cameras—but the staff made an exception after grilling me on some trivia. I was a terrible student who flunked nearly every subject in school, but I'd skipped a lot of classes and spent hundreds of hours in the library reading everything I could get my hands on about Hemingway's work and life.

After the revolution they'd converted Hemingway's home into the Hemingway Museum. Bullfighting posters, animal heads, horns, and antlers were everywhere, but far and away the most dominant feature was the personal library of 8,000 books along with his typewriter. The contents of the bookshelves represented one of the most profound displays of curiosity I'd ever encountered. I saw piles of first editions: Fitzgerald, Faulkner, Mailer, T. S. Eliot, Thomas Wolfe—even *The Catcher in the Rye.* I wanted very badly to steal that book. During World War II, not long after the liberation, J. D. Salinger had met Hemingway in Paris. It was a meeting that changed Salinger's life. Salinger had continued to write to Hemingway after the war. Hemingway knew who Holden Caulfield was long before the world did. However interested the world was in Hemingway, his library demonstrated he was even more interested in the world. The great seducers are always suckers. And what I loved about his home was feeling that Hemingway was the biggest sucker who ever lived; the world had never seduced someone so completely. And that mutual seduction put such smiles on the visitors I saw that day.

Everything in the house was left untouched since he'd died. There was alcohol still inside a handful of bottles in the living room lying beside a vast pile of magazines and newspapers he subscribed to. You were surrounded by his passion for bullfighting and the hunt in paintings and trophies hung all around the house. The bathroom had his chicken-scratch handwriting on the wall showing his battle with his weight and high blood pressure over the years. Beside the pool visiting Hollywood starlets like Ava Gardner swam naked in, there was an understated cemetery for his beloved cats and dogs.

Every step I took on his property felt as if he could come back through the door at any moment. It was a little eerie combing so much of a man's life left pristinely as he'd chosen to live it in his adoptive home. Havana's marina had been named after him. Why not? He'd donated the Nobel Prize and the Pulitzer to the Cuban people. His Pulitzer had been stolen from the shrine where it was kept near Santiago de Cuba. The staff guarding the house told me that it was eventually returned. Back in Havana, the room where he started writing *For Whom the Bell Tolls* at the Ambos Mundos was roped off. There were old women guarding it who had met him as teenagers. Apparently he wasn't stingy with compliments for pretty girls and they still blushed remembering them.

I'd admired Hemingway's work for a long time, but his effect on so many of the Cubans I spoke with in his adoptive country added a great deal to my appreciation of the man. Cubans by and large are a tremendously respectful people, but they aren't easy to impress. Héctor had shrugged once after mentioning he'd fought around the world for crowds but never *felt* (not heard) anyone respond like his own people. "Everybody deserves to have Havana as a hometown," I heard again and again.

Alfonso lined up for me a meeting with Gregorio Fuentes, Hemingway's former captain of his beloved fishing boat, the *Pilar*, which he kept in Cuba. Nearly half a century after the last novel Hemingway ever saw published in his lifetime found its way into readers' hands in 1952, the inspiration for *The Old Man and the Sea*, Fuentes, with his 103-year-old birthday around the corner, still lived in Cojimar, the tiny fishing village from the story. While Castro was up in the Sierra Maestra, Fuentes supported the revolution by smuggling explosives inside his boat. He still worked for the revolution by speaking with foreigners about his life and friendship with Hemingway. He asked for fifteen dollars from visitors to his home, which he donated to the Cuban government. Fuente's tale of going up against a marlin was Hemingway's comeback after the disastrous reception of his World War II novel, *Across the River and into the Trees*. Critics had savaged the book and relished their ad hominem attacks against Hemingway. The common wisdom was that he was shot as an artist and had become nothing more than a third-rate caricature of a bloated legend.

Hemingway responded by sitting down at his typewriter. After a handful of weeks writing inside his San Francisco de Paula home, he sheepishly approached his wife, Mary, with the pages of his manuscript. She read the book in one sitting and returned to him with tears in her eyes and told him she forgave him for *everything*. For different reasons, others seemed to be able to relate:

readers weren't far behind Mary's reaction, snatching up over five million copies of *Life* within two days of the novel being featured in the magazine. Forty-five years later I carried a beaten-up copy across Europe, and in every country men and women would stop me, tap an index finger on the cover, and shake their heads smiling. The critics awarded it the Pulitzer Prize in 1953 and the following year it was specifically mentioned when Hemingway took home the Nobel Prize in Literature. "All the works of Hemingway," Fidel Castro once said, "are a defense of human rights."

Montalvo picked me up outside Trejo, with Alfonso and Lesvanne in the car. Alfonso, who was riding shotgun, winked at me as he took a sip from a twelve-year-old bottle of Havana Club from his left hand while waving with his right, a copy of *Romeo y Julieta* wedged between his fingers. His eyes were bloodshot and his face had a sickly pallor.

"You okay?" I asked.

"Don't look at me like that." Alfonso laughed. "Get in. Today we have a good day. A very, very good day. So what if I'm already celebrating how you're going to remember this day. I live for days like these."

As I got into the backseat with Lesvanne, Montalvo rubbed Alfonso's shoulder and we began to drive.

"My friend, celebrating all these days you live for is going to put you in the ground," Montalvo said.

"I won't live for long anyway. That isn't the point. I leave to go home to a place where everyone reaches old age, and how many really enjoy the life they have? A midlife crisis is the *best*-case scenario. Of all the species on this planet, you know how many expect to live to old age? Only those that reside in captivity. All the rest are eaten when they no longer have enough life to fight."

"So why don't you move here?" I asked him.

"My favorite thing is to miss my flight from Havana." Alfonso laughed, reaching back and slapping my knee in the backseat. "I hate leaving this place. Brinicito, do you have any idea how many flights I've missed attempting to leave Havana?"

"It must be a record." Montalvo shook his head.

"Even now when I can't fuck the pretty girls I always visit, they're still sweet to me. We still have a good time. Life has always been sweet to me. The only cruelty is saying good-bye. Which reminds me—" Alfonso handed his cigar to Montalvo, who whisked away the smoke from his face and held the cigar at arm's length out his window. "Brinicito, I want to give you my card before I forget for after you leave so you can always reach me if you need anything here or there."

I took the card and put it in my wallet. But of course the next time I tried his number several months later to see if Alfonso wanted to meet in Havana again, he couldn't answer because he was already there, buried in the Colón cemetery after his liver finally gave out. He'd gotten his wish and never had to say good-bye to Havana ever again.

"After we visit the old man in Cojimar I will show you all the books I am bringing back. It is a crime to part with them, but for the price I'll get I will. eBay has made the life of a bookseller so easy. If I collected baseball cards down here, I'd make a fortune. And, by the way, I have figured out a way to pay for your trip and every trip you make down here. Montalvo can get you several Cuban Olympic tracksuits on the *mercado negro* and you can sell them on eBay to Cuban Americans in Miami. For three hundred dollars apiece, you could sell a handful for fifteen hundred. You get these tracksuits and a couple boxes of Cohibas from the cigar factory, and you've paid off all your airfare and rent. Let me show you just a few books I have with me from this morning. First editions! London's *White Fang*!"

The international book fair in Havana was nearly over and moving on to spread out over the rest of Cuba. Alfonso had cleaned up at the old eighteenth-century Fortaleza de San Carlos de la Cabaña, where the fair attracted tens of thousands of book lovers and collectors. Even an international book fair in Cuba is a touchy thing (beyond the fact that it is permitted to sell only state-sponsored books). After La Cabaña was built by the Spanish in 1774, it was used as a military base and prison for the next two centuries. When the rebels seized the fortress in 1959, after Batista's troops surrendered without offering any resistance, Che was installed there for five months to oversee a military prison and revolutionary tribunals, which resulted in extensive executions of informants, Batista's secret police, war criminals, political prisoners, and traitors. These events turned a lot of supporters against the revolutionary agenda. Later on La Cabaña was converted into a historical park with a few museums and a famous cannon, which explodes across the Havana night at 9 p.m. each evening. Then again, a lot of the prettiest plazas in Madrid where tourists sip coffee were once public execution grounds or impromptu bullfighting rings.

After we reached Cojimar we got temporarily lost. The town was too quiet, almost somber, and both Lesvanne and Montalvo immediately sensed something was wrong. The few people we saw in town refused to make eye contact with our vehicle except for strange men inventorying all movement from street corners. *"Joder,"*

Montalvo moaned, "secret police. Something went down here last night. Can we visit this man another day, Alfonso?"

"It's not a crime to visit Fuentes. We're not doing it in secret. What happened here?"

The streets were almost completely empty. Lesvanne spotted a face he recognized walking with some waiters in uniform to La Terraza, the most famous tourist bar in town. When Lesvanne hollered to them out the window none of them stopped walking. We pulled over and Lesvanne got out to ask some questions and to double-check our directions to Fuente's home. When Lesvanne returned to the car he reported that a delegation of three hundred people from across the United States had been visiting and doing volunteer labor in Cuba. Most of the delegation stayed in the dorm facilities athletes had used during the Pan American games near Cojimar. A couple of days before, a young woman with her friends from California had visited a beach outside of town with a video camera. Three men approached her and demanded the bag with the camera inside. She refused. One of the men struck her in the face while another snatched the bag. The police were called. Within two hours Cojimar and two other areas the boys were suspected of living in were under complete lockdown. Scores of police and special police invaded the towns and searched each home, door to door, until they found the perpetrators and the girl's property. The boys were quickly arrested and the government notified the girl's family back in the States that the camera, along with the girl, were promptly being sent home.

"Those boys who took the camera are *fucked*." Lesvanne shook his head. "Even a thief could get the drawers. But to attack someone before robbing them?"

"What the hell are the *drawers*?" I asked.

"It's like a morgue, only they put living people into the space of a coffin and push you into the wall. You're left there for one day, or two days, or three. You shit all over yourself. You lose your mind. Striking a woman is terrible. There is very little violence here and they should know how that will be treated. They must have been truly, truly desperate for some reason. You can be arrested in my country for not carrying your ID card. You can imagine how bloodying a tourist is handled. The tourist dollar is the breathing hole in our little cage."

We found Gregorio Fuentes's small apartment on the corner of a narrow, hilly street, and the 103-year-old man answered his own door. He was puffing away on a cigar and refused to wear glasses, but his grandson held his elbow for support just in case. After he sat down, Gregorio looked healthy and alert, his chair surrounded by photographs and paintings of himself and Hemingway. The gift shop feel of the living room didn't seem to be his idea, but he wasn't embarrassed by it, either. He was giving you his time for the fifteen dollars and a bottle of rum you were expected to bring. The money went toward the revolution, the rum stayed on the premises.

I knew that Gregorio Fuentes, who could fish before he could walk, had stopped fishing for the remainder of his life the day he found out Hemingway had committed suicide in 1961. I knew it, but I can't say it really prepared me for *feeling* the intensity of that bond in Gregorio's living room, with him sitting there.

I told him the day before I'd seen his old boat the *Pilar* for the first time, and he nodded. "Isn't she beautiful? I don't think she's very happy away from the sea."

Which was true. I didn't think *Pilar* had much interest parading herself around as a centerfold beside the swimming pool in Hemingway's backyard. You could tell she missed the action. She'd helped Hemingway catch some of the biggest fish ever caught, was rigged to spot U-boats during World War II, had hidden explosives for the rebels during the revolution, but now she continued to work for Fidel winning him all those cover charges from tourists eager to pose in front of history.

"I don't know anyone in the world as identified with their profession as you," I clumsily began. "But after Hemingway died you never wanted to fish?"

"After we got news of his death . . ." Gregorio stared at me, adjusting his ball cap. "I had no desire to fish anymore. I was captain of the *Pilar* for twenty years. I had fished all my life. I have loved the sea. I have loved all that lives in the sea. But this man was my friend. I had no desire to fish after I knew he was gone. I miss him. He was such . . . *fun*." His crinkly lips curled into a smile as he relit his cigar and took some more drags from it.

For the next ten minutes his grandson cut into the conversation and elaborated on Hemingway's love of Cuba, Gregorio's allegiance to the ideals of the revolution, how the embargo was harming the island, and a few other perfectly interesting things I wasn't really paying attention to. Gregorio's face, while he was quietly smoking and thinking, was too captivating to take much else in.

The last thing I ever asked of Gregorio was why he thought Hemingway had such an effect on people. Especially Cubans.

His blue eyes looked like cracked, half-frozen puddles. He stared at me and puffed on his cigar for a while. Then he put down the cigar and cleared his throat before saying, and smiling with that century-old face, "He knew who he was."

11

ELEVATOR MUSIC

The heaviest of burdens is therefore simultaneously an image of life's most intense fulfillment. The heavier the burden, the closer our lives come to the earth, the more real and truthful they become. —Milan Kundera

"I WANT TO TELL YOU my favorite story about Che," Videliah, Jesús's seventy-four-year-old mother, told me over coffee on one of my last nights in Havana. "Before his death three years ago, I was married to the love of my life for fifty years, God bless his soul. My husband played the piano, was close friends with Ernesto Lecuona, one of my country's most beautiful composers. I fell in love with my husband at first *listen*. I could hear we were soul mates even before I could see his lovely face. Wherever he is, I hope he cannot hear this confession. The only man I would have cheated on him with owned the most beautiful eyes I have ever seen in my life. I saw them when I shared an elevator with Che when I was still young and beautiful. He was with two soldiers, but he couldn't pay attention to their conversation as the elevator climbed in that office building. He leaned over to confess my beauty was too distracting. It wasn't a dirty compliment—it was warm. Che never cheated on his wife. He was very respectful of women. He passed very unpopular laws where powerful men were forbidden from sleeping with their secretaries. No other Cuban would ever *think* to pass such a law. Fidel had many lovers and many children from different women. Che wasn't that way. But calling me distracting was all he had time to say before it was time for me to leave the elevator. I worked as a secretary in the building and my stop was before Che's. You have no idea how many times I've returned to that brief little climb in the elevator with him. Even as an old woman the wound is fresh. But the story I wish to tell you is when Che left Cuba for the last time. He changed his identity and radically altered his appearance in order to sneak out to Bolivia. It was a suicide mission from the very beginning. He had no illusions. Che was never going to live to be anyone's grandfather. And the irony of Che's downfall is that a peasant betrayed him to the police. The police passed on the information to an American-trained and funded army. Che could have been drinking mojitos at the Nacional, but instead spent his last days nearly starving to death trying to help these oppressed people, only to be betrayed by a peasant and executed on the CIA's orders. The wristwatch Che was wearing when they murdered him is now worn on the wrist of a man in Miami as a trophy. But before Che left he had dinner with his wife and family one last time. His wife introduced him to his children as Ramón, his new identity's name, and they didn't recognize him. The disguise was so well done even Che's children were all fooled. When dinner was served, out of habit, Che sat at his usual place at the head of the table. Instantly one of his small children confronted him and grabbed the chair. 'You cannot sit here! My *father* sits here.'"

Videliah smiled and reached a hand across the table to place over mine. "You don't have the hands of a boxer, do you?"

I had to look away at her *quinceañera* portrait placed over a bookshelf. Along with free birthday cakes for all children delivered to their door by bicycle and a free wedding day, the state offered a party for all girls on their fifteenth birthday celebrating their transition into womanhood. A banquet hall is rented along with a feast and they receive a dress and fancy dress clothes for their family. All the boys in attendance wear rented tuxedos. Fourteen couples dance a waltz around the *quinceañera*, who is allowed to select a boy of her choosing to dance with. A photographer is hired to commemorate the day. Every Cuban lady lives with an arrestingly beautiful portrait of herself posing dreamily somewhere on the premises of her home. Videliah's portrait was the most lovely I've seen.

My time left of that first trip in Havana was nearing its end. I've always been terrible with good-byes. I've tried to sneak out of everything before it ends all my life—family, relationships, friendships, even life itself. Cuba as these people knew it had been coming to an end for fifty years, yet it just never actually *happened*. Castro's obituary has been on file at the *Miami Herald* for decades, yet at this point he might end up living longer than that newspaper.

After my last training session with Héctor on a rooftop in Old Havana (he got tired of having to give a cut to the Macbeth witches

at the front), I paid a visit to Montalvo's house a few blocks away
from the gym. At Alfonso's suggestion, I'd bought some cigars
and tracksuits through Montalvo's contacts on the black market
·to help cover some costs of the trip and maybe make it a little easier to come back. His street, like a lot of streets in the baked Old
Havana maze, has a vise-like squeeze. The streets are potholed
and dusty. The sidewalks are filled with dog shit and trash. Many
windows on the homes are barred, with old men and women assuming poses gripping the bars and staring out with docile eyes
at the neighborhood. There's never a bustling morning commute
here, everything is clotted and fading or giving out. From the rooftops you feel a lot of eyes watch your movements. There's no home-
lessness anywhere, but what roofs people have over their heads leak,
the plumbing doesn't work, food is terrible, electricity is finicky—
everything everywhere is continually breaking down.

I banged on Montalvo's rotting front door just as I heard a nee-
dle drop on a Barry White record inside. Lesvanne was deliver-
ing the tracksuits and cigars soon. Typical of Lesvanne and
Montalvo, the only cut Lesvanne wanted was a tracksuit for Montalvo to enjoy, and Montalvo wouldn't take more than a bottle of
rum for his father-in-law. They were both insulted at the idea of
anything more.

"*¡Oye!*" Montalvo hollered. "*Te gusta*, Barry Blanco?"

Montalvo's wife answered the door with their grandchild in
her arms. I received and gave a kiss to both while spying Montalvo from the corner of my eye, wearing his pristine Cuban Olympic tracksuit, responding to Barry Blanco with the relish of Bill
Cosby cleaning off a spoon of Jell-O.

"He cheats on me every afternoon with Blanco." His wife shook
her head. "Look at this? I'm not homophobic but to have to watch

your husband of thirty years have an orgasm in your living room to Blanco every day? This man has no shame."

"You cheat on me with Jorge Miguel," Montalvo volleyed, under his breath, as he swayed. "'Careless Whisper'? *¡Qué va!* Don't tell me about Blanco. In our open marriage I have my Barry Blanco and you have Miguel."

"Lesvanne already delivered everything?"

"Yes. He just stepped out. Thank you for this tracksuit. Aren't I a flashy *papi chulo* in it! Ay! Ay!" Three Cuban wrist snaps accentuated this point. "Brinicito, I have something for you while I cheat on my wife for the next four minutes with Blanco."

He reached over and grabbed a massive photo album. Montalvo dropped it like an anvil in my lap but quickly reclaimed it to inspect the pages. For a reason I had significant difficulty determining, he began to show me pictures of people he had known in school or in track who had died. After pointing out four recent deaths, Montalvo gestured at another and shrugged, then almost sang, "Heeeeee's dead, too." I looked to his wife for some explanation and she held up her hands and paced off to the kitchen to make some coffee on the stove for us. After he'd introduced me to twenty more dead people, he didn't bother to lift his finger anymore, simply slid it across the images. "*Él también.* Dead." Turned the page. "*Él* . . . hmmm . . . *momento.*" Montalvo turned toward the kitchen and leaned back in the sofa until I could feel the backrest about to snap off. "*¡Mi amor!* Marco Antonio Reyes? Four-hundred-meter runner."

His wife sang back, "*Muerto, ¡mi amor! Dos años atrás.*"

"*¡Graaaaacia!*" Montalvo turned back to me and paused. "He's dead, too. *Vamos a ver quién más.*" He flipped over some more pages and inspected the faces with the tip of his finger against his cheek.

"Montalvo," I asked, grinning in the perverse delight of his weirdness. "Why are you showing this to me?"

"Because Alfonso has just left and I miss my friend. And now you are leaving. I hate good-byes. Good-bye is death. So my revenge against that is to listen to music I love and find all the people of my generation who are dead so I gradually get cheered up realizing how happy I am with everyone still alive in my life. Have you had anyone close to you die?"

"There were three suicides in school. But I wasn't close to them."

"No, no," he corrected. "They count. When a good-bye makes you sad, open up your school photos and find them. Keep score. This is better than pretending about heaven. That is the most beautiful thing I can ever offer you to understand about Cuba. If there is a heaven, even as bad as things are here, everyone would know who all the Cubans are."

"Why?"

"They would be the only people asking to go back home."

And as we stared at each other in silence, for the first time, I was aware of Montalvo's ancient father-in-law in a rocking chair across the room from us. I had never seen him in the living room before. His daughter had been nursing him in his room for all of my visits. He stared intently into my eyes while he fanned himself with an exquisite peacock feather. After we made eye contact he nudged his head toward the cabinet.

"*Hijo, ¿quién es él?*"

"Don't worry about him," Montalvo said, without looking up. "My father-in-law is *crazy.*"

"What does he want?"

"Who cares? He wants to drink. Photos! *Muy importante.*"

"Right."

I had trouble calibrating myself to that room. I leaned back in the couch for a second and grandpa was ominously pointing his peacock feather at me. It might as well have been a rocket launcher. He slowly dragged the tip of his feather in the direction of the cabinet. Keeping the feather pointed, he turned his head toward me, with his straw fedora at a maniacal angle all his own.

"Montalvo," I pleaded. "What is he trying to show me?"

"Nothing. He wants the rum we got him. He's crazy. Even at ninety, all he wants to do is fuck and drink. He was tortured by Batista. After his torturers got the firing squad, he celebrated with his first drink and has been a drunk ever since. He's crazy. You and your peacock feather are *crazy*, I tell you," he said to his father-in-law.

We spent the following hour going over all Montalvo's track medals, ribbons, trophies, and press clippings from his glory days. His favorite possession was a photo of Fidel beaming proudly with his Pan American silver medal from the early sixties.

Lesvanne entered the apartment wearing the searing bright outfit he laundered every day. As he stood in the open doorway with his sideburns as perfect as Cadillac fins, the sun blazed off his fake Versace belt buckle and glazed his freshly polished shoes. He found the cheek of every female in the house to kiss before joining us in the living room.

"Please tell me why I'm being shown everyone who has died in his album," I pleaded to Lesvanne.

"Ah! ¡Él también! Dead. ¡Mira, mira! Chico, ¡mira! Look!"

Montalvo yanked Lesvanne down beside us on the couch to behold yet another victim.

"Why is he showing us friends of his who are dead?"

"It's his favorite game."

"Why does he seem so . . . *festive* about it?"

"He used to do this somberly. But Barry Blanco puts him in a good mood."

Montalvo closed the book suddenly and hollered for his wife to get his track medals from his room to show us all again.

A cab dropped me off on the Malecón near the Hotel Nacional. An old woman and a little boy were arguing about which direction they wanted to go. It was that strange hour between the time when the sun sinks out of view and the streetlights turn on, while it's still muggy out as the colors drain and begin to smear against the rooftops and balconies throughout Centro Habana. From a distance, all the apartments along the Malecón unfold like a Christmas calendar of hurricane-bruised colors. As usual, it felt like a drive-in movie experience to watch the day bleed out.

The Malecón was crammed with families greeting friends and I watched the handshakes far too closely because I had been told that if you shake hands with someone's wife and clandestinely run your thumb against her palm during the gesture it meant that you're asking if she'd like to have an affair. I knew this because I had done it by accident after meeting a boxer's wife to whom Héctor introduced me. It was roughly the same look I got when at a fruit stand I asked an eighty-year-old woman if she had papaya available, not knowing I was requesting pussy by its slang term. On my second day in the country, I got lost near the Malecón near the Habana Libre hotel—a popular cruising area for gays—and asked if anyone knew where the *maricón* ("faggot") was by mistake. Even a stone-faced policeman broke down laughing.

Bike taxis hustled rides while the fishermen worked barefoot and shirtless, smoking unfiltered cigarettes next to a bucket of the day's catch. Some worked alone with rum, others in groups with conversation. *Jineteros* kept their eyes peeled for an easy wallet while their female counterparts arched their backs and hissed, "Warr joo frawm?" Thousands of teenage silhouettes sat flirting on the Malecón like it was one collective sofa. Some people paced, turning over decisions made a little easier by their proximity to the sea as itchy stray dogs roamed in search of handouts. Old women with sacks of candy held out fistfuls of lollipops and bags of popcorn to families sitting against the wall near solitary musicians honing soliloquies on trumpets or guitars, while cruise ships approached the harbor. Somewhere beyond the perfect line where the sky and sea kiss, the shark-infested passage spanned, a three-day float—if you make it—to pay dirt.

Somebody once said that at the end of the world there's always a tourist and a whore fucking in a hotel. If that's here, that whore's mother probably made the bed and had coffee ready for them. The girls with price tags always ask me why I look so sad and offer me company, but I'm always too shy to accept their advances. Femininity here in *any* permutation—wife, mistress, mother, grandmother, daughter, friend, stranger—overwhelms and intimidates me. Where I come from, any woman worth her salt knows how to break your balls, but they're so worn down by a culture perfected to make them feel like shit that hardly any know how to truly break your heart.

One more day until flying home. . . .

12

IF SPANISH LACKED A FUTURE TENSE

)

It's a soccer ball covered with ants, to which an unknown
player has given a tremendous kick, sending it spinning
through space without the ants having the slightest idea
where they came from or where they're going or why. That
doesn't stop the little animals from clinging to the surface
or from killing each other so as to keep holding on to the
ball and their dreams.

—Carlos Loveira, *Juan Criollo*

⌄

MAYBE EVERYTHING *HAS* BEEN SAID, but how much of it has been
heard?

Of the eighty-two revolutionaries crammed onto the leaky boat
that shipwrecked onto Cuban shores on December 2, 1956—
twenty-nine years after Loveira's novel—no more than twenty
survived the initial encounter with Batista's army and succeeded
in escaping to the Sierra Maestra mountains. Only twelve men
from this group survived to see victory when, on January 1, 1959,
Batista fled Cuba for Spain with an estimated three hundred

million dollar fortune stolen from the Cuban people. Since that time, some estimates say that there have been 638 attempts on Castro's life organized on American soil. In 1979, on a historic trip to address the UN General Assembly in New York, Castro was asked about the constant need for protection in light of the assassination attempts.

"Everybody says you always have a bulletproof vest," the reporter Jon Alpert remarked on the plane ride.

"No." Castro smiled.

"No?"

Castro leaned back and struggled to unbutton his shirt and reveal his soft, sparsely haired fifty-three-year-old chest.

"I will land in New York like this." Fidel beamed. "I have a *moral* one. A *moral* vest. It's strong." He held up a fist. "That one has protected me always. It's too hot in Cuba to have a bulletproof vest."

On the afternoon of my last day in Havana, I saw a little girl get bit by a dog in Parque Central in between the tournament fight cards at Kid Chocolate. I watched her from a stone bench beside the Esquina Caliente crowd of men arguing baseball just down the street from the Capitolio. She tried to pet one of these Goya-nightmare stray dogs and it snapped at her hand. She went off like a car alarm, but it was the *way* she screamed that made the old men give up their arguments and rush over to console her. I had been hypnotized by these men's bickering my entire visit. I'm convinced that that girl's ability to distract them from their shouting is the only bona fide miracle I've ever witnessed in my lifetime. You'll have to take my word for it, but if the Hot Corner heard Slim Pickens himself was falling from the sky straddling an atomic bomb, slapping his cowboy hat against his hip and yee-hawing his way down onto their heads . . . there wouldn't have been a flinch. "We're talking *béisbol* here, *coño*."

The Esquina Caliente finally cheered her up enough that she smiled and jammed her head against her mom's shoulder. The men went back to baseball and the mom carried her baby home.

I closed up my notebook and followed the little girl and her mother to Calle Neptuno, where they caught a cab and disappeared.

The last thing I had planned before flying home was to catch an Industriales game at Estadio Latinoamericano with Jesús. It was nearing the end of the Cuban National Baseball League's ninety-game season. Television in Cuba only has three channels and when baseball or Brazilian soap operas are on, the city shuts down to watch. As much as these people loved boxing, if Teófilo Stevenson came out of retirement to fight the heavyweight champion while a little league game was telecast from any corner of the island, people would riot if anyone dared replace it with boxing. I've never loved Americans more than when I see them up close watching a baseball game. It distills one side of their culture and national character in a way nothing else does. It's like they're watching their daughter at their first dance recital. And the only people on earth who loved America's game as much as Americans were these people.

And this was Jesús's going away present to me. We were going to stop at his dad's house on the way to say hello. He looked so proud on his way to work, pulling his Industriales cap over his little shaved head after he kissed his wife and boy. That's when his wife came over to me and told me his dad had terminal cancer and nobody had the heart to tell Jesús yet. It was in his pancreas and there wasn't much time left. The dread of keeping this information from someone who had been as kind to me as Jesús had been during my stay hung over the rest of my last day. But it's impossible to hold on to any one feeling for long given the speed that this town dishes them out.

I'd had a laughing fit at the gym that afternoon because I'd mentioned I wanted to meet Félix Savón, the three-time Olympic heavyweight gold medalist, before I left, if it was possible. Most of the coaches at Trejo were either Olympic or Pan American gold medalists themselves or had coached Olympic gold medalists on the national or Olympic team. They knew and enjoyed Savón—everybody knows everybody in Havana anyway—but he was like a sweet little boy, they said. I got the impression that Cuba's answer to "the baddest man on the planet" was more like Lenny from *Of Mice and Men*.

"Sure you can meet him!" one coach hollered. "We've already talked to him about you. He told us he'd like to meet you in the Presidential Suite at the Nacional this evening. He'll bring his medals to show you but be careful, he probably won't wear them around his neck!"

While I was smiling to myself about this, I got to a street corner and noticed a sweaty, filthy old man crawling on the ground like a crab across the intersection. I wasn't high. I'd been offered plenty of weed by people who, for some unclear reason, insisted on smoking it from their nostrils rather than lips. But I was aware of the years in jail many have spent for so much as a joint and wasn't keen to tempt fate. Yet, this guy, stone sober as I was, wasn't evaporating like any mirage under closer inspection. All he had on was a loincloth. It was a busy intersection. Out of maybe two hundred people walking on the sidewalk—the fifteen taxis, ten Chinese bicycle taxis, forty cars, and two horse-drawn carriages on the road—I seemed to possess the only pair of eyes *staring*. I appeared to be the only person remotely concerned with this man's role in the universe.

In New York people had arguments with their horns; in Havana they had operas. As the man progressed to the center of the intersection, still in the middle of the street with the cars patiently waiting for him to pass, I noticed there was a rope attached to his ankle tied to something that remained offstage behind a lamppost. I reached into my breast pocket and took out a cigarette, waiting with my match until I saw what he was dragging: a truck's tire.

Maybe everybody was too busy to notice because, like every other day in Havana, it's Valentine's Day year round. You can't walk anywhere without somebody blowing kisses or whistling or hissing at somebody. If this were the States it would be a sexual harassment lawyer's wet dream. Yet hardly anybody seems to mind. Cupid was supposed to be a screwed-up kid settling scores with grownups anyway, so it makes sense he'd be mistaken for a local patron saint in this place.

I made my last walk home as I always did, with the sunset glinting off American hubcaps and putting the finishing touches on a stickball game played down an alley, with everyone pleading for just one more out. The sunset got its hooks into the whole overwhelming dripping-wet painting of everything in Havana, and I turned over the same thought I had from the beginning: maybe Cuba is just one dictator's heartbeat away from becoming like everywhere else. But what if it's not? How long could this possibly last? How long *should* it last? It's a lot easier to theorize about human behavior than it is to look at it.

In the darkness Jesús lit a match and we started down thirteen flights of stairs inside his parents' apartment complex's barren stairwell. The elevator had been broken for years and the power had gone out an hour before we arrived. We kept passing whole families sullenly panting up the stairs toward home. They gasped their hellos.

"The opening first pitch is only a few minutes away." Jesús laughed. "We have to hurry!"

We'd spent twenty minutes with Jesús's clandestinely dying father and mom in their apartment. Jesús massaged his mother's feet while pleading for stories from his father about heroic team feats at ball games they'd attended through the years. "Did you bring me any cigars?" the father asked his son.

Jesús handed over three from his breast pocket and offered a match as his father bit off and chewed the end of a cigar. Halfway through each feat detailed in the story the cigar went out and Jesús had to light another match for his father.

"So." His father grinned at me devilishly. "My son's entire life he's offered me this service. Don't think I raised him to be my slave. You can ask my wife, I lost my mind when I saw this boy's face for the first time and I never got it back. He still convinces me I invented for all the world the pleasure of having a son."

"Then you should come with us to watch the game." Jesús kissed his cheek.

"I'm a little tired, Jesusito. Another time we'll go."

"This man never missed a baseball game I played in my entire life." Jesús laughed. "Not a stickball game or a pickup game in the park. Never."

"I told him already." He slapped his cheek gently. "I was a slave to this boy. Now go enjoy the game while I take a nap with my queen and our ugly-as-sin dogs."

Right then we all heard the roar of air raid sirens coming from Latinoamericano's ballpark.

"*Vamos, ¡Jesusito! Venga.* I don't care how poor my country is, if you catch a foul ball you keep it and bring it home to me."

When we finally got outside bicycle spokes whirred by as boys accompanied their girlfriends or younger siblings to the ballpark. Hitchhiking families crammed into wheezing jalopies or whining Ladas for the stadium. While I was evaluating again the old man's choice to keep his illness from his son, Jesús clapped my shoulder. "You know what El Duque told the Americans when they asked him if he was nervous about pitching at Yankee Stadium?"

"What did he say?" I smiled with relief.

"He said how could anyone be nervous about Yankee Stadium after pitching at Latinoamericano. That's what he said *after* he'd left. This experience is going to ruin the rest of sports for all your life. It is going to molest you like a priest! Baseball is the highest religion in my country."

We joined the immense crowd marching its way into the entrance, liquor and cigars in hand. Latinoamericano could hold over fifty thousand fans and there was not a parking lot in sight. After we paid two Cuban pesos (about ten cents) for our seats, a vendor pushed two raffle tickets toward us from a barred window as if they were crack pipes. "Good seats?" I asked.

"No designated seats inside." Jesús laughed. "No luxury boxes. No commercial breaks. You'll see."

Before we'd gotten inside another clap sounded: tin cans being smashed together, echoing throughout the stadium. A drum started pounding and thousands more people clapped behind its thud. Another siren wailed. We crammed through a narrow tunnel with hundreds all around us and then the expanse of the diamond and outfield unfolded before us, sprinkled with that immaculate constellation of ballplayers and their mitts standing under several furiously burning lights extended by concrete at the angle of fire engine cranes toward a burning building. A three-story logo of Industriales dimly shone from the side of a blue-painted building just beyond the outfield. A ribbon of camouflage green uniforms circumnavigated the crowd where the military had been called out in case anything beyond the usual rioting occurred. As we found our seats behind the reserved government seating, the beat of the drum reached a crescendo and three well-built teenage girls in spandex turned their backs to the field and stuck their asses out to twerk with abandon. Those around them laughed and hollered approval.

"You see that man?" Jesús asked as he raided a tray of peanuts from a vendor. "The only one out of uniform, in the opposing team's dugout?"

"Yeah."

"Does his profile look familiar?" Jesús laughed.

"No," I confessed. "I have no idea who he is."

"Their team doctor is Fidel's son."

"*Him?*"

"Oh yes." Jesús giggled. "None of Fidel's children followed him into politics. I wonder why that is? None of them wanted anything to do with this mess confronting the United States."

At that point I gave up entirely on trying to follow the game in front of us.

"How hard is it for you to stay here, Jesús?"

"Some of these athletes, when they first got to Florida, did things that amused Americans." Jesús smiled, cracking open some peanuts. "They bought dog food for their children because they saw a child smiling on the can and had no idea there was special food just for dogs or cats. Some fainted the moment they walked into an American supermarket. Some kept million-dollar checks in their back pocket for days because they didn't understand anything about banks."

"You've never been away from Cuba?"

"I left with a delegation of engineers to Toronto once. For a week."

"Was it what you expected?"

"Is Havana what *you* expected? I was born the same year as the triumph of the revolution. My father was always so proud of this. What he risked his life for in so many ways came true. For the first time since Columbus we were in control of our own destiny. Extreme poverty does not exist. Have you seen any homeless on our streets? I saw many homeless in a rich city like Toronto. . ."

"I'm waiting for the *but*."

"The *but* is two very precious things. My father and my son. Two very powerfully opposing forces in my life, Brinicito. My father was able to provide me a better life than he enjoyed in so many ways. Can I offer that to my own son here in today's Cuba?" And then Jesús took a deep breath and concluded the topic the way I'd hear so many fathers sum up the calamity of their albatross. "The greatest joy any Cuban man can know is becoming a father, and our deepest anguish, no matter how hard we try, is not being able to provide for them here. I have never told my father this, but I send in our family's names to the lottery each year."

"What *lottery*?"

"Every year the United States lets twenty thousand of us enter through a lottery to avoid the rafts that leave. All those horrible deaths from the *balseros* or smugglers' boats. It's all so *feo*. So each year I send in a letter with our names. And if they ever select us I will have to live with the betrayal of my father, which I don't know how I will ever do. He might never forgive me. But the alternative is betraying my son. And that is something I could never forgive *myself* for."

Someone from Industriales hit a home run and everybody in the stadium but us jumped to their feet to see how far it would go.

13

SAND CASTLES

I had nothing to offer anybody, except my own confusion.
—Jack Kerouac, *On the Road*

As the plane made its final descent and sunk beneath the clouds, the first lights I could discern coming from Toronto were bank insignias atop skyscrapers. There was relief in being home, trading in the hysteria of communism for the perversion of capitalism. Exchanging the uncertainty of questioning everything that happened, was happening, and *would* happen in Cuba for where I came from, where people could accept the world blowing up sooner than any real change to the status quo.

Cuba had José Martí, Che, Camilo Cienfuegos, and Fidel on their culture's Mount Rushmore. It's exhausting sizing those people up. My culture's Mount Rushmore growing up was seemingly carved by Andy Warhol: Britney Spears (sexpot masquerading as a virgin), Michael Jackson (the strangest man on earth as most successful mainstream star ever), Hulk Hogan (fake athlete in a fake sport and the Make-A-Wish Foundation's number-one-requested celebrity for dying kids ahead of Michael Jackson and Mickey Mouse), O. J. Simpson (the fifth estate's wet dream), Lance Armstrong (Cancer Jesus selling his inspirational lie while raising half a billion dollars in cancer research), and Mike Tyson (our favorite world-class victim posing as victimizer). How many Cubans had I met ashamed of not being able to live their culture's broken dream? The culture I came from was constitutionally incapable of shame.

The French Canadian plumber sitting next to me on the flight home spent three hours, uninterrupted, detailing how he got over his divorce by regularly flying to Cuba to binge drink, fuck, and "look after" a series of eighteen-year-old girls—with their family's full support after being paid off—until one got pregnant and he could *safely* marry her off the island and have her to himself back home. He looked like the bloated, heartbroken Kerouac from his famous William F. Buckley interview.

"None of this bullshit back *here* with women," he continued. "*Tabernak!* Our way of life is fucked up. All the pressure to have enough to offer a girl to get married until you do, and then everything around you, day after day, conspires to get you divorced. You're suspect if you aren't married and once you get married you can't seem to find anybody married who is happy. Your wife blames you for everything and she takes everything. Fuck that. I threw away half my life on that scam. You're young but you could learn a lot from me. It's why our society is so scared of prostitution. The institution of marriage is far less honest a transaction than spending a couple hours with a whore when you feel lonely."

It's not hard to identify the people who fall for the kind of beauty that subtracts rather than adds something to their lives.

When I got back home from Havana my father had something terribly wrong with him. He'd been collapsing to the ground again and again with mysterious "attacks." Nobody knew what it was and he refused to do anything to find out. Because of a real estate crash he'd battled a mountain of debt throughout my childhood. We all knew how much he smoked and drank every day. But like all highly functioning addicts, it had always felt like a tease. No smoker's cough or hangovers. Like so much between my father and me, everything hid in plain sight. How much does the line between privacy and secrets really matter if the only secrets you keep from people are the ones everybody already knows? He'd drink daily and I was resigned to the fact that he'd never stop, but then he'd never officially *started* in the first place. His alcoholism was always treated as a kind of tourism of the place where *real* drunks doing damage to their loved ones lived. The self-destruction he carried out without obvious consequences gave him a strange power over his own life and mine.

That's why for so long it was okay when I went to get fruit with him at the market as a child and he ducked off to the liquor store, leaving me a twenty to pay for the groceries. We both pretended to ignore the brown bag inserted into the plastic grocery bags: his crudely conspicuous sleight of hand. We both pretended to ignore my role as witness to his ritual. We ignored how his shame of my witnessing this spiked the punch bowl of his process. We *couldn't* ignore how much fruit went rotten by neglect in his house. But nobody launched any inquiries into why. We just always had another reason to get more. And then more. And more.

As soon as I got back from the airport my mother told me my father might be "leaving the earth plane."

"*Might?*" I repeated.

"Darrr-ling," she said. "It's just he might be ready to leave."

Translation: he was dying. All scary things for my mother were spun into a positively reinforced excuse to discuss how compassionate the universe was. That was the law. And the law wasn't for her the same as the one my father explained to me when I first asked him to define his profession. "The law is artificial order from total chaos." He laughed. My father, a child protection lawyer, married a Hungarian gypsy refugee who looked into crystal balls and probed into the endless desperate lives that rang our doorbell and sat with her in our living room, channeling spirits from the *spiritual plane*. Day after day I'd answered our door while my mom meditated and aided all these wounded souls who'd exhausted every other conventional remedy to their problems and reluctantly found their way to our doorstep.

"What's wrong with him?" I asked her.

"Bwinny, we don't know what it eez."

"What did the doctor say?"

"Zat is zee zing!" She snorted. "He won' zee a doctor."

"He lives across the fucking street from a hospital."

"You know your father."

It was as though knowing someone meant tolerating everything that might kill them. She said he'd fall and complain that it felt like an elephant was on his chest. He wouldn't let her call an ambulance. He said if he was dying he didn't want to die in any fucking hospital.

"You should go see him, Bwinny."

So I did. Before he let me in the door, I had to swear an oath not to tell him to cross the street and go to the hospital. An hour later he suffered the same mysterious "attack," collapsing and complaining of the elephant on his chest. Then more every hour or

so. Each time I had no idea whether I was witnessing a dress re-
hearsal of his actual death or the real thing. Each time he asked
for my hand and I held it until whatever it was gradually subsided.
We tried to pretend everything was normal until the next attack.
After a half dozen attacks my father suggested we do an inventory of the possible culprits. Cigarettes triggered it, walking up
the stairs, masturbation, the miscellaneous-spontaneous variety.

"Don't worry, Brinny, I think I have a remedy to lick this thing."
He smiled reassuringly.

The "remedy" consisted of two frozen towels, one for his forehead and the other for his chest, that he had stored in the freezer.

I don't remember how long this went on for. Obviously nobody could live in a constant state of emergency so, at some point
the following morning, he announced we required groceries. Not
pricey groceries from the closest supermarket, mind you; our destination was reasonably priced bulk items from Costco twelve miles
away. *He'd* drive.

When we got there my father handed me a shopping list after
announcing his intention to get the eggs. The world could go on
spinning. He was getting eggs and I had a list for the remaining
items we needed.

Things were going to turn out okay. I started walking down
an aisle but found I couldn't read anything on the piece of paper
my father had given me. Even before I realized I was crying, a
woman working in Costco offering samples to customers asked
me what was wrong. I didn't know where to begin so I turned
around to point toward my father, by way of explanation, but instead saw an avalanche of Lucky Charms boxes in mid-collapse
burying my father, who was laid out on the ground. He was try-

ing to protect himself from more boxes falling on him, so he wasn't dead.

Hemingway said the only difference between people is the details of how we live and how we die. Gaudí got hit by a bus, Nick Drake overdosed on antidepressants, Lennon was shot in the back outside his apartment by a *Catcher in the Rye* fanatic, Plath stuck her head in an oven—you can't look at their lives or their art the same way ever again. My father was going to die under a pile of Lucky Charms.

I ran over to him.

"Go!" he gasped, like a soldier dropped at D-Day. "Don't worry about me! Go back. Get the milk. *The milk!* Keep going. Milk is the priority!" Then came my breaking point and his life's moment of triumph. "Not the regular bullshit—get the 2 percent milk!"

"I can't do this anymore," I told him. "I tried. I can't. I can't do this."

"Okay," he whispered, glaring at the new marshmallows Lucky was offering in the cereal box. "Help me up and we can go to the hospital."

It turned out one of his arteries was almost entirely clogged. I couldn't stay with him in the hospital, even though the rest of my family arrived immediately. After I took him to the emergency room, I went back to his house and slept for two days. While I slept, doctors opened his chest and catheterized his artery, saving his life.

When he got out, he stopped drinking and smoking for almost a year. Within a month, the most perverse thing my family discovered about him during his dry period, which none of us spoke about, was just how much *easier* he was to deal with loaded up on all the things that were killing him.

I took whatever work I could find to make enough money to leave town and get back to Havana as fast I could. I taught boxing in parks. I worked for a few weeks in football pads as an extra in a Disney TV movie called *Angels in the Endzone* but was fired for reading books in the locker room instead of hurrying out in front of the camera. I hustled tourists at speed chess downtown. I worked, sheepishly, as the only bouncer at nightclubs in Chinatown without a Kevlar vest (they were expensive). I collected garbage until I backed a truck into someone's roof and was fired. Nothing panned out so I gave dealing drugs a whirl and lasted all of three days before I chickened out and gave the backpack with two pounds of weed back to the guy who'd originally handed it over. The person who'd hired me to deal drugs, miraculously, took pity on me and offered to stake me a couple grand a month to turn professional at boxing. That scared the hell out of me. All I wanted to do was leave.

I borrowed some money from my uncle to run away to Spain where a fighter had written me about a possible job helping a trainer at another boxing gym in Madrid.

14

WET MATCHES

You can't fix it. You can't make it go away. . . .
Maybe a small. part of it will die if I'm not around
feeding it anymore.
—Lew Welch, "Chicago Poem"

I'D FOUND THE ONLY ROOM I could afford in Madrid sandwiched between the Prado museum and the Atocha train station in a pension that was being run as a transvestite brothel. It was a cheap place to stay and the boxing gym where I got the job was only a few stops on the train, and on the way back you could walk with El Greco, Velázquez, Goya, and Salvador Dalí easily accessible at the Prado and Reina Sofía before you got home.

The transvestites and I shared a bathroom. The boys called me *el guapo* when they passed me in the hallways. They worked outside the gates of the Parque del Retiro while the Moroccans sold hash inside the gates or near the pond with the rowboats. The Moroccan dealers even had business cards. It was all very civilized.

Then it was four late one night or early one morning. I hadn't talked with anyone or slept for so long I'd lost track. There was another argument cooking up from behind a wall in my room. The police had come the night before and left after a few minutes.

I leaned out the window looking over the little courtyard and lit a cigarette, staring at the dresses belonging to the skinny South American boys hung on the laundry line. There was an ashtray on the windowsill with a train wreck of cigarettes scattered in its palm.

I'd fallen for a girl back home and written her a letter and she'd promised she'd come see me. On the night I'd first met her I'd thought she was a little nervous to sleep with me because she was a virgin.

It only lasted three days.

The last time I saw her was on her porch:

"What's wrong, Brin?"

"I don't know. I just don't have anything to ask you and I don't have anything to say to you. I don't know why."

"Well, that's when you say good-bye."

She was right.

The night I met her I'd been working on a story about someone with the awful luck of falling for a prostitute. When we were eighteen and first visiting Europe, a painter friend of mine had sketched a portrait of a haunted and haunting girl standing behind a window in the Red Light District and had given it to her. The real girl didn't especially care, but the girl in my story did. And I was trying to figure out a way for them to kiss and have it mean something because I liked the poetry of prostitutes withholding a kiss and giving up all that other stuff. I wasn't even really sure if they really did.

The girl behind the counter at the café followed me outside where I was smoking and asked what I'd been writing about, giving me a startled look when I told her. I asked if I'd said something wrong and she asked if I could walk her home when she got off at 3 a.m.

Along the way she told me she enjoyed the walks to the boys' houses more than the boys.

Sometimes the wrong people have your number and I needed to put some miles between us.

I hadn't told anyone when I borrowed some money from my uncle and flew over to Madrid and stayed out all night Christmas Eve until that strange hour when the Chinese step out into the copper streetlight haze and huddle on hundreds of street corners across town clutching dozens of shopping bags full of to-go food for a few bucks. Chance being stuck over a toilet for ten hours and go sightseeing through the nighttime streets that get started around 3 a.m. Walking until the Chinese have abandoned the street corners and turn off the Gran Vía and head down to Puerta del Sol along a path where all the Africans are waiting for you, peddling movies and music and scarves and sunglasses on blankets, so that if a whistle echoes down a corridor that *la policía* are approaching, the blankets are packed up by the hundreds, swept up as quick as dominoes tip over, and two seconds later a thriving black market economy is a ghost echo of footsteps haunting eighty different directions, weaved into all the other squeaky Windex-scrubbed reflections on storefront windows of urgent men casting glances at their fake designer watches.

A lot of strangers close in on one another to nurse their respective hangovers with scenic strolls down the streets near the statue of a bear reaching up into a tree, looking just like a boy going for his first kiss. For entertainment I gave reading *Don Quixote* another half-assed try in Spanish on a bench nearby, until the tourist buses rolled up and the Gypsies moved in like a kicked-over ant nest and set up their coordinated strikes.

Then someone knocked on the door of my room.

"¡El guapo! ¡Correo!"

I opened the door to one of the transvestites with half her makeup off. I was pretty sure her name was Daisy. She handed me a letter. I opened it.

Just a date and a time and a place. A little quote beneath as a flirtatious fuck-you:

> *"I'm a romantic; a sentimental person thinks things will last,*
> *a romantic person hopes against hope they won't."*
>
> —F. Scott Fitzgerald

She had cigarette-stain eyes. I prefer dark eyes even though most girls who possess them dismiss them as common. They aren't. You look *into* brown eyes, while you look *at* all the other colors. With no buildup or wind-down, apart from us nearly fucking, we'd said good-bye. She'd just finished doing some handstands for no particular reason.

I went to see her at the café but she'd stopped working there. I was leaning over a table writing in a notebook when I heard some roller skates smack the pavement. I looked up and saw her.

"Can I sit down?"

I stood up and we looked at each other for a while. I pulled out her chair and she sat down.

"The first time we met you were writing a story about a guy who falls in love with a prostitute."

I nodded.

"It's strange, it happened to me."

"Hold on a second." I tried to process this. "You fell in love with a *gigolo*?"

"No." She smiled. "I was the hooker."

"When?"

"For the last five years."

"You were a hooker when we met?"

"Yeah."

"But you were working *here*."

"Part time."

"But you were in school."

"How do you think I paid my tuition?"

"Your stepdad was a dentist!"

"It's creepy you remember so much. Are you in love with me or something? I came so close to telling you but, you know, it just sort of took care of itself."

"Well," I said, "I still don't even know your name."

In Madrid my phone rang.

"You know who this is?"

"You're the only person who has my phone number."

"I'm at Plaza Mayor."

"Okay. You're close by."

"I'm high on ecstasy."

"That's great."

"I'm drunk, too."

"Come over."

"You're sure you know who this is?"

"I already answered that question."

"Where do you live?"

I gave her my address.

"I'll call you when I leave."

4 a.m. Phone rings.

"Still up?"

"No, I'm fast asleep."

"I've been dancing all night. I just got out of a swimming pool five minutes ago. I stink. Still want me to come over?"

"Get over here."

"Positive?"

4:15 a.m. Phone rings.

"I'm getting the heebie-jeebies. I haven't talked with you in a really long time. This is really weird."

"Don't worry. I have strawberries. It's fine."

"You have . . . *strawberries*?"

"Exactly."

"You have strawberries?"

"Exactly. Nothing weird. Bowl of strawberries. Very wholesome arrangement. Everybody's happy."

"Okay."

"Just come over."

There was a pause and I felt something in my brain creak.

"I don't think I—" Raped, pregnant, aborted pause. "Okay. I'll be there in a second."

A few minutes later I saw her get out of a cab on the Gran Vía. I dug into my pocket and pulled out my keys and flicked them out the window. I heard them connect with the pavement.

She entered the room and sat on the floor and grabbed a handful of strawberries and smoked from a pouch of Drum tobacco.

She didn't say much at first. Every ten minutes or so she'd go to the bathroom and leave the door open while she pissed. After the first time I leaned over to watch her.

"Why don't you close the door?" I asked.

"Why should I?"

This seemed to me a very sensible answer.

"I don't know."

"I'm peeing."

"I know that."

"We*lllll*?"

"Well, do you ever close the door?"

"Do you want me to?"

"No. It's just weird you're so . . ."

She wiped herself and flushed the toilet.

"What?"

"I don't know," I said. "It's intimate."

She came back over to the carpet and sat cross-legged, facing me.

She wouldn't say anything.

"Tell me how you got into it," I asked, feeling like a jackass.

"Julia Roberts in *Pretty Woman*."

I gave her a look.

"My sister."

"Is she still working?"

"No," she said, pressing a strawberry against her lips. "She was a meth addict. So was my mom. But my sister kicked it and got out of turning tricks."

"So you worked on the street?"

"No. I worked at places they have set up for it."

"Which ones?"

"A bunch."

"What kind of type goes for it?"

She smiled. "There's no type. It's everybody. Nobody."

"Did you fuck celebrities?"

"Sometimes. Sure."

"Only Vancouver?"

"No," she said. "Other places. They give you an apartment. They set you up with a room. I'd write my essays or study and the johns would come over and I'd buzz them in. They'd leave and I'd go back to the books until the next one arrived. I worked at a place in Japan for a while. Hostess thing. I didn't go over there for it. But it finds you."

"How'd you get out?" I asked. *Are we on Larry fucking King?* KISS HER.

"Roll me another cigarette." She waited until I'd finished and handed it over and lit it for her. "You do that nicely. I always was a little crazy for how you roll and prepare those things. Well, a john approached me and I could see it in his eyes."

"See what?"

"It happens to these guys. They fall for you."

"But you never fall for them?"

"Anyway—this guy was gray, gray but not ugly. He was wearing an expensive but all wrinkled-up suit. And he came over to the bed and sat down beside me. He told me I didn't belong there. And I was pretty cold about it and told him if he was feeling something for me it was probably a useful thing to know that for me love was money."

"You still believe that?" I asked.

"No," she responded. "But he said that was all right. It was fine. He took a second looking at the ground, then turned back to me while he reached into his briefcase. He told me he had money. Then he asked what my price was to get out. I asked him to repeat himself—just to be a bitch about it—and he found the checkbook in that *at-ta-ché* briefcase of his. I couldn't breathe when I saw it. Sorry. I have to pee."

She tried to get up but stumbled. Behind her I saw a wallet drop from her pocket. She struggled to get to her feet and made it, albeit a little woozily. When her back was to me, I swiped the wallet. She had the bathroom door open so I couldn't case it.

"Had you ever put a price on getting out before?"

"Roll me another one," she said, flushing the toilet. "No, I'd never put a price on it. Not before that moment. But I thought about it. And I just, you know, crunched the numbers."

"What'd you come up with?"

"I told him I wanted him to pay my full tuition up to a doctorate in whatever I wanted. I wanted a car. I wanted an apartment for a year. I wanted twenty grand upfront."

"And he tore off a check?"

"He tore off a check. We walked out the door together."

"You were with him?"

"No. I *saw* him. But I wasn't *with* him. It was just your average sugar daddy arrangement for a while."

"You think so, huh?"

"*Anyway*, then I met somebody. And I fell in love with that somebody. That had never happened before. Or since. And I told the guy who'd gotten me out of the game and he was good about it and backed off. He gave me space with it. And the guy I fell in love with fell in love with me. We played house. I was with him. And it was—I'm not sure how to put it—it was *true*."

I reached over and took the cigarette from her mouth.

"Why are you looking at me like that?"

"Is everything you're telling me made up?"

"Maybe."

"Okay." I put the cigarette back between her lips. "Keep telling the story."

"I played it straight with this boy and a lot of stuff was around the corner. Playing house was nice. But one night I'm out walking my dog and I bump into that john. The sugar daddy. He offers me fifteen grand for one night. I took it. Turned the trick. And the next morning I go back to the guy I was living with and confess it."

"Why?"

"Because I loved him."

"I got that part. I meant, why'd you turn the trick?"

"Anyway—I told him it was a horrible mistake. I told him that I loved him. And he said he loved me and that we were done. That's why I left the city to come to Europe. Biggest mistake of my life."

"So the john bought you out and bought you back in?" I felt like a CNN ticker.

"I'm getting tired."

"Did you kiss the john?"

"I'm sleepy."

"Sleep here."

"Umm . . . I don't think so."

"Not with *me*. Just sleep here. I can't sleep on the bed anyway."

"Why?" she asked.

I shrugged. "It intimidates me."

"I can't stay here with you. I can't stay here."

"Why?"

"Because this is better. For *you* I mean. It's a good little memory to gnaw on as it is."

She got up off the floor and looked at me, tilting her head to one side.

"I have your name," I said.

"Do you now? You know my name?"

"I don't *know* it," I corrected. "I *have* it."

I pulled out her wallet and stood up and gave it to her. We both held on to it for a second before I let go. She leaned over and I pulled back and everything was fine until she kissed me hard for a few moments, then slipped off my lips as softly as snow falling from a branch. Then she was gone and I went over to my window and watched the dawn breaking until she came out the entrance of the apartment and disappeared onto the Gran Vía, a suicide's leap below my window.

15

MUSICAL CHAIRS

Marco Polo describes a bridge, stone by stone.
"But which is the stone that supports the bridge?" Kub-
*   lai Khan asks.*
"The bridge is not supported by one stone or another,"
*   Marco answers, "but by the line of the arch that they*
*   form."*
Kublai Khan remains silent, reflecting.
Then he adds: "Why do you speak to me of the stones? It
*   is only the arch that matters to me."*
Polo answers: "Without stones there is no arch."
                    —Italo Calvino, *Invisible Cities*

A COUPLE OF MONTHS LATER I scrounged enough money to take a
direct flight from Madrid to Havana. I sat with a girl named Ría
on the edge of the Malecón, with Miami somewhere off in the
sunset behind us, ignited against the horizon like a lit cigar dropped
into a puddle of gasoline.

Ría was a pen pal who had just graduated from the university of Havana. Some Cubans I'd met in Madrid, who had married off the island, had put me in touch with her. They told me she was in love with the same books I was: Cervantes, Calvino, Kundera, Duras. Through her work designing Web sites for the government she was in the coveted position of having access to the Internet. This was exceedingly rare for Cubans. We wrote each other e-mails almost every day. It's always strange finding someone on the page before you know them anywhere else. Sometimes you get lucky and start off with a curious mutual understanding— "landsman" is the lovely word to describe that sensation. She insisted we write in English so she could improve her grasp of the language. She'd taught herself English by learning the lyrics to seemingly every song ever written. She'd never left Cuba before yet knew, in great detail, about everywhere I'd ever traveled from literature, film, art, and history books. When I told her about my mother's background she knew all kinds of details about the Hungarian revolution. After Hungary supplied Cuba with all their horribly unreliable humped Camelo buses, she'd gotten curious about the land that gave birth to those monstrosities of dysfunction.

We broke the ice with Ría's idea of small talk.

"The tourists my friends meet from Gringolandia always try to seduce us with the cars they drive back home." Ria giggled, wiping dark locks from her black eyes. We had corresponded for months, but I'd never seen a picture of her before. She was waif-thin, swimming in an oversized Terry Fox Marathon of Hope T-shirt, a little pair of battered tennis shoes beneath a white skirt patterned with purple lilacs she'd sewn on herself. She reminded me of a Cuban Audrey Hepburn, hopelessly beautiful in all her delicate features and almost apologetic grace. Over the years I would have the chance to meet several very important people in Cuban society, but I had the most luck in meeting Ría.

That day, she introduced me to her smile that involuntarily tilted her head to one side like the girl Picasso captured in *The Dreamer*. She'd brought along some peso submarine-sized cigars for us to smoke. After she'd gushed about how much she enjoyed quality cigars, I'd felt too ashamed over our correspondence to confess that I didn't care for them. For a present I'd brought her some Romeo y Julietas from the gift shop of the Habana Libre hotel. As she bit off and spit out the end of her cigar she discovered that her lighter had run out of fluid and spiked it on the pavement at our feet. "*Cubaneo,*" she growled. "Whatever isn't broken here will be soon."

I reached over with the flame of my match while she puffed her cigar to life. After she filled her lungs with smoke, she filled her cheeks until they expanded in Louis Armstrong proportions before exhaling. "Oh how I've missed this smoke! As I was saying, in Cuba cars themselves tell you very little about us, but you can tell everything about someone by their license plate. License plates are the Cuban people's Rosetta Stone."

"Decode all these drivers for me." I cast my hand across the lanes of traffic racing along the Malecón.

"In one glance you can tell if they are a foreigner, their job, how important they are, where they're allowed to go. Even if you had a million dollars sent to you from Miami you can't drive your car for five minutes without the government allowing you to. We stole the same system of license plates from the Soviet Union. My cousin was a secret policeman before they put him in jail for sell-

ing materials from the airport on the *mercado negro*. Soon they
will have cameras all over the city monitoring all movements."

"What was he selling?"

"Fuel. Cigars. Food. *Anything.*" She took a long draw from her
cigar and inhaled deeply. "I can't even concentrate because this
cigar is giving my lungs an orgasm. Even my asthma is behaving
and isn't attacking me because of how *luxurious* this Romeo y Julieta is. I'm not even upset you lied to me all this time in our letters about cigars. How many other things did you lie about also?
All writers are such liars."

"I didn't lie to gain an advantage," I told her. "Maybe I did. I
just wanted to hear your description of how much you enjoyed
them."

"That *is* an advantage over a stranger. Cigars were the only
sensual pleasure I had as a teenager."

Ría's uncle worked in a cigar factory as an inspector and brought
home good stolen cigars for his family. It was the only luxury Ría's
family enjoyed until the uncle was caught and lost his job. Ría and
I were the same age and during the Special Period, when she was
a teenager, the food shortages were so severe it was a bigger crime
to kill a cow than a person. She told me her boyfriend became a
"cat fisherman" from people's yards. There was no other source
of meat. People went to prison for having an American dollar in
their pocket. Santa Claus was illegal. But through all that awful-
ness her family had the best tobacco in the world whenever they
wished.

"I felt like a fairy-tale girl lost in a dark forest." She laughed.
"But with cigars I had my magical little fetish tune to whistle, to
forget my troubles."

Ría pointed to the blue government-owned plates. She explained how the letters and numbers on the plates were indications of whether the car could be used for personal travel and where it could go. The first letter indicated which of the fourteen provinces the car came from. A "K" signified a privately owned car. Caramel plates for those higher up in government-run firms. Maybe they could only transport visiting officials during business hours or perhaps had more leeway for private use. Mint green plates were for military personnel, placed only on the rear of their vehicles. Olive green for Ministry of the Interior—issued plates, including Fidel's motorcade of armored 1980s-made Mercedes. Black plates were for foreign diplomats who mostly lived in old abandoned mansions on Havana's jarringly opulent Fifth Avenue. They were free to ignore traffic laws. Cars with white plates were for Cuban ministers or heads of state organizations. Maroon plates for rental cars. Bright orange plates for Cubans working overseas, religious leaders, or foreign journalists.

"Yellow plates for all the old American cars held up by bubble gum and Popsicle sticks," Ría went on. "Those are the only cars Cubans can legally trade and buy and sell. Only cars before 1959, when our revolution began. And for those the government has not yet decided which plates to give you, 'provisional' red plates are given. Isn't it all so egalitarian?"

"How does anybody purchase a new car?" I asked.

"With permission."

"Permission?"

"This is our version of a catch-22. To gain permission you must explain how on earth you could ever afford a new car, living on the government wages that over 90 percent of us do. Let's change the subject. I believe in the principles of this crumbling revolution, but I find it inconceivable that on your first visit you never slept with one of our women."

We'd come from the apartment she'd found me in Calle Neptuno to sit on the Malecón where the U.S. battleship *Maine* had mysteriously exploded and promptly sank, setting off the Spanish-American War just before the turn of the twentieth century. This was the "war" in which William Randolph Hearst invented yellow journalism for the American public. "There will be no war," one of Hearst's employees telegrammed back from Cuba. "Please remain," Hearst telegrammed back. "You furnish the pictures and I'll furnish the war." In 1898, for twenty million dollars, Spain handed over Puerto Rico, Guam, and the Philippines to the United States and in all but name took over Cuba, signing into Cuba's new constitution the right to intervene and "supervise" the treasury and foreign relations. Gitmo was handed over indefinitely with the signing of the Platt Amendment soon after, with an annual fee of four thousand dollars to be paid by the U.S. Treasury, which no Cuban was involved in negotiating, and which was never to increase. But all this had come after the Spanish troops had crushed José Martí and the Cuban rebel army and wiped out between two hundred and four hundred thousand Cuban civilians in an eerie foreshadow of the concentration camps that would haunt the new century across Europe.

I'd tried to track down Alfonso and coordinate meeting him in Havana again, but his phone had been disconnected and he never answered any of my e-mails. I didn't know he had already been granted his wish of never having to leave Havana again since he'd been buried in the Colón cemetery for over a month at that point. Montalvo didn't have a phone or a computer, so Ría had offered to meet me at the airport. We'd shared a gypsy cab back to my original block near the Plaza de la Revolución and discovered nearly everyone I'd met during my first trip had abandoned Cuba altogether. Two houses had been sold on the black market to finance escapes out of the country. The old man who had worked as a doorman at the Nacional had died in his sleep. Ernesto had reunited with his wife in Barcelona. The family of Jesús had gotten lucky in the annual lottery of twenty thousand visas and relocated to Miami. Only Doogie Howser remained on the block, and he'd taken a mistress to Varadero and wouldn't be back for a week.

Ría had helped me work out an alternative plan, through a friend of a friend of a friend, with unregistered accommodation in Centro Habana, a little dingy neighborhood called Cayo Hueso (Bone Key). She found me a room on the roof of a four-story walkup across the street from a building that had recently fallen down. After Ría rejected the traditional 15 percent referral fee from the married couple illegally renting me the room, they were entirely convinced she was a spy. Their mutual shock made it clear no other plausible explanation existed in their minds.

"We're happy to pay you for bringing him to us," they reiterated nervously. "This is a reasonable custom."

"I'm not opposed to the custom." Ría smiled. "But it doesn't apply here. I won't accept money for helping a friend find accommodation. If I did this in service of a *stranger*, I would. *Claro?*"

"We know times are very hard," the husband renting me the apartment reasoned. "I respect what you're saying. Don't be stubborn here."

"Then this extra money will help your family and I'm happy for that. Thank you for looking after my friend."

The husband and wife, Arnaldo and Ariana were their names,

still looked petrified accepting Ría's explanation. But they had no choice. Ría had nothing left to say about it.

Back on the Malecón some kids were diving into the ocean while a trumpeter serenaded them. A fisherman clubbed his first catch with the heel of a ratty Nike sneaker as a policeman stopped a young black local girl walking hand-in-hand with an old sun-burned tourist. She didn't have her papers and was taken away in a squad car to the station. The tourist hailed a taxi and gave pursuit. The nearby, supremely well-guarded U.S. Interests section was almost entirely obscured by fifty flapping Cuban flags beneath a vertical phalanx of poles pointed at the heavens. If anyone inside could see past the flags, a sign had been freshly painted, proclaiming WE DON'T WANT SLAVE OWNERS HERE. A family huddling beside us stared off at another cruise ship slugging its way across the horizon into the harbor. We got up and walked for a while under the curled streetlamps before sitting back down on Havana's collective sofa and windowsill to the world.

Eventually we walked the length of the Malecón as kids glazed the cement in sticky embraces, the waves just over the edge of the seawall. Sometimes just below their feet other people would be fooling around against the rocks, but all you could see were shadows folding like origami against the dim light of the horizon. We turned onto the Prado promenade toward some fights being held at Kid Chocolate that I'd invited Ría to watch. A pack of boys chased after a soccer ball under the trellis of trees overhead while *jineteras* smoked cigarettes on stone benches waiting for business. Stray cats sat and stared predatorily at the birds perched on the branches overhead. Artists were taking down their afternoon displays and packing up their canvases.

"Hundreds of years ago," Ría said, smiling, "the most beautiful women in my city could only be seen stepping in or out of carriages along Prado. Some of the first foreigners who wrote about their visits never got past just how stunningly beautiful the women's feet were."

"My boxing coach Héctor sent me to Prado to observe the women after our first lesson together," I confessed to Ría. "When we were finished for the day, I asked what made the Cuban style of fighting so much more effective than anywhere else in the world. He told me to come here and sit on a bench in Prado and to study how the women walk. 'It's all right there, Brinicito. That's our secret. We try to box the way our women move. Have you ever seen women who can do more with each step than ours?'"

"He is probably a *puerco*." Ría laughed. "But it's an intelligent observation."

The natural light was almost entirely gone when the streetlamps flickered on and hummed beside us. Distant smokestacks rose into the last embers of glow hovering over old Havana's skyline. I'd forgotten about the mood that always seemed to haunt the Prado and so much of Havana with nearly each step. Something like catching the gaze of a beautiful teenage girl with every fuse on her body lit by sexuality while smiling at you with rotten teeth. Both for Havana's beauty and its decay, it's nearly impossible to restrain yourself from staring at everything you see. I was told before my first trip that no city in the world offered the dreams you could have sleeping in Havana. However, nobody warned about how it also feels like an exhausting nightmare that never quite fulfills the promise of that with which it's threatening you.

A pack of *jineteras*, all uniformed in spandex, walking arm in arm with a group of much older, drunken, overweight, sweaty European tourists, strolled past us. Ría watched them from the corner of her eye until they were by us. She turned to me.

"I wondered when you first contacted me if that was the arrangement you were looking for."

"It worried you?" I asked.

"It *amused* me." She winked, reaching over to squeeze my wrist.

We walked in silence for a while. Along the Prado they used to sell slaves on the auction block. Before Fidel, when segregation was in full swing, the Cuban apartheid meant many clubs and parks still refused black Cubans entry. Famously even President Batista couldn't gain membership to a country club because he wasn't white enough.

"How many boyfriends do you have now?"

"*¡Qué va!* I'm innocent. So *dime*. Before you drag me to this boxing match I would like to know what movies do they like where you're from, Brinicito."

"Superheroes and comic book stuff are the most popular. Hollywood makes a lot of movies about America being attacked or blowing itself up that people seem to enjoy watching. Distraction. Escape."

"They're sad?"

"Not even sad. *Depressed.*"

"Movies to me are as close as we have to dreams. What do they wish to dream about where you're from? *Por ejemplo*, what is the most popular movie of all time in Gringolandia?"

"*Titanic* made the most money."

"I saw it. We get pirated DVDs of American movies from the black market."

"What did you think of it?"

"*Titanic* doesn't sound like escape or distraction to *me*. Fidel *loved* the film *Jaws*. He said it was capitalism attacking every citizen with nowhere to hide. I'm sure Fidel would say *Titanic* describes a lot about America."

"The doomed, supposedly unsinkable ship?"

"Bah!" Ría slapped my arm. "Forget politics. *Emotionally. Existentially.* There's poetry in what that ship's failed journey meant. Have you read Neruda?"

"*Listen,*" I said. "Forget Pablo Neruda and start talking about Leonardo Di-fucking-Caprio."

"*Titanic* has different significance here. We don't go on cruise ships anywhere. We can't go anywhere. We know why we're miserable—we're stuck *here*. Why do your people care so much about an unfortunate accident with *Titanic* during a pointless transatlantic crossing?"

"Where I come from more people believe in angels than climate change. The *unsinkable* ship is how we see our own lives."

"I must tell you, the only part I liked about *Titanic* was when the orchestra played after they found out they will all die. *That* Cubans would like."

"Do you think it was true?"

"Everyone has the same death sentence as those doomed people on that big boat making all their plans for what they will do when they arrive in New York. It's uninteresting. The men who played their instruments were beautiful."

"Do *you* play an instrument?"

"Several."

"So what would you play?"

"Under *those* circumstances?"

"We're all living those circumstances, with an iceberg on the way sooner or later, aren't we?" I asked.

"I don't know. Just a melody of some kind. I like little melodies. When Orpheus went into hell to retrieve his bride he had to play a melody for the devil to get her back. I like to think it was a little melody he played. We're all just melodies in the lives of every person we know."

"So what's your melody, Ría?"

"How can I know that answer? I don't think you get to choose. It's played with everyone else's orchestra. I'm sure I'm just elevator music for most people, but maybe a symphony for the people who love me."

"You don't think you get to choose?" I asked.

"Maybe you can. I believe you can. But that very idea that I believe you can choose just becomes part of mine! Maybe that's my fantasy."

"For you is my melody sad or happy?"

"Oh Brinicito." Ría looked over and through me. "I think your melody is that very question."

"I always read how primitive things are here relative to everywhere else. You might get around to adopting this glorious invention called 'small talk' one of these days. You sure know how to go for the kill, don't you?"

"Military service is mandatory here. I'm a good shot with a rifle. My point is just, even with us, it is strange. Do I have the same melody in person as in writing when you read me before? Are both melodies playing for you and you're guessing which is the real me? Do they play nicely together or give you something you didn't expect? Less or more? Maybe you were curious and attracted to me but you aren't now. Maybe it's the other way around. This is a little more complicated than maybe you expected with your question. I don't even know if my melody or my country's deserves to be a happy one to someone like you. Maybe we seem very sad and this gives your own sad feelings some comfort."

"How would that possibly give me comfort?" I asked.

"Because unlike the *Titanic* our voyage isn't a luxury cruise. And even if it failed there's beauty in some failed journeys. We're sad for reasons many of us remain proud of. And from what I see of many who come from where you do, you can't even put your finger on what makes you sad. That is a sadness none of us understand. It's incomprehensible to not know why you're sad here. That's a strange gift, isn't it?"

We were nearly at the lion statues at the end of the promenade. Cabs were parked on the corner of Calle Neptuno overlooking all the hotels Ría was forbidden to enter. Hotel-approved bands were playing Buena Vista Social Club standards on several of the patios while doormen and security stared off. We crossed the street over to Parque Central and Ría snickered at the mob of Esquina Caliente raging at one another over the merits of this or that Cuban pitcher's dominance if they had a chance to pitch outside the confines of the island. "*¡Yo discrepo!*" one ancient man cried out. "There are not two opinions unless you are a fool, old man!" "*¡Yo discrepo!*" "*¡Usted está senil!*"

"We should stay here and listen." Ría laughed. "Listen to the formality of these people. This will be much more interesting and informative than the boxing at Kid Chocolate. This is better than the Brazilian *telenovelas* that shut down Havana. Who knew?"

I pried Ría free and we walked down the block to Chocolate's entrance, yet while I paid two Cuban pesos for tickets, all I could hear from inside was a barely intelligible speech over a broken-down loudspeaker. As we entered the gymnasium the voice made one final pronouncement overrun with churning feedback that echoed off the walls and suddenly everything fell silent. Inside they had problems with most of the lights and the scene was lit like van Gogh's *The Potato Eaters*, the shadows smeared and lathered all over the room. The packed audience was quietly standing at attention before a lineup of Cuba's pantheon of great revolutionary boxing champions, a murderer's row of legendary fighters. Their heroes were all a little grayer and paunchier than in their primes, all wearing a mishmash of various Cuban jerseys or tracksuits, but the silence had no stuffy formality. The boxers' faces had scars from their battles, though the audience had many scars of their own from daily battles, too. The capitalism grenade the fighters had smothered was the same grenade everyone else received the same shrapnel from. Boxing is the only sport where the score is hidden from the competitors while competition rages on. Life didn't seem all that different a lot of the time, considering the circumstances. But not knowing the score imbues the moment with a horrible tension that's only relieved when one arm is raised in victory and the other is left hanging.

In the silence we all saw the Cuban Olympic team's famously grumpy head coach for the last forty years, Dr. Alcides Sagarra, look down the line of champions and not be able to contain a smile. He clearly couldn't contain the smile while his countrymen in the stands admired his life's work. Sagarra was soon to step down and retire as Cuba's coach, and no small portion of the silence was offered in homage to his contribution and for his fighters' contributions to the revolution's struggle: thirty-two Olympic gold medals and sixty-three World Amateur Championships. No country on earth could touch Cuba's achievements in that realm. And in Castro's symbolic war against the United States, these soldiers to the cause had trounced a country with infinitely more wealth and thirty times the population. Even more, they'd all done it while turning down every offer of riches to leave. My sense witnessing this ceremony was that the silence wasn't just in gratitude for that sacrifice, it was equally an attempt to impart that what they had done on behalf of Cuba wasn't in vain. La Lucha—the struggle—in the ring was irrevocably intertwined with the struggle of all Cubans. There was no way to illuminate anything about the struggle of Cuba's boxers without exploring all Cubans' courage and humanity. I'm still not sure if that silence I witnessed lasted a few seconds, or an hour.

Teófilo Stevenson was the centerpiece of the group, still handsome and effortlessly composed, grinning almost bashfully as he magnetized the auditorium's collective wonder yet again. Nobody could look away. Stevenson's grin made him seem like a Cuban Cool Hand Luke, but this version hadn't just rebelled against every temptation America had offered him and been crushed by way of reprisal, he'd gained some measure of satisfaction. It was as if he knew that it was all the people watching who had given him the strength to stand up to the forces and temptations that had conspired against him throughout his life. He'd spent his life climbing pedestals to accept medals and trophies and accolades, but after all his battles were over, he was on no pedestal. Little separated Stevenson from anyone there and that was by Castro's design, after all. Distilling the interplay between Stevenson and the crowd that night was easiest to understand as an inside joke, which was as impenetrable as Mona Lisa's smile to an outsider. Stevenson looked out and giggled at the smiling faces in the crowd with as much admiration for them as they had for him.

Next to Stevenson stood Félix Savón, Cuba's second most famous champion, who had just returned from the recent Olympic Games with his own third Olympic gold medal in tow (which he was wearing), finally achieving what only his idol beside him and Lázló Papp of Hungary had. Just before his thirty-third birthday, Savón's final fight representing his country at the Sydney games had been a brutal, bloody affair. But what had caught my eye more than anything about his final match was what happened when the final bell sounded. Savón's historic career was over, having spanned fourteen years of unparalleled dominance on the international stage, and he paced back to his corner with blood dripping from one eye like a teardrop. Instead of looking for any validation from the crowd for his achievement, he instead looked out to spot the Cuban flags in the audience and hollered out through his mouth guard, "*¡Gracias, Cuba!*" He radiated gratitude. Back home in Havana standing in that lineup, Savón, a six-foot-six hulking heavyweight with one of the most lethal right hands in the history of the sport, wore the expression of a little boy who'd just learned how to ride a bike for the first time standing next to Stevenson, his hero, and being counted with him. Nobody in the room looked more adoringly at Stevenson than Savón, even though, after all these years as his successor, despite all his bravery, he still only managed to shyly peek.

And down the row the next face I recognized straight away was my trainer, Héctor Vinent. Of all the heroic boxers standing in that line of champions, Vinent was the only one who seemed uneasy and double-parked in his role. His best friend,

Joel Casamayor, only four years before, had become the first Cuban Olympic gold medalist to defect during the Atlanta games. Casamayor had left after being rewarded for his first gold medal with nothing more than a Chinese bicycle. For him it was the final straw. Vinent was the superior boxer with the far more marketable puncher's style. Far more money was on the table for him to accept his friend's pleadings to defect along with him, and he'd not only turned them down but urged Casamayor to remain in Cuba. Despite this fact, the state had punished Vinent, at the age of twenty-four, in his absolute prime, with never being able to pursue the craft he'd mastered on the island. Every fighter in that line, save Vinent, represented Cuba's past. Vinent was the only one there who pointed both to Cuba's troubled present and uncertain future.

Vinent spotted Ría and me and nodded just as the crowd roared an end to the ceremony and ushered in that night's fights with the clang of a wrench against a rusty fire extinguisher.

Vinent walked over to us and offered his hand for me to shake hello, and kissed Ría's cheek.

"So did you bring me back any books?" Héctor laughed. "You can both sit with me and the Havana team and their coaches. After we can get dinner in Barrio Chino and talk."

"Who is the best boxer right now?"

"*La mejor?*" Hector smiled. "Guillermo Rigondeaux. I have never seen anyone with his ability in my life. Savón gave him the captaincy after the Olympic Games. Fidel gave him a house near the airport. It's more than he gave me for both my medals," he said.

Ría shook her head and laughed.

"What's so funny?" Héctor asked her.

"Maybe it's not so funny." Ría shrugged. "I was just thinking about the next great athlete in the crowd who is just a little boy, watching all of you with his dad. What's going through that boy's mind staring at all of you?"

Héctor laughed. "It's not going to be easy convincing this generation to follow our path. Time will tell."

16

ROSETTA STONES

But if that flower with base infection meet,
The basest weed outbraves his dignity:
For sweetest things turn sourest by their deeds;
Lilies that fester, smell far worse than weeds.
                    —William Shakespeare, Sonnet 94

SOMETIMES IT TAKES STARING for a while to really know what you've been looking at. It took a long time to understand that night at Chocolate and bring the blur into focus. After the fights I went with Ría and Héctor out to dinner at a restaurant in Barrio Chino. Héctor was always in a good mood going out to eat. I finally got around to asking him the question I'd wanted to ask since I first met him.

"What was the temptation like for you with so many people outside Cuba willing to pay so much to have you fight for them?"

Héctor turned to Ría and winked.

"We've drifted away from sports and jumped into politics." Héctor smiled, refilling his glass from a can of Hatuey beer. "But

I'll answer your question. The U.S. is like a beautiful girl who is in love with you, but you don't like her. You have to ignore her. You have to resist and lament and live the rest of your life based on memories."

Boxers entered the ring in defense of their families, their neighborhoods, their society, and then—and only then—their own self-respect. Most stayed, but soon some left. The first defection took place five years after Fidel's ban, when Enrico Blanco, at fifteen, won a gold medal at the Pan American games in Canada. Shortly after his match he snuck off and vanished. In 1993, a year after Héctor won his first Olympic gold medal in Barcelona, Giorbis Barthelemy swam eleven miles to Guantánamo Bay's naval base. He failed to reach Gitmo and was captured and jailed on his first attempt. After he was freed from prison he made another attempt and succeeded. The following year, in 1994, five more Cuban boxers defected. Eliseo and Elieser Castillo, two brothers, watched in horror as sharks attacked their raft while they drifted for days. Diosbelys Hurtado defected during a layover in Miami. Alexis Barcelay wandered across a minefield to get to Guantánamo Bay. Mario Iribarren snuck off from a competition in Denmark. Two years after that, Héctor's best friend and Olympic champion, Joel Casamayor, and an amateur light heavyweight champion named Ramón Garbey abandoned Cuba. As times got more desperate, the floodgates were opening. Cuba's heroes transformed into traitors overnight and Fidel removed any trace of their legacy he could find. As much as the state could muster, they ceased to exist in their homeland.

That night in Havana at Kid Chocolate, with Héctor and Ría beside me, was the first time I'd seen Guillermo Rigondeaux, Cuba's next great champion, fight before his home crowd. It was obvious Rigondeaux had accepted the baton as Teófilo Stevenson and Félix Savón's successor in Fidel's continuum of symbolic weapons against the United States. What *wasn't* so obvious was what he was going to do with it. Héctor hadn't exaggerated his abilities. Rigondeaux wasn't only calibrated like a five-foot-five, 118-pound Stradivarius of a fighter, he was even more impressive as an artist. He inflicted violence with balletic grace, flawless balance and timing, and an almost mournful disdain for his opponent as he fluttered across the ring barely landing on his toes while lashing lethal blows, which struck and evaporated from view as quickly as he unleashed them. He'd been a prodigy since he was a boy and now, at only twenty, this strange gargoyle-faced Cuban was Mozart with a pair of gloves. But was that going to be enough for him to resist the temptation of defecting? Castro had given him a house; for the next medal he might get a decent car. Small potatoes compared to what he could get elsewhere, but there were other factors to consider, like how much money or fame was worth losing your family forever.

Like Héctor and many of the other great Cuban boxers, Rigondeaux came from the east, born in Santiago de Cuba on a coffee plantation with eight siblings. He grew up with no running water in his family home, so each day he walked a few miles to load up on water and transport it back to his house. He was born the same year as the Mariel boatlift. When barely in his teens, he was discovered for his potential by the Cuban industrial sports complex and sent to train in Havana at La Finca, the most elite sports academy on the island. The collapse of the Soviet Union and an end to their billion-dollar subsidies sent to Cuba led to the Special Period, during which Rigondeaux spent the remainder of his teens. And now he was Castro's official face of boxing on the island in the turbulent time of Elián González.

Rigondeaux's face, like all the other fighters' faces that night, was obscured by headgear until he claimed victory. But even then, as soon as his coach removed the headgear, he held a photograph of Fidel aloft, which concealed his face. How token was this act of public glorification? Was he truly grateful for what the revolution had provided him, or was he simply looking after his own survival?

I kept waiting for him to turn so I could study his face, look into his eyes, but almost immediately he was whisked out of the ring by his coaches and ushered back to the dressing room. It would take six years, another Olympic gold medal, and one of the most notorious failed defection attempts in Cuban history for me to cross paths with Rigondeaux again.

The following summer, in June of 2001, thousands of miles away from Havana in Belfast during the World Amateur Boxing Championships, Rigondeaux would meet someone eager to support his professional dreams and set him free to claim them. Rigondeaux and several other Cuban boxers had managed to sneak away from their fortified hotel rooms to have a drink at a local Irish pub. An Irishman named Gary Hyde, who owned a few pubs but had never had a drink in his life, remembered the handful of Cuban boxers lined up at the bar "like sitting ducks." Hyde zeroed in on Rigondeaux and warmly began to exchange words in broken Spanish. Six years later, Hyde promoted a boxing show in Cork, which his friend, Michael "Lord of the Dance" Flatley, attended by his side.

"You're missing a superstar in the making," Flatley chuckled in Hyde's ear. "Somebody we can all get a feel for, and follow through to big titles."

"Where you going to get one of those?" Hyde replied.

"Maybe go to one of the poorhouses of the world."

Rigondeaux's sad face instantly flashed in Hyde's mind. "Why skip Cuba?" Hyde thought to himself.

It was ten years in a Cuban prison for each athlete you so much as *discussed* defection with. And Hyde, like Rigondeaux, had his own wife and kids to potentially never see again. But Hyde crunched the risk versus reward calculus and two weeks later, in March of 2007, he was in Havana and had arranged through contacts at La Finca boxing academy to meet Rigondeaux next to the Esquina Caliente arguing baseball in Parque Central. Rigondeaux knew exactly what the meeting was about without it being told in advance. He simply asked Hyde what he was doing in Cuba. "Writing a book," Hyde lied.

"On what?" Rigondeaux asked.

"Boxing."

"*Professional* boxing?"

Not long after that meeting, Rigondeaux signed his name to a contract with Hyde as his manager, written in a language he couldn't read. By then the joke in Havana I was told about Cuban athletes was that they signed more contracts than autographs. Only after many lawsuits filed in Miami after he'd escaped on a smuggler's boat did Rigondeaux understand the importance of his signature on *this* contract. He'd traded in Castro's spider web for another in professional boxing.

After Hyde had signed Rigondeaux, he wandered down to the Malecón and pondered the logistics of escape. He sorted through every means imaginable: rafts, speedboats, jet skis, *submarines*—

anything he could think of. He looked up at the moon. "This was
the same moon I look at when I'm looking up in Ireland," he told
me years later. "How can I get from here to there without going
through airports, without going through security. All we had to
do was get them twelve miles away; once you were twelve miles
off the coast of Cuba, you were in international waters. I didn't
think about the consequences after that."

Hyde couldn't identify the ideal escape route so he flew home
to Ireland to give it some more thought. But in the meantime he
left his signed boxers with cell phones. He also left behind his
daughter's debit card, which he promised to replenish regularly
once he returned home, and to send over more money hidden inside the pages of printed material via DHL.

Every year I returned to Havana after meeting Rigondeaux
that day at Chocolate, so many boxers and ordinary Cubans I'd
known disappeared, or were in the desperate process of doing everything they possibly could to flee, that it was impossible to take
for granted any casual good-bye anywhere, because it could mean
a good-bye forever. Security cameras sprouted up all over the city,
tracking millions of footsteps from above street corners, only in-
tensifying the Cuban version of *1984* that always felt rewritten by
Charles Dickens. Everywhere you looked people's eyes looked
bloodshot from how exhausting this reality made interpersonal
dynamics. I saw people laugh themselves to tears or fight themselves back from sadness almost every day. People either had no
time to spare to get close to life or they had to pull back so far it
was like they'd fallen out of orbit with their regular lives and into
some poisonous constellation of dread. Both extremes only highlighted the difference between you and them, all the while with
the sinking awareness that, sooner or later, even with the lucky

ones, they all had a different train to catch from yours. More than ever before Cuba began to sharpen and snap into focus as some kind of nightmarish Grand Central Station, divided with such cruelty between those with tickets and those condemned and resigned to purgatory for the remainder of their lives.

17

CHASING THE AMERICAN DREAM FROM A SMUGGLER'S BOAT

I couldn't bear to think about it; and yet, somehow, I couldn't think about nothing else.

—Mark Twain,
The Adventures of Huckleberry Finn

THE PERVERSE IRONY with increasing numbers of Cuban boxers, ballplayers, and ordinary citizens being trafficked off the island was that the same waters had transported their ancestors on slave ships *to* Cuba almost five centuries before, starting around 1520. Slavery continued to flourish in Cuba for the next 366 years, until it was outlawed in 1886.

The transatlantic slave trade tore between ten and fifteen million Africans from their homes and grimly deposited them into indentured servitude in the New World. More than two million more, shackled together in cramped, disease-ridden spaces, died making the horrific seven-week passage. Recent estimates suggest as many as one in ten voyages underwent a slave mutiny. Africans attempted suicide, tried to jump ship, or refused to eat. Slavers were known to remove the teeth of slaves so they could force-feed them. Even before any slaves entered and perished on the boats, perhaps twice as many died being marched hundreds of miles to the awaiting ships or while being held in confinement in dungeon-like con-·ditions. In all, for every hundred slaves that reached the New World, forty perished somewhere along that excruciating journey.

Havana's port used to be home to one of the biggest slave markets on earth. The port was protected by El Morro, which was built by the Spanish in 1589 as a fortress to guard Havana against invasion and raids. A chain was spread out across the waters. In 1762, the British captured El Morro after they landed in Cojimar, attacked from land, and mined through a bastion to seize control. The following· year England returned Cuba to Spanish control and La Cabana was built as insurance against further invaders. The lighthouse was added in the mid-nineteenth century.

Importation of slaves was outlawed in the United States at the beginning of the nineteenth century and Spain officially did the same twelve years later in 1820, the same year the American government ruled that bringing African slaves to the United States was an act of piracy, a capital offense. However, the trade hardly slowed down. Seven years after the American ban, twice the amount of slaves arrived in Havana. The number of slaves *doubled* again the following year. Slaves would continue to arrive on Cuban shores, unabated, for the next fifty-six years. By the turn of the eighteenth century, nearly one in four people living in Cuba was a slave. Hundreds of thousands more slaves continued to arrive by the boatload. In 1886, Cuba's population had exploded to nearly a million and a half people. The global demand· for sugar and tobacco, and the extraordinary labor force required to produce both, contributed to the ever-growing slave class. By that time three U.S. presidents had offered to buy Cuba from the Spanish, offering a lot more money for the island than they'd offered France in 1803 for Louisiana ($15 million) or the Russians in 1867 for Alaska ($7.2 million). In 1897, President McKinley offered Spain $300 million. No dice.

The following year, in 1898, when war broke out between the United States and Spain after the U.S.S. *Maine* sunk in Havana's harbor, the United States finally had their island. On December 10, 1898, following four months of fighting, Spain and the United States signed the Treaty of Paris. After Spain relinquished control of the Philippines, Guam, and Puerto Rico to the United States, Cuba took down the Spanish flag and raised the stars and stripes.

"What's a million dollars compared to the love of eight million Cubans?" Teófilo Stevenson famously replied to an offer of millions of dollars to leave his island. But since Castro took power in 1959, over a million Cubans *had* left. Castro called anyone who wanted to leave a "worm" or a "traitor," and most of the Cubans who had escaped looked at anyone who agreed with Stevenson's position as being brainwashed or scared for their lives to voice any dissenting opinion to the party line. What most compounded the ambiguity of this dynamic for me was watching the boxers who defected— mostly black Cubans (although, unlike African Americans, I've never met a Cuban who didn't refer to himself solely as a *Cuban*)— proudly wearing the Cuban flag on their trunks and on their robes in the United States. I could never determine exactly *which* Cuba they believed they were fighting for. It was never clear if they were fighting for the Cuba *before* Fidel or the one they hoped would come after. And what Cuba was that supposed to be?

18

TOURIST INFORMATION

As Castro lay on his deathbed, his brother Raúl was hold-
ing his hand. A crowd had gathered outside the win-
dow chanting up to their leader, "Fidel! Fidel!"
"What are those people doing outside?" Fidel asked.
"Saying farewell," Raúl replied.
"Where are they going?" Fidel asked.

—Cuban joke

IN THE SUMMER OF 2006, not long after Fidel suddenly stepped
down from power and handed over the reins to his brother Raúl,
I went back to Havana to see how much had changed. It doesn't
take long to hear from the people you meet that Havana is the
biggest small town on earth. I'd experienced it from almost the
first day with tracking down boxing heroes. Finally Cuban kis-
met brought it home with the Castros.

The plane began its descent over the last handful of haunted
miles dividing Cuba from the United States. Out my window the
sunset glazed over the surface of the ocean and glinted off the slits

and nicks of wave creases like fresh wounds. Up and down the plane I heard the slap of blinders yanked down over the windows while the rest of us eagerly took in the view. It's this last home-stretch that fleshes out the tourists from the locals on flights to the island.

An announcement came over the speakers on the plane that we'd begun our descent into Havana and the bald woman sitting next to me tapped my shoulder.

"Are you okay?"

I shrugged while an advertisement on the screen lauded some company's corporate responsibility and philanthropy: *The future is friendly.*

"Do you—," the woman began, smiling magnanimously and pointing at my heart. "Un-der-*stand*—English?"

I couldn't figure out if her overenunciation implied I might be deaf, a foreigner, or suffering from some severe mental handicap. Maybe she had me pegged for the trifecta.

"I flunked English in ninth grade."

"I don't mean to sound presumptuous, but I wondered if you'd like to know why the stranger sitting next to you on the plane was returning to Havana."

"Shoot."

"I have a *score* to settle with Havana."

I looked around at some of the other passengers on the plane. Healthy mix of agendas on all the faces.

"I'm guessing you're not alone on that front," I told her.

"Well, it was exactly one year ago today that I discovered a lump in my breast while I was taking a shower in an Old Havana ho-tel. I wanted to come back here, to the same hotel, in the same room, for the anniversary as a *fuck you.* . . ." She seemed to be trying to cling to the anger but losing traction. "I wanted to come back here as a *fuck you* to what I've gone through the last year fighting cancer. Because, well, I may have lost a breast and I may not be able to conceive a child anymore, but guess what?"

I let out the rest of the air in my lungs and shrugged as an American Express ad glared at both of us from above my meal tray. She paused and stared at me. Suddenly she reached down and unzipped her bag, revealing a large box of condoms.

"I can still get *laid*! I'm going to meet someone over there. I'm going to meet a few people maybe."

She looked out the window with the island finally in view and smiled. "Did you know that Cubans say life is a joke to be taken very seriously?"

"When Columbus arrived they told him the island was infinite, too."

"You know, we should have dinner some night. . . ."

We touched down on José Martí Airport's runway. I'd been following the news since Castro entered the headlines with his illness, which was supposed to be an official state secret. They were throwing a party on Calle Ocho in Miami to celebrate the old man's impending demise. Many journalists assumed he was already dead.

I took a gypsy cab from the airport over to a wedding Ría had invited me to in her home town of San Antonio, a suburb outside Havana. The old Ford that picked me up was doing just fine until she began to overheat halfway back into the city.

"I knew she was angry about me listening to reggaeton at this hour." The driver shook his head, scrambling around the radio dial until he found the classical composer Ernesto Lecuona. "Even at her age she requires a little seduction at night. Now she will punish us for denying her. *Cubaneo*." The driver shrugged and grinned at me in the rearview.

"Only in Cuba" was the translation of the driver's last remark, tearing at the old scab of daily life. Each new circumstance put its own new slant on the meaning.

And about thirty seconds later, when a father and son pulled over with their horse-drawn carriage to offer a hand, I wondered if Cubans had an expression for the converse: the positive things that happen here that would mostly never happen anywhere else. The closest word I know in Cuban slang is *palanca*, meaning when someone helps you out of a jam. And nearly *every* aspect of life here could constitute a jam. Survival itself literally depends on daily *palanca*.

Other people came by to help. First some cyclists and then a motorcycle pulled over to the side of the road. Every Cuban is a proud mechanic. You wouldn't last long without being one. Everything that hasn't broken down soon will. The result of this condition is that while nobody has any money to replace anything, nearly everyone who sees trouble will stop and help.

I'd never been to the town Ría was from before, so I asked one stranger after another for directions to the little courtyard where the wedding was being held, got lost over and over, then saw Ría on the street waving at me before I even spotted her. Right after we sat down, out of nowhere, a sonic boom exploded over our heads as fighter jets broke the sound barrier. I jumped out of my chair until several people came over to laughingly explain that on Tuesdays and Fridays, the same time every night, the Cuban Air

Force conducted test flights. "*¡Tranquilo, chico!* The gringos are not invading our island tonight. Relax, man!"

And then, surprising me even more, I did.

Weddings have always spooked me. I was looking around the room going over my usual refrain: Love is chemicals. Love is junk. Love is being addicted to someone's *brand* of junk. I'm surrounded by junkies. I grew up a twenty minutes' drive from the worst area in North America for drug use, a ghetto that the rest of my town was ashamed to admit existed, but here we were happy to celebrate an institution attempting to reinforce a union of addiction as best we can.

People were sweaty and relaxed at the wedding. Despite the festivities being outdoors, the bathroom stunk out the whole place. The plumbing, as usual, was shot. Maybe it was strategic. It's hard to concentrate on the past or the future with that kind of stench permeating everything. The whole occasion wasn't dictated by a wedding photographer capturing the Hallmark version. Nobody was posing for history. Lots of easy and hard tears came down on their own, without the usual cues prompting them. All the attendees had a certain amusement relating to how death and birth embroidered everything, with the different generations brought together. All that stuff just felt very human, with the burden of the joke shared by everybody.

Then a bird shat on the groom while he was reciting his vows. Everyone except me exploded in cheers. I was confused until Ría explained to me that if shit lands on you in Cuba (or you step in it), you're regarded as *lucky*. Good fortune and wealth was on the way! When it was clear Ría hadn't meant this statement ironically, I looked at the faces all around me. Nobody at the wedding had ever *dreamed* of owning a car. None of my Cuban friends or their parents had ever opened a bank account in their lives. Ría had used a rag after she got her first period and her mother showed her how to rinse it out and use it again for the next month. And there was her boyfriend, the cat fisherman. "Cat cooked in lemon sauce was not *that* terrible," she had said.

After the vows everyone got up to dance to Elvis singing "Love Me Tender" while I sat down in an open chair and lit a cigarette.

After the wedding, around three in the morning, I got dropped off at a hotel in Miramar. Half an hour later Raúl Castro's grandson strolled through the lobby like Hugh Hefner returning to the Playboy mansion. I noticed him enter—along with the entire hotel staff—with two bodyguards and three towering blondes in slip dresses and heels. I didn't know who he was at the time, but while he was making the rounds shaking hands, the bartender tipped me off about his identity.

"He travels around with *three* models for girlfriends?" I asked him.

"Two of the models are his girlfriends. The other one—the one you keep *staring* at—is actually Fidel's granddaughter. I would stop staring if I was you."

It took a while for the information to sink in before I regained my senses and turned back around to face the bar and buy a pack of cigarettes from the bartender. I felt a hand on my shoulder.

"*Yuma,*" Fidel's granddaughter addressed me. *Yuma* is one of the more derisive terms certain Cubans attach to American tourists behind their backs. But she used it with such unabashed provocation I couldn't keep a straight face. "I'd like to have one of your cigarettes."

"*Yuma?*"

"Yes, *yuma*."

"I've never been called a *yuma* by a girl who looks as much like a *gringa* as you do."

I reached over for my pack to give it to her when, in one horribly drawn-out sound, she cleared the phlegm from the back of her throat so forcefully I dropped the cigarettes on the ground. Cubans refer to this common gesture as "scratching your throat," but Fidel's granddaughter's effort sounded like heavy machinery working in a gravel pit. I was about as nauseated by the sound as I was turned on by the rest of her. The look on my face made the bartender blow Diet Coke through his nose. I got out of my chair, knelt down, and picked up the cigarettes as she glared down over me.

"Why are you picking them up, *yuma?*" she moaned.

The bartender's face contorted in abject shame and I saw him put his hand to his brow.

"*Yuma*, I'm not smoking anything you dropped on the ground. Here's an elegant solution: *buy another pack*."

I followed her suggestion while the bartender conveniently hid his laughter by wiping the Diet Coke from his face with a towel. I shook the pack toward her to free up a loose cigarette and she leaned over and pursed her lips over the butt. When I went to light the cigarette with my Zippo, she did the truck driver throat-scratching thing again.

I looked into her eyes while the flame danced over her pupils.

"Thank you for the cigarette, *yuma*."

For the rest of her thirty minutes in the hotel bar she completely ignored me until she left with her group. She gave me a quick glance, followed by the shrug of one shoulder as she swung her purse over the other and strolled out the front entrance.

The next time I saw her, at a New Year's party in Centro Habana, she didn't have her entourage in tow. A lot of Cuban TV and radio personalities were there. It turned out she worked for Radio Havana as a writer. I didn't ask anyone at the party to confirm the bit about her being Castro's granddaughter. We noticed each other while she was dancing with another pretty girl in the cramped apartment.

After midnight of the New Year, I followed her outside to the balcony for a cigarette. She'd just been outside the country to visit Venice and told me she never wanted to travel again after the experience. I asked why.

She asked me if I'd ever read *Invisible Cities* by Italo Calvino. I shook my head. She told me a story from it about several men around the world who had an identical dream. They all saw the same naked girl from behind, with long hair, running through an unknown city. They chased after her, twisting and turning down the streets, but eventually lost her. After the dream all these men set out in search of that city where they'd seen her. They never found the city, but they found *each other*. So they decided to build a city like the one from their shared dream. Laying out the streets, each followed the pathways they took in pursuit of the girl. At the spot where they lost the fugitive's trail, they arranged spaces and walls differently from the dream so she would be unable to escape. They all settled in the city waiting for the scene to be repeated one night, but none of them, asleep or awake, ever saw the woman again.

New men who'd had a similar dream arrived to this city. They, too, changed the streets, arcades, and stairways so that at the spot where the woman vanished, there remained no avenue of escape. But they never found her, either.

Then Castro's granddaughter stopped telling the story.

I asked her to finish, but I also wanted more privacy to take my revenge against her for that night at the hotel. She agreed to go for a walk.

We walked from the party toward my apartment, where I had access to a rooftop overlooking the busiest street at night in Centro Habana, Calle Neptuno, where I could hear rum-soaked dominoes being played deep into the night. When we climbed the stairs several floors to the roof looking out over the other rooftops in all directions and the Juliet girls on their balconies talking down to their Romeos and the chorus line of taxis below us, instead of trying to kiss her I chickened out and went back to fishing for the end of the story.

"Tell me what happened with that city in the end," I asked her.

"Stop pretending like you brought me back here for the story when I can tell very easily you're already looking for a place to fuck me on this roof. Have some dignity, *yuma*."

She took off her shirt and glared at me. The dogs on the roof next door sounded the alarm and woke up the rooster to join in.

"Are you worried about Fidel finding out? You were quite bold when we met at the hotel. I wasn't sure if you knew my little secret or not."

It turned out nobody else had the dream of the girl and everyone else who saw the city left immediately because of the ugliness of such a place invented and designed as a trap.

Fidel's granddaughter asked me the next morning in bed if this was helpful tourist information.

19

SHADOW BOXING

*Who controls the past controls the future. Who controls
the present controls the past.* —George Orwell

TEÓFILO STEVENSON WAS A CHAMPION of the Muhammad Ali–
dominated 1970s, before my time. Mike Tyson was my era's champion. The most mysterious opponent who was ever mentioned to
challenge Tyson for the heavyweight championship was the Cuban boxer Félix Savón. Most of the world was only able to watch
Savón every four years when he steamrolled through competition
with a stunningly lethal right hand.

One afternoon I was sitting in the bleachers next to a father
and son for the first of three sets of boxing competitions taking
place all day at Kid Chocolate. My high school gym might have
cost more to build, but with hundreds of millions of dollars you
couldn't re-create what Chocolate looked, let alone *felt*, like the afternoon when I saw Félix Savón enter the place. For a second he
was framed by the murals and quoted passages from Fidel, the

chipped paint and haywire scoreboards, the rafters and leaky ceiling . . . but then some of the faces in the crowd spotted him and smiled, nudging more and more people to share in the fun of spotting Savón.

The father next to me had just offered me a cigarette and was telling me that one day his son would fight here and make him proud. His boy was around ten and rolled his eyes.

"You need a light?" the father asked me.

Cuban tobacco in most cigarettes off the street is obscenely strong and vaguely sweet. I felt a little self-conscious smoking in front of his son, but I had forgotten that self-consciousness hadn't been invented in Cuba yet.

He asked if I was a boxer myself and flexed his muscles while his son laughed. The boy raised his fists to his face and glared menacingly at me until my laughter obliged him to give me a friendly shove.

Just then I heard the cheering subside for the fight that was going on and noticed an enormous, towering man in Cuban track pants stroll across the gym floor alone. I didn't have a good look at him.

"*¿Quién es él?*" I asked the dad, to make sure it was who I thought it was.

"Oh that's just Félix. He's a good friend."

"*Savón?*"

Savón, like Teófilo Stevenson, was a three-time heavyweight Olympic champion. Don King had offered him a lot more than the five million Teófilo Stevenson rejected to fight Muhammad Ali, for Savón to turn pro and fight Mike Tyson. The figure was somewhere in the neighborhood of twenty or twenty-five million. He turned it down flat. I'd seen an interview with him where he slowly made his way, speech impediment and all, to explain, "I may not be a millionaire because of what I turned down, but it's possible I made a million friends with my decision here."

Félix Savón was famous for being a little slow, but also the sweetest and baddest man in the country. There he was, all by himself, waving graciously to a few people who called out his name.

"Félix is working with one of the teams?" I asked.

"*Claro.*"

"He's a friend of yours?"

"*Familia.*"

"*¿Familia?*"

"Jes," the father broke into English, to emphasize his point. "I will introduce you. *FÉLIX! ¡OYE!*"

"Fuck! Man, *don't.* What are you doing!"

"*¡OYE! FÉLIX!*" Then leaning over to me, "*Familia.* My berry goo' frien'. Berry goo'." Félix, still in stride toward an empty chair near the ring, raised his hand to acknowledge the piercing scream of the man sitting next to me in the stands. Clearly he had *no* idea who he was looking at.

"I really think Félix wants to be left alone."

"*¡Qué va!* Bullshit. Félix i' like my *hermano.* Let's get him over here and you can have a photo with Félix. Félix! *¡OYE!*" The pitch of this *oye* was pleading and defiant at the same time.

"Man, I don't even have a camera," I pleaded. "Let's leave him alone."

"*I* have a camera."

Félix waved again, but you could tell he dreaded what was to come next. Though it was unlikely he dreaded it half as much as I did.

The father abandoned his son's hand and got to his feet, shoved both hands in his mouth, and whistled with such ferocity Félix stopped, turned, and glared in our direction. It was a glare I had never seen Félix offer any opponent during the fourteen years he was flattening *everybody* in his boxing career. Right then Félix flashed the Lenny dreaming-of-the-rabbits grin.

"Please God stop," I pleaded with this man. "For the love of your child."

"*¡OYE!*"

"Your son."

"*MADRE MIA, ¡FÉLIX!*"

Félix squinted until he spotted us and frowned.

The father waved him over and grabbed me by the arm. "*Coño*, grab my fucking camera."

I did as he instructed, though I didn't even want a photograph with Félix Savón.

"*¡FÉLIX! ¡OYE!* Don't pretend like Miguel Antonio Torres has not known you since you were a child of seven! Get over here, you!"

Félix Savón, all six-foot-six and 240 pounds of him, one of the greatest fighters the world had ever produced, dropped his head and began the walk of shame over to us. The child of Miguel Antonio Torres could not have been more pleased with this glorious day, the day his father regained the heavyweight championship for daddies *everywhere*.

"Miguelito, wait here for us. Papi must take care of this."

I was grabbed by the elbow and hauled down the stairs toward the first row. We were on a platform as Félix arrived, so I was eye level with the Cuban legend.

Félix sheepishly apologized and Miguel, five-four in sandals, reached up and slapped his cheek gently. I was introduced as a close family friend and Félix extended his hand, which looked as though it could palm a beach ball. As we shook hands I tried not to feel like a Muppet in the exchange.

Félix asked softly how I'd liked the tournament. His speech impediment wasn't quite a stutter, though he did have trouble enunciating his words.

The father mentioned a photo, and Félix warmly put his arm over my shoulder, which cued me to put mine over his. We had a considerable section of the crowd enjoying my awkwardness over holding Savón hostage. Miguel Antonio Torres stood before us with his camera pointed, and both Félix and I smiled at him. Our fixed smiles extended to nearly a minute until Félix, not breaking his grin, asked if there might be a good time to take the photo.

"*¡Hijo de puta! ¡Mierda!*" Miguel screamed.

I asked if the disposable piece-of-shit camera was broken. Félix looked over at me and clenched his massive jaw, striations spread out over the cheek like a cracked windshield.

Click . . .

The comedian Mitch Hedberg once opined, "I think Bigfoot is blurry, *that's* the problem. It's not the photographer's fault. Bigfoot is blurry, and that's extra scary to me." So are certain freakish moments in your life. Miguel's blurry photo of Félix and me standing together captured the moment crystal clear.

I asked Félix if I could speak to him after the fights and he gave me a strange look and took my notebook to write down his phone number. As he strode off toward the ring, he said he was free that evening and to call.

I went outside Kid Chocolate for some air. The portrait photographers who worked the front steps of the Capitolio with their century-old cameras were packing up for the night when a fleet of bicycles carting birthday cakes raced down the side of the road in front of them. Every kid in town was entitled to a free cake until they reached fifteen (plus a free cake on their wedding), and the state delivered the cakes to your door. It was always one of my favorite sights around town. But they also reminded me of a very strange day in my life, my twelfth birthday.

Months before that birthday, I had asked my parents for a poster of Muhammad Ali for my room. He was the bravest person that I knew and I wanted to see his face looking at me every day. When they took me to the poster shop, I couldn't decide between my two favorites. There were six or seven Ali posters in the store that I liked, but the choice was easy to narrow down to two. I had nearly saved up enough money on my own with my allowance to buy one, but I couldn't shake the premonition that I'd only end up obsessing over the one I didn't choose. I used to visit the shop all the time and drive the owner crazy asking him to unfurl the posters and hold each of them up for me. And then my bullying incident at school happened and I was afraid to leave my room, let alone step outside my front door. By the time my twelfth birthday rolled around, my family wanted to help cheer me up and gave me enough money to buy *all* the Ali posters at the shop. I didn't even have to choose anymore. After I handed over the vast fortune of $75 in my hand and bought all the posters in the shop, I felt something I'd never felt before. Maybe it was a child's version of buyer's remorse being channeled into something existentially more troubling that blew all my circuits. At first, I tried to pretend I was excited as I always imagined I was supposed to feel, not having to make an awful choice between the two things I most wanted in the world. In my magical thinking, the posters were going to fix everything that had gone wrong in my life. But the day after I put up all the posters in my room, I got so upset I tore them all down

Nothing about his house stood out from any of the others on his block; it looked like any residential, suburban home you might find in Edison, New Jersey. Evander Holyfield, about the same age but with about half the punching power of Savón, had been able to purchase a 109-room mansion in Atlanta. Keeping that mansion, however, was a different story, since he lost hundreds of millions of dollars in earnings and promptly went bankrupt, his home going into foreclosure.

Savón had grown up in Guantánamo, the son of a bricklayer. Boxing hadn't come naturally to him, but he worked at it. He was turned down three times by the Gitmo boxing school before they let him in as a teenager. Savón went on to win 362 amateur fights for his country, 6 world championships, and 3 Olympic gold medals, never suffering a defeat that he didn't avenge. According to Cuban media reports, he used to shadowbox while staring out at the U.S. naval base, dreaming of victories against Americans. Some Cubans joked that if the United States gave Guantánamo Bay back to Cuba, then they could have Miami back.

I opened the gate of the rickety fence outside Savón's front yard just as his front door opened and music splashed out into the neighborhood. A child spotted me from inside the foyer and ran down the main hall, only to return holding the enormous right hand of a smiling giant.

"¡Oye, campeón!" Félix howled.

He insisted that he had some things he could sell me. He said he had a book and a film others had helped him with about his career and life. He had an *agent* I should talk to. I must have raised an eyebrow at the prospect of a man who'd turned down a multimillion-dollar career hiring an agent to look after his financial interests, because Félix laughed.

"An *agent*?" I asked. That was an interesting occupation in a communist state.

"A friend who helps me with things," he clarified.

"Okay."

"Come inside. How much time do you need?"

"Not long."

"Is a hundred dollars for thirty minutes okay for you?"

"Yes."

"Then I start my watch now." Félix reached over to fiddle with what looked like the world's first digital watch. Finally it beeped to his satisfaction and he winked at me. "Please come into my living room."

Savón's severe speech impediment was probably not helped much by the effects of twenty years of boxing, which made each syllable of the words he spoke remarkably difficult for him. His mouth and jaw worked impossibly hard just to complete brief sentences in less than thirty seconds, so I wasn't sure how much ground we could cover in thirty minutes.

Savón's living room sat next to his extensive, glassed-in trophy room. He refused to allow me to look it over and tapped his finger on his watch.

"We're on *your* time, my friend. What would you like to talk about?"

I took a deep breath as I set up my small camera on Savón's coffee table and began filming him.

"Guillermo Rigondeaux," I said, naming the most recent and highest-profile defection in Cuban boxing history.

"The same boxing promoters interested in him came here." Savón smiled, lifting his fist and poking his index finger toward his carpet.

"The same ones?"

"The same."

"What did you tell them?"

"My wife answered the door when they arrived." His wife came over and stopped for a second at the doorway to listen. "My wife told them, 'Félix is more revolutionary than Fidel.'" As I laughed with him, Félix looked back at his wife, they smiled to each other, and she went back into the kitchen to be with their children.

"*¿Entiende?*" Félix asked coyly, grinning.

"Rigondeaux left this country. What are the reasons that you stayed here and turned down the money?"

"I have many reasons why I'm a Cuban boxer." Savón lifted his chin and pondered them fondly. "The love of my family. My love of the motherland. In Puerto Rico I was offered five million to leave. In Mexico ten million. Even more later—"

"These offers were to fight Mike Tyson?"

"Yes, that was part of it. But none of it mattered to me. They tried other times to convince my wife to speak with me. But I've always said I'm not a millionaire in Cuba, but I have millions of friends that can always lend me a peso or a piece of bread if I need it. *¿Entiende?*"

"How do you feel about Rigondeaux?"

"As time goes by, the younger generation loses values." Savón paused and gathered himself. "They lose the will we had in my time. When Rigondeaux was a boxer here, I was the captain of our team. Due to the confidence I had in him, I left him as a captain of the Cuban national team. He betrayed his principles. I'm sure he had his reasons for doing that. But life's motives for most people nowadays are giving more value to money than honor."

After another fifteen minutes Savón's watch sounded its alarm and our time was up. He shrugged sheepishly and indicated for me to shut off the camera. Once the camera was off he reached over to collect the agreed-upon price for the interview. I paid and Savón smiled and spoke the only two words I'd ever heard him speak in English: "Thank *you*."

When I got back to my apartment I packed up the rest of my belongings along with the footage from the interview and caught the next flight out of Havana.

20

WAITING FOR RIGONDEAUX

Show me a hero and I will write you a tragedy.

—F. Scott Fitzgerald

IN THE SUMMER OF 2007, two-time Olympic champion Guillermo Rigondeaux and his teammate, Erislandy Lara, had been arrested in Brazil after going AWOL from the Cuban team during the Pan Am Games. The defection attempt made international news and quickly became a national soap opera, regularly appearing on Cuban news and in round table discussions. Castro, though largely out of public view since stepping down from power because of his secret illness the year before, spoke out in the state newspaper *Granma*. Castro branded Rigondeaux a "traitor" and "Judas" to the Cuban people. "They have reached a point of no return as members of a Cuban boxing team," Castro wrote in *Granma*. "An athlete who abandons his team is like a soldier who abandons his fellow troops in the middle of combat." And then Teófilo Stevenson, despite his legend being built on the foundation of having turned down every offer to leave Cuba, defended Rigondeaux and Lara. "They are not traitors," Stevenson declared. "They slipped up. People will understand. They've repented. It is a victory that they have returned. Others did not."

Only a few months later, one afternoon in the autumn of 2007, I was training with Héctor at Trejo when I spotted someone out of the corner of my eye at the gym's entrance.

"*Mi madre*," Héctor whispered, dropping his hands slowly, looking in the same direction as me. "It's *him*."

"*Him?*" I asked.

"*Sí*," Héctor confirmed, then repeated gravely, "*él*."

When any Cuban refers to "him" in conversation, with little to no information or context provided, it invariably refers to Fidel.

"*Mi madre*," Héctor groaned again.

"*¿Cómo?*" I asked. "*¿Quién?*" Who?

Héctor remained frozen. It was one hundred degrees out that afternoon training in the open air of Rafael Trejo. I nudged him, but Héctor wouldn't come to. I looked around us as the silence took hold. All the proud coaches refused to look at the problem straight on, instead glancing sidelong at the entrance to the gym. A profoundly disturbing thing you discover very quickly traveling in Cuba is that the most dangerous person for Cubans isn't the police or even the secret police; it's their neighbor. Anyone can report you for anything "outside" the revolution—even if you haven't done it yet. Héctor himself had been banned from boxing before he'd ever attempted escape.

So what was this?

Was there news that Fidel died or was *él* paying a visit?

"It's *him*." Héctor repeated, this time even more softly, nodding in the direction of the entrance. "This is very dangerous for us."

"*¿Cómo?*" I asked. "*Who?*"

"*Rigondeaux.* There, hiding in the shadows."

All I could see was a child near the entrance. Kids came in off the street all the time to watch or hang out at the gym. I hadn't noticed anything special about this one.

"*That's* Rigondeaux? That child?"

"*Claro,*" Héctor grunted. "That child is twenty-seven and per-. haps the greatest boxer Cuba has ever produced. Fidel has said he will never fight again. He has nowhere to go. Anyone in sports can no longer be seen talking to him. We could lose our jobs. *You* can talk to him."

It was as if a Cuban version of Mr. Kurtz had stepped out of his own version of *Heart of Darkness* to haunt our gym. I'd never seen Rigondeaux's face without it being obscured by headgear or a photograph of Fidel he was holding up after winning a tourna-ment. Finally I saw him, only to recognize the saddest face I'd ever seen in Cuba. He stood aloofly in the shadows wearing a Nike ball cap and jeans, with a fake Versace shirt that had the sleeves ripped off.

Without realizing it, I started toward Rigondeaux. As I ap-proached him, in the shade under the bleachers of the entrance to Rafael Trejo, I reached out a hand and introduced myself. He did what he could, under the strained circumstances at the gym, to muster a smile. Up close I noticed his right eye showed dam-age, slumping slightly from his left. Rigondeaux's attempt at a po-lite smile betrayed the gold grill over his front teeth for a brief moment as he took another drag of his Popular cigarette.

"So where did you get that gold on your teeth?" I asked him.

Rigondeaux snickered, dropped his head, and smirked, tak-ing a last long drag on his cigarette before flicking it on the ground and stamping it out with his sneaker. For a moment his face assumed the same hopeless expression as Lee Harvey Oswald bemoaning, "I'm just a patsy." Then it vanished and he sighed. "Oh, you know, I melted down both my gold medals into my mouth."

I didn't know where to go from that statement.

"I used to fight in this place. . . ."

I met Rigondeaux that strange day in Rafael Trejo in November of 2007, and for the first time Cuba ceased to be an abstraction—it finally had a face.

Rigondeaux survived in Cuba as best he could—living under house arrest after his failed defection in Brazil during the Pan Am Games the previous summer—until his escape on a smuggler's boat in February of 2009. After his escape, his father back in his hometown of Santiago de Cuba disowned him for betraying Fidel and the revolution. But his mother supported him. According to jokes told around the Trejo, he'd signed more contracts with foreign promoters promising to fight in the United States than he'd ever signed autographs for fans. Maybe he lived off a few foreign money drips secretly sent to him to help support his family and build some trust to take the leap of his life. He'd owe all those people every dime once he took the bait and at least *physically* left Cuba behind.

Rigondeaux and I arrived in America to start new lives at about the same time fifteen months after our first meeting. He was installed in Miami while I'd moved to New York. His journey required abandoning a wife while I'd found one. When I caught up with him in Los Angeles in March of 2010, he looked even more distraught than when I'd first encountered him in Havana.

He finally found the stage he wanted. It was hard to imagine how anything in America could be worse than the situation he'd escaped back home. His sixth professional fight was the following week. He was making more money in a fight than he would have made in a lifetime fighting in Cuba.

But that wasn't the issue. His mother had just died back on the island and he was forbidden to attend the funeral. He was told if he set foot back on the island he'd be arrested on sight. Back in Cuba, the eighteen months Fidel had taken boxing away from his life forged an overwhelming bitterness in his heart, but he would describe the voyage on a crowded smuggler's boat to Cancún—surrounded by thirty other terrified human cargo—as the most traumatic event of his life. The boats capsized, smugglers threw their cargo overboard, people were held hostage at gunpoint until a ransom was paid. I didn't have to pull back all that far to see that a badly wounded canary in the coal mine for Castro's Cuba had emerged on the opposite side of the Florida Straits.

Boxers have a notoriously limited shelf life and Rigondeaux was making up for lost time, of which he had little left to cash in on his talents. Rigondeaux's only path to success was to hurtle toward the American Dream like a runaway ambulance through traffic. I spent the next three years chasing my own version behind the hurtling ambulance of his life.

The first fight of his I witnessed was in Tijuana. His manager wanted publicity and had invited me down there for an interview and offered to let me inside the dressing room and enter the ring with Rigondeaux to soak up the atmosphere. The promise of total access at the ground floor of Rigondeaux's professional career in the States, on the way to a world championship, was the bait. But gangsters had threatened the manager about entering Tijuana, where they had connections to the mafia. They could arrange police planting drugs, hire a hit man, or just have us kidnapped. For as little as fifty dollars, any of the three were at their disposal. So these were the risks and rewards about heading down across the border. Rigondeaux's manager, Gary Hyde, got on a plane after leaving an entire family in tears begging him not to. My wife was too angry about my recklessness and stupidity to muster any tears when we said good-bye.

I was going to turn the offer down when my old trainer Ronnie Wilson found a pretty miraculous way to give me one final push out of my own way. I received a letter several months after I'd published a story about how Ronnie had helped me and others clarify our paths, while succumbing to his own addiction.

Hello Brin,

I'm not at all sure where to begin with this. I am Ronnie Wilson's daughter. He did also have a son, my older brother Dean. Silly as it sounds, I Google my father's name from time to time, looking for stories such as yours . . . yearning to know more about him. Your article touched my heart. He was such a kindhearted man, who would give the shirt off his back to anyone in need. However, drugs and alcohol are horrible friends to keep. They turned him into an ugly person . . . he was a totally different person when under the influence. I want you to know his family loved him to death and I personally time and time again tried to help him. I took him to rehabs and attended AA meetings with him, pulled him out of bars and got him home safe to get some sleep and food. I could go on and on. I'm still so saddened by his disease and refusal of any help. My husband and I have even offered him to come live with us on many occasions, but he has always declined.

I have three beautiful children, Ronnie's grandchildren. It's heartbreaking to know they will never get to know the wonderful man he used to be. I was always daddy's girl and still feel that way at age thirty-four. He was my hero and I'll forever wonder what I could have done to save him from this horrible addiction. I appreciate the time you took in describing the kind, selfless, gentle man he once was. Those are memories I cling to and choose to share with my children. If you do have any other memories you might have of my father I'd be extremely grateful if you shared them with me. I have very few articles and photos left of his boxing career. At one point when he began to clean up a bit, he asked me to send him what I had because someone was writing a biography about him. He soon ended up back on skid row in downtown Vancouver, so I don't know what became of it all. I still have a couple of Ring magazines and some old black-and-white photos. Thank you for sharing such kind words about my dad.

Warm regards,
Jennifer

Jennifer lived in San Diego with her family, back where Ronnie began his professional career as a teenager. I tend to conflate a spiritual need for destiny with what's on offer in horoscopes and numerology and other spiritual junkie track marks, but I'm a Gypsy mother's son. I had watched my mother, whom all my friends told me was crazy, make a living for thirty years trying to heal people through means I could never accept for my own wounds, the ones that healed her. Jennifer's message in a bottle—and the fact that she lived ten minutes from the border I was meant to cross—was enough of a karmic tap on my shoulder for me to push my chips in and agree to head down to Tijuana for Rigondeaux's fight.

I wrote Jennifer back and she suggested we meet in Old Town the night before I crossed the border. I showed up in the spooky little neighborhood and quickly spotted the tall "slightly awkward" blonde she'd warned me she was. But the first thing I noticed about Jennifer from a distance was how she shared her father's disarming confidence, the kind that reminds you that anyone who doesn't feel safe in some essential sense could never be generous even if they wanted to. As she got closer, Jennifer had her dad's same shy, caring eyes. I was so distracted, I didn't even register that she was carrying a pair of her dad's brown Everlast trunks in one hand and a folder of clippings in the other, until she held them up for me to see.

21

WRITING IN THE SCRAPBOOK
OF A TYRANT

*I believe that on such an issue as this no one is or can be
completely truthful. It is difficult to be certain about anything except what you have seen with your own eyes,
and consciously or unconsciously everyone writes as a
partisan.* —George Orwell, *Homage to Catalonia*

FOR THE NEXT THREE YEARS I dropped down the rabbit hole, following Rigondeaux around the world for each of his fights while
spending the rest of my life chasing down everyone I could find
in journalism, film, boxing, academia, and publishing who
contributed definitive work on Cuba. I bumped into Leon Gast,
director of *When We Were Kings*, filming a Manny Pacquiao
documentary while Rigondeaux was on his undercard. Leon said
he hadn't seen footwork like Rigondeaux's since Muhammad Ali.

Ann Louise Bardach had interviewed Fidel Castro for *Vanity
Fair* and written *Cuba Confidential: Love and Vengeance in Miami
and Havana.* "Maybe the most corrosive legacy that Fidel Castro
will leave behind is that of the broken family," Bardach told me.

Larry Merchant, a former boxing writer and longtime HBO boxing commentator, invited me over to his home in Santa Monica. "Boxing is every man for himself in and out of the ring." Merchant laughed. "It's a slightly more civilized version of the jungle. It itself symbolizes the rawest form of free enterprise. You're on your own. To come here just to be a fighter and not be able to go back to the ground where you came from is something relatively new and strange. Of course in America where the streets are paved with gold . . ."

Carlos Eire, author of the National Book Award–winning memoir *Waiting for Snow in Havana* and *Learning to Die in Miami*, had his office at Yale. Eire had left Cuba, along with fourteen thousand other children, during the Operation Peter Pan exodus of 1960–1962. He said when he'd heard the first reports of Elián González's arrival in Miami, he "lost his mind" reliving his own childhood trauma. "There are many, many people who admire Fidel Castro and who think his revolution was a good thing. Including just about every professor down my hallway." I was fascinated that such a confession in no way gave this man pause toward his convictions for even a second.

Steve Fainaru, the Pulitzer Prize–winning journalist and author of *The Duke of Havana*, was in Oakland. "It's just such a difficult choice. I think the fact that people are *forced* to make that choice—that there's this either/or—it says so much about the Cuban government and their political situation. And it says so much about the *United States* government, frankly, and our continuing ridiculously anachronistic views toward this small island. It's really sad."

His partner on the book, Ray Sánchez, the only U.S. newspaper reporter based in Havana at the time of Rigondeaux's defection, now lived five blocks up the street from me in New York. He had a child of his own in Havana. "If the Cuba story is about *anything*," Sanchez began, echoing Bardach, "it's about the separation of families. For the last fifty years we've seen this tug-of-war that has just torn families apart and plays out every day, in virtually every Cuban household."

Several months later Leon Gast mentioned that Don King, who'd offered tens of millions to Félix Savón and Teófilo Stevenson to defect, was passing through Brooklyn and offered me an introduction. King repeated the same lines from a script he'd said at a press conference for one of Rigondeaux's fights several months before: "Rigondeaux is *Cuba libre*, and that's fighting for freedom from Cuba. He had to get on the boats, the rafts, and brave the hazards of the ocean and the shark-infested waters to seek freedom. Where did he seek that freedom? *Old Glory* right here." King pointed down to an American flag button on his jean jacket. "This is the only country in the world that people try to break in rather than to break out."

Enrique Encinosa, the Cuban American author, radio host, and boxing historian, lived in Miami. Before I flew out to interview Encinosa, he told me over the phone that the greatest pleasure he could ever experience in his life would be putting a gun to Fidel's head and pulling the trigger.

Just over a decade since I'd read his book on my first flight over to Cuba, journalist and author S. L. Price passed through New York City and we arranged to meet at his hotel room, across the street from Madison Square Garden, at two in the morning. I'd brought along a bottle of some vile coffee-infused tequila. Price looks like Jimmy Stewart and sounds like he narrated *The Wonder Years.* He had spent four years working for the *Miami Herald* and traveled to Cuba repeatedly to work on his book *Pitching Around Fidel* from 1991 until he was told he could never return, shortly before I first arrived in 2000.

"*Cuba*—" I laughed a little nervously, setting a glass before Price and reaching over for the tequila to fill it for him. There wasn't another chair in the room so I flipped over his hotel wastebasket and sat on that. Before I could hit record on my tape recorder, Price was off and running.

"I moved to Miami in 1990. I grew up in Connecticut, went to school in North Carolina, I lived in New Mexico, lived in Memphis, lived in San Francisco and Northern California, and then I moved to Miami and it was literally like moving into a different world. There are many Americans who will say, 'Ugh, Miami is a foreign country.' Many Anglos from all over the country have that opinion. I actually look upon that as a great plus. I thought, 'Fantastic!' You know, I get to go to a place where Spanish is a majority language, where there's an entirely different culture. It was an amazing transition. I went to work for the *Miami Herald*, which of course is sort of the enemy of Castro. I found it fascinating that there were plans in place for when Castro would die, what the *Herald* would do—the game plan for covering the story. And in some ways I realized the most important person in Miami was Fidel Castro. Not the mayor. Not the President of the United States. But *Fidel Castro*. What I love most about Miami is that it's a city still in the state of becoming. So when I got down there, I suddenly realized that the second capital of Florida was Havana; that psychically Havana was in the mind of Miami almost all the time. I didn't want to wall myself off from that. I thought it was fascinating.

"I got the opportunity to go to Cuba for the first time in 1991 for the Pan Am Games. You have to understand, a journalist wants a story, and Miami's one of the great news towns in the world—you can't write a bad story about it. It's simply too extreme and colorful and interesting and conflict-ridden.

"So I get to Cuba for the Pan Am Games and in Miami I'm told everybody's miserable in Cuba. Everybody wants to get out and everybody hates Castro. Then when I get to the Pan Am Games, it's not just that Fidel was doing the wave. His boxers are having a record-setting day against the Americans, the sworn enemy of the Castro regime. Fidel is standing up and throwing up his hands like any boozy fan in the cheap seats. But the fans are really proud. The fans, the people in the street, they're telling me 'This has got to change here. I don't like it . . . *but we kicked your ass.*' And then they'll go on to detail to me the problems with the U.S. Congress. And of course the literacy rate there is over the top.

"This was 1991, and I still have never been to a place like Cuba. Cuba disturbs *you.* It's funny, because as a traveler you often think, 'Well, I want to relax. I want to go on a trip and in a sense, just *be.*' Cuba doesn't let you just *be.* You go down there and you are heartbroken. You feel intensely both positively and negatively every single day, sometimes hour by hour, and minute by minute. By the time you leave, you're exhausted and you never want to see the place again. And then about a month or two months go by—it depends on the last time you were there—and you start thinking about it again. I've never felt that way about anywhere else.

"It's so easy if you stay in Miami or in Havana to have a black-and-white view of the world. I happened to live in Miami and be entranced by Cuba, but I wasn't in love with the system. It isn't like I went down there and thought, 'Oh, communism is great; socialism is the way of the future.' But when I went to Cuba, it confirmed for me probably more than anything else the idea of the gray area and of *living* in the gray. There were people who criticized Castro, who were incredible critics of the regime. They wanted Castro to die tomorrow and they couldn't leave. But they couldn't bear to leave Cuba. Couldn't even *think* about getting on a raft. And then there were people who left and actually believed in many of the principles in Cuba, but left because of financial reasons. They wanted to take care of their family, so they left. And when they got to Miami they said, "down with Castro." There are people who—who just didn't fit into any of the boxes.

"When I met these people I thought: This is human. It's not neat. It's not reduced to some box where they're bad and we're good. And you know, there were heroes in Miami who had left behind families, children, their wives—penniless—and wouldn't send them money. Teófilo Stevenson gave every sign to me of being a full-blown alcoholic. In some ways, even though he was mouthing pieties about the revolution, he seemed to have his soul damaged by being a flag bearer for the revolution. It wasn't clean.

"In *Lawrence of Arabia*, Jackson Bentley asks Lawrence, 'What is it about the desert that so appeals to you?' And Lawrence says: 'It's *clean*.' The thing about Cuba is that it's *dirty*. It's *not* clean. And the relations between the families in Miami and the families in Havana aren't clean. It's dirty. And I don't mean dirty like filthy or corrupt—although all that is there. I mean it's *gray*. You will go there and *all* your preconceptions will be upset. And if you're any kind of human being, you will allow them to be upset.

"At the Olympics, when we competed against the Russians, they were *enemies*. But there was something about the Cubans that American kids that I knew thought was very, very cool. And Teófilo Stevenson was that way. I didn't understand the politics of it.

At that point I was a real kid. But there was something about that pride that was unmistakable. When we watched the Russians as kids, against the U.S., they were the enemy and they *looked* like the enemy. They were steroid-ridden, unhappy, blunt. The Cubans weren't like that. They were stylish. They were proud. They carried themselves with a feeling of love—love is sort of a strange word to use—but you knew they were tough and they were proud but you could tell that they loved what they were doing and who they were. They were proud to have the Cuban flag on their chest. And that was disconcerting because they were supposed to be the enemy, to be communist and therefore deep down hateful of their country.

"There are plenty of people in Cuba who want their system to change. I need to be as clear as possible on this. Everybody I met thought, '*We* built this thing. Castro's gotta go. This has got to change and I need a better life for my child.' There's that, too. This system is bankrupt. And then there's also this embargo, which has got to stop. 'You're hurting *us*, you're not hurting the guy on top,' they say. So, it's all very mixed. And then at the same time, there are people who say, 'Before Castro, my father had no education, had no health care, and couldn't read. And now he can do that. There's something good about that.' I've been trained to assume that there's *nothing* good about the Cuban revolution. So I'm getting these mixed messages, and that's thrilling. Because it confronts me with all my preconceptions and makes me throw them out the window and start again."

For the next four and a half hours, I didn't move off my waste-basket until we both noticed out his window the sun had come up.

22

MISADVENTURES

*I see it all perfectly; there are two possible situations—
one can either do this or that. My honest opinion and my
friendly advice is this: do it or do not do it—you will regret both.*   —Søren Kierkegaard

"*MALA SUERTE*" WERE THE FIRST WORDS uttered by the formidable
stepfather of a Cuban girl I'd fallen for, after casually placing his
bishop to pin my queen right in front of my king. He removed
the unlit Winston Churchill Romeo y Julieta cigar from his
lips that he'd been chewing on since we'd begun playing an hour
ago. He gulped the last of his mojito and refilled the glass with
a bottle of mud-colored Havana Club. "Another zugzwang.
What a *feo* position, but with such a sensual name it's hard not to
savor it."

It was the third game in a row he'd taken off me and he'd been
playing for both of us every move along the way. It was an ugly
feeling to be that easily toyed with, but I was a little more concerned

with the interrogation about my relationship to his daughter
Sofía that inevitably loomed.

After three years of clandestinely meeting her in hotel rooms
around Toronto, on my way to or from Cuba to film the queasy
documentary on Rigondeaux I'd begun, it was the first time Sofía
had invited me to her home. Thirty minutes earlier she had left
us alone to talk while she grabbed some groceries for a meal she
wanted to cook that evening. "See you soon, *papi*!" she hollered
innocently from behind the front door. But after her stepfather
and I instantly glared at the door to acknowledge her good-bye—
and then even faster at each other—I assumed he was going to
flip the table and start swinging at me. We both knew he was *papi*
by rank while I knew, and he seemed to suspect, I was *papi* by
sexual confession.

After winning a lump sum of cash a couple weeks before in
Ireland by betting on a Rigondeaux victory at twenty to one odds,
I convinced Sofía to join me on my next trip to Cuba. Sofía and I
were leaving the next day to visit what was left of the Havana their
family had left behind ten years earlier, when she was fourteen.
She'd left Cuba only a couple years younger than my mother had
left communist Hungary. My mother and she had a little more
in common, too. They'd both spoken up as kids in school when
the Youth Communist League recruited new members to announce their belief that communism was, in fact, bullshit. In other
words, they were both preternaturally stubborn and gutsy.

Her stepfather and I were sitting fourteen hundred miles away
from Havana, huddled over a chessboard in the dining room of a
small apartment in a quiet Toronto suburb. While I was struggling with another zugzwang on the board, I knew from his

daughter that he was still reeling from the life back in Cuba he'd chosen to abandon. We were in the same apartment where, his stepdaughter had told me, he had sent his wife, son, and her to live a year ahead of his arrival, a decade before.

After securing a *tarjeta blanca* (white card) from the government to leave the island, he'd sold on the black market their beautiful Havana family home, just down the street from the Habana Libre hotel in Vedado. He'd sold the house to finance his family's departure and look after their needs in Canada the best he could until they could gain a foothold. The plan was to give his family a head start in their new life, free of all of Cuba's crushing restrictions, until he could join them. He had to wait a year after he'd sold the home to not raise any suspicions with the government and endanger any of their extended family. But when he arrived in Toronto the following year to reunite with his family, they weren't the same people he'd said good-bye to at the airport twelve months before. He couldn't recognize them from how much they'd changed adjusting to life outside Cuba. His marriage never recovered and his wife eventually left him for a man she'd met online who lived in Miami. Now his teenage son had suffered a nervous breakdown and lived with him down the street while Sofía took over the family's old apartment after graduating university, working two jobs, and living with a roommate.

"Do you mind if I smoke this?" He held up the cigar between his fingers. "It reminds me of nice things. Proust had his madeleines, we exiles have our cigars to retrieve the past."

"I don't mind." I smiled, tipping over my king.

"Gracias," the stepfather said, placing the cigar between his teeth while reaching into his pocket for an old Zippo. He made

kissy-faces in my direction sucking in the flame while his eyebrows arched teasingly. "You give up so easily."

"It's pretty obvious I've brought a knife to a gunfight."

"I'm not bored." He grinned, chewing on an ice cube. "But I've been meaning to ask you since my daughter first mentioned you to me. Wife or mistress?"

"Come again?" I asked.

"Is your preference for a wife or a mistress?"

"You went easier on me with chess."

"And you left the field of the battle." He laughed. "So I'm giving chase. Sofía told me you have a wife in New York."

I nodded.

He nodded back to me, absentmindedly replenishing the chessboard's rank and file.

"I must admit . . ." He laughed, flicking some ash off his cigar and resting his fist against his cheek with the smoke curling toward the ceiling. "I find your dynamic quite strange. Three years ago you met a Cuban boxer who told you he melted his Olympic gold medals into his mouth. Even if you made that up, if he didn't say it, he *should* have said it. But you've been chasing this tortured boxer around the world and to finance this pursuit, Sofía told me you've maxed out four credit cards and a line of credit to do this."

"Maybe the wife or mistress thing is a better question for her to answer," I suggested.

"Last week our family—what's left of it—watched Rigondeaux fight in Ireland on the Internet. Sofía told me you bet your last thousand dollars on him winning in the first round at twenty to one after some thugs robbed you of your camera and your footage filming him."

"Just before the fight I gave Rigondeaux my phone in the dressing room, with Sofía on the other end of the line. I wanted him to hear a friendly Cuban voice before he went out to fight."

"We were in this dining room when she spoke to him. Do you know what she told him?"

"No," I admitted. "But whatever it was, I've very rarely seen Rigondeaux smile the way he did."

"She asked him to win so she could see you. And now the proceeds from Rigondeaux's victory have given you and my daughter a trial marriage in Havana for two weeks."

I shrugged.

"I see," he said. "So, wife or mistress?"

"You first."

"An old communist joke has Marx, Engels, and Lenin asked their preference. Marx immediately said, 'Wife.' Engels countered, 'Mistress.' Lenin answered, 'Both.' Like *you* have chosen."

"Why did he choose both?" I asked.

"Because he wanted them to know about each other. That way he'd be free to spend more time *learning*."

"One more game before Sofía gets back?"

"Of course." He reached over and held his pawn suspended over the board. "You're following one of Fidel's pawns with Rigondeaux, aren't you? This boxer trying to escape Cuba in a smuggler's boat and make it in professional boxing has more in common with a pawn than at first glance, doesn't he? Pawns are the only pieces on the board that can't go backwards."

"That's true," I agreed.

"But they're *also* the only pieces on the board that, if they can make it all the way to the final row of the enemy's side, can transform into something more powerful. All the boxers and athletes of tomorrow must be tuned into *radio bemba* to see how he does. I'm sure Castro's traitor is Cuba's martyr for most people."

"He's already won a world title and made some serious money. He might earn a million dollars within the next year or so. As his life and career keep unfolding, I'm trying to explore if leaving his whole life behind was worth it."

"Stories are like sexuality." He grinned mischievously. "All that matters is the flammability. Whatever the tale is—moral or immoral, tragic or farce, ambiguous or black-and-white—the potency is all in how hot it burns. How hot does this Cuban stranger's story burn for you?"

"Well," I said. "I'm bringing all the footage I've shot with Rigondeaux to his family so they can see him for the first time since he left. If they'll speak to me and I'm not arrested interviewing them, I'll take that footage back to Rigondeaux in Miami."

"So answer my question," he persisted.

"Maybe I reject the premise of the question."

"All the precious things we have in life are fragile. We'll lose them all one way or another soon enough. Sometimes we'll lose them for the right reasons, often for the wrong reasons, and occasionally for no reason. Whatever you intentions are, I think you appreciate how precious my daughter is."

"Yes."

"I tried to save my family from the suffering we endured in Cuba by bringing them here." He swept a hand across the room. "In the process I unwittingly destroyed everything I had. I lost everything I cared about. This boxer you follow confronted his own Faustian bargain abandoning his family. But like a lot of writers you remind me of a bullfrog. Do you know what a bullfrog does?"

"I don't know what a bullfrog *is*," I confessed.

"During mating season a bullfrog finds a pond in the swamp to sing his song to lure any females who can hear his voice. And many female bullfrogs turn into groupies the moment they hear it. But nobody falls for his song more deeply than himself. So much so, in fact, that he forgets the reason why he began singing in the first place."

"Sofía's a bigger romantic than I am."

"And romantics pretend they love the hopeless chase when really they're addicted to suffering. The only woman who really saw me for who I am told me that I was someone who would fall in love ten thousand times. She accepted that before she gave in to being one of those ten thousand, rather than trying to force me into being someone else by stopping with her. She didn't waste any time trying to prevent me from being who I was. I think you have the same curse and it's much uglier to see my daughter falling for this than it ever was looking in the mirror."

"Maybe if you find the right girl you don't have to fall in love with ten thousand other ones. You can just fall in love with *that* girl ten thousand times and you sort of fulfill the quota of the curse, no?"

"Okay." He slapped his forehead. He reached down and picked up his pawn and set it gently back down. "*Bueno.* Let's be civil before she gets home and return to some chess. Your move."

23

SLIDING DOORS

*Probably for every man there is at least one city that
sooner or later turns into a girl. How well or how badly
the man actually knew the girl doesn't necessarily affect
the transformation. She was there, and she was the whole
city, and that's that.*

—J. D. Salinger, "A Girl I Knew"

PRETTY MUCH EVERYTHING I'd lined up in Havana to complete my
documentary fell apart almost immediately after we arrived. *Split
Decision* was meant to explore all the reasons behind why Cubans
remained on the island or fled, examined through the consequences endured by Cuba's heroic boxers who turned down fortunes or, like Rigondeaux, escaped. Increasingly it became clear
the only story I could tell was how I couldn't tell that story. I wanted
to interview as many notable Cubans and experts as I could find—
artists, journalists, athletes, coaches—knowing meanwhile that all
the interviews would have to be conducted illegally. There was
no way to *officially* line anything up unless you knew the right

officials to bribe. And everyone I spoke with assured me I'd have to bribe everyone who went on camera to get them to talk about how money had no value.

I wanted to shoot my footage as fast as possible and remain below the radar for as long as I could. I had an ambitious list of people to interview on camera. Banned authors like Yoani Sánchez, the controversial blogger whom *Time* magazine had named one of the world's most influential people in 2008 and who'd interviewed Obama not long before. Yoani's blog was translated into more languages than *The New York Times* and she was quickly beginning to symbolize a controversial role as something akin to Cuba's Anne Frank.

I wanted Teófilo Stevenson to talk about his role in the revolution and Rigondeaux's "betrayal," which he'd ultimately spoken out in defense of. If Stevenson and Félix Savón represented Cuba's past, and if Rigondeaux's story was emblematic of its present, a young teenage boxer named Cristian Martínez caught my eye as someone representing the future. He'd starred in a documentary about elite young boxers on the island called *Sons of Cuba*, and many people viewed him as the next great boxer emerging to assume Rigondeaux's abdicated role as Cuba's dominant champion. *Sons of Cuba* was the first film for which foreign filmmakers were allowed into La Finca, the elite boxing academy where all of Cuba's great champions had trained.

Last, if at all possible, I wanted to interview Rigondeaux's wife and children: the collateral damage. Even knocking on their front door represented crossing a Rubicon. Or *worse*. An American, Alan Gross, had just been imprisoned for illegally working as a covert U.S. operative supplying satellite equipment to people on the island.

After we drove to meet Sofía's grandparents near Playa del Este and unloaded all the supplies we'd brought, I went over to the Habana Libre to check on the status of the people I wanted to meet and discovered nearly all of them were spooked about the risks and asked that I make no effort to contact them again. At the other hotels around Havana where I'd arranged to discuss the possibility of other interviews, I was stood up by every contact I'd had lined up through journalists in New York. Cars began to drive past with strangers smirking and pointing up at the cameras hanging over the streets, heightening my paranoia. My desperation still had a step on my fear, but it was pretty evident that things were falling apart.

"Beeeg brother eez watching, gringo," I was warned by the people renting me the apartment in Centro Habana, where Sofía and I were staying. "Welcome to Hotel California! Leezon to Mr. Henley's words. 'Check owwd aanee time bhat joo can never leave. . . .'"

Any country takes on a sinister hue once Don Henley's lyrics begin to carry any significance.

I made more calls around Havana to sort out something— *anything*—and salvage the two months I had already committed to being there. I'd borrowed a lot of money and maxed out every credit card and line of credit I had, and the only way out of bankruptcy was getting a story.

My attitude at that point was that my debts were an asset, because anybody else chasing after this story with a budget would steer clear. Bad cards or not, I was all in. Pretty soon the warnings I received from the people who were renting me the apartment escalated to begging on the lives of their children that I cease anything that could get their families in trouble. Everyone was petrified to talk about anything related to Rigondeaux or other defected fighters. "You're on your own," I was told repeatedly.

I heard the same things over and over: *Security knows everything. Taps the phone. Checks your e-mails. Talks to your neighbor. When your boxer tried to defect, Castro wrote about Rigondeaux himself. This is not a man to ask questions about. Officially he is a traitor.* Surveillance had escalated since Castro had stepped down from power. Cameras were on most of the street corners now across the entire city. More uniformed police. More secret police. The CDR on every block had stepped up their vigilance. More informants. The government was clamping down on everything, especially an issue as touchy as defecting athletes. *Leave this situation alone. You can leave. We cannot. We live with the consequences of your actions. If you are not careful you will not leave or ever be able to come back.*

After I went back to Playa del Este to pick Sofía up, the time with her grandparents had left her sealed off. They were two sweet people who lived in a small apartment after they'd traded in their house in Havana for two apartments in this suburb. Relatives lived in their other place. Sofía's grandfather had been a wealthy man who managed three sugar refineries that were all seized by the rebels. A couple of strokes had left his speech very limited, but he was open to talking about the circumstances of the complete overhaul that his life and country underwent during that time. He acknowledged the many struggles and missteps of the government's maneuvers.

When he touched on the impact of the U.S. blockade he was nuanced and explored it from several sides. The Cuban American vote in Florida had largely been responsible for the results of both of George W. Bush's elections, while Castro had a scapegoat for his own blunders, he said. He had no bitterness about losing his own station in life prerevolution in exchange for the improvements he saw for so many others from how life had been pre-Castro. "Do you really imagine the Cuban people would hand over the wheel of our country and abandon our whole socioeconomic system to a pack of bearded kids if all the greed, corruption, and unspeakable cruelty hadn't made life in this country a living hell for millions of our citizens? Castro was created by those conditions. The new generation never saw what was before. Those who did are dying off."

After we left and headed back to Havana, Sofía was very quiet in the car. She stared out the window at the sea and finally shook her head. "After they're gone I'll never come back here. I hate returning to Havana more each time. It only reminds me I don't belong here any more than I do where I live now. All of my beautiful memories just rot away while I'm in Toronto, but here the stench makes me sick. I'll never ever come back after they die."

This was the backdrop of our trial-run honeymoon from hell.

While the rest of the world's attention had turned to the struggle against dictators in Syria, Egypt, and Libya, Sofía and I landed in Havana just as the celebrations on behalf of the fiftieth anniversary of the Bay of Pigs failed invasion were picking up steam. As a tidal wave of antigovernment protests swept the Middle East, Havana was caught in some kind of bizarro Fourth of July, collectively celebrating their greatest victory against imperialism and their maximum leader outliving ten U.S. presidents and counting.

I brought a camera along and we marched with the masses. It was a weird and convoluted mix of the deadweight of so many other things Cubans had endured along with that half-century's opposition to the United States. But along with all the mandated hypocritical bullshit summed up on billboards proclaiming it was all *¡VAMOS BIEN!*, thousands more people were lost in their pride like kites blown out of their souls scratching the sky. It was like being on the field for the Super Bowl with a hundred thousand players from one team. In between the little flags, blown whistles, and chants, I saw faces bracing all around me, struggling against an unknown future and turbulent past to create a spectrum of emotions that spanned from panic to exhaustion. The surreal spectacle was held in the Plaza de la Revolución with Russian MiG fighter jets straight out of *Top Gun* soaring through the clouds and scaring the hell out of a flock of vultures circling over our heads. Hundreds of thousands of *habaneros* took buses, hitchhiked, biked, or simply walked out their front doors and struck out across the city on foot to join the crowd in the square.

Once we got near the Plaza, thousands of immaculate, olive-uniformed and white-gloved soldiers marched in formation, row after row, with rocket-propelled grenade launchers slung over their shoulders. Behind them dozens of military trucks with forty red-tipped rocket payloads drove next to other bulky vehicles rumbling by, with .50 caliber cannons and gleaming tanks bringing up the rear. The huge building-high stencils of Che and the newly built Camilo Cienfuegos stared down over another procession of soldiers following the last pack, with automatic Russian guns held against their chests. Framing the festivities were hundreds of silhouetted citizens on the roofs of the various ministry buildings enclosing the square, waving diaphanous Cuban flags against the sky. Then the navy marched into view with their rounded hats and bayonet-tipped rifles pointed up at the sky. Far off, we could

see Raúl Castro waving a beach hat in front of the José Martí monument surrounded by other government heads. Fidel's name was
chanted and posters featuring his face at various ages were held
aloft. Some Cuban troops fired a cannon while the fighter jets
made another pass over the throngs.

As we got closer to the crowds, Sofía and I were jammed in
against everybody like a packed snowball. We saw a procession of
schoolchildren in their colorful uniforms wave their scarves over
their heads as a replica of the *Granma*, the leaky boat that brought
eighty-two revolutionaries to the island, was pulled on a float behind them. The kids, as usual, caught my attention because innocence in Cuba does not resemble the Disneyfied kind that I was
accustomed to back home. Cuban childhood has its own intricate
character and coding. Fidel was welcomed by the children as a
kind of cute grandfather figure compared with the hyperpater-
nalistic view their parents always seemed to have of him, whether
they loved or hated him.

As we slowly churned toward the bottleneck of the main procession, with hundreds of home-painted placards held high—
¡*VICTORIA O MUERTE*! and ¡*SOCIALISMO*! and ¡*VIVA FIDEL*! and ¡*VAMOS
BIEN*!—next to Camilo's smiling face, Sofía leaned over to me in
the crush of the parade. She had been seething through all of this.

"Why did we come here, Brinicito? This is fucking excruciating. They're just doing this to pretend that if Cuba can stand
up to the United States it can deal with how much worse life is
about to get after Raúl lays off a million government workers. Everybody's only here because 80 percent of them work for the government! They *have* to come here. It's the same old bullshit,
scapegoating the U.S. for all our problems. It makes me sick to
my stomach. Over fifty fucking years to turn one page from this

same comic book they offer us. Let's get out of here. I've had enough of *all of this* to last a lifetime. Please, I can't be here anymore."

After Raúl waved his hat over us from a platform surrounded by his entourage of stooped yet supremely powerful political old men, Sofía yanked me out of the parade and dragged me down a nearby side street where someone just turned a pickup truck's engine. Another person waved us over to the bed of the truck and we climbed in and sat alongside a dozen Cubans eager to get back home after perfunctorily paying their dues at the *great celebration.*

After being rebuked for trying to console her, I sat holding Sofía's hand while everyone in the back of the truck took turns bemoaning their flawed country with as many jokes as earnest complaints. Despite looking furious for the same reasons as everyone else in the truck, I noticed that Sofía didn't bother to chime in or participate in the grousing. Nursing her own grudge brought on an agitation in her that was so overwhelming none of the people around us even tried to cheer her up with a joke. As much as was possible crammed into the bed of the truck, the others stayed clear. Instead they looked at me apologetically while Sofía closed her eyes and breathed heavily as the wind played with her hair. Without her having to say a word, they knew she'd endured what they had, but they also mysteriously determined she wasn't staying long.

We drove back into town down a long, hilly street with the sidewalks mostly empty. I was trying to think of a place we could go to cheer Sofía up. Havana was all but abandoned, even more of a city of ruins than usual for the next few hours. We'd have the Hotel Nacional to ourselves for a drink or the Museo del Chocolate without the forty-five-minute wait to get in next to an open sewer or Coppelia for an ice cream. Maybe hitchhike out to Playa del Este on a deserted section of beach, with the tropical water and sand so bright it was almost neon. But one look at Sofía's sullen face and it was obvious that I was to leave her alone for the rest of the drive in.

Like most of the Cubans on the flight over, Sofía had brought a huge amount of supplies to deliver to her grandparents and extended family: medicine, a walker for her grandfather who'd just suffered a stroke, vitamins, toothpaste, foot cream, tampons, an mp3 player, soap, and a slew of other basic necessities well beyond the reach of average citizens. Sofía had been hassled by customs officials, being forced to explain and then defend each item, as with many other Cubans returning home to help their families. It was clear that she'd been through the routine so many times already that the only emotion she had left was disgust. She told me after we got in the cab outside José Martí Airport that once her family had raised enough money to survive in Canada, all their resources went toward sending Sofía back to the island to deliver what they could provide back home to family members buried by increasing needs as things continued to deteriorate in Cuban daily life.

From the beginning, unlike most Cubans I'd met who had defected or found other means of leaving, for Sofía nostalgia for anything relating to *home* repulsed her. Her sentimentality was reserved only for the decidedly unsentimental stories she'd left behind. Mainly stuff she trotted out to demonstrate how elusive she was from my grasp and best to keep at a distance.

The first time I met her in a Toronto hotel lobby on King Street, she'd laughed in my face before confirming to herself the suspicion that she'd had since we'd begun writing each other: that she was completely out of my league. She announced this finding at such volume that most of the hotel staff took my measure and nodded agreement. Naturally, any hopes I had collapsed on the spot and I assumed at any second she would turn around and disappear forever, all with the indifference one might bring to throwing away trash. "Listen, Gypsy, maybe we can just grab a drink first since you came all this way, but don't get any ideas. . . ."

Some snow was falling outside and clung to her hair and jacket collar, and the rest of her looked like some tropical princess. Before she'd left Cuba, all her life she'd wanted to see the snow, and on the day she finally arrived to Canada, Toronto was under siege, battling a blizzard. She'd traded one excruciating extreme for another, and that was before she had enough English to contrast Cuban men with their Canadian equivalents. Leaving home as a teenager, Cuba was like a bear trap where the only means of escape required amputating vital portions of her soul. Food and music were the only safe areas to remain connected. Everything else seemed to bring into focus how the two worlds she straddled had left her life completely off-balance. And because our meetings after this one had all been restricted to fleeting marathon fuckfests around Toronto—behind the backs of our respective partners—there was always a kind of wartime urgency compounded by a tacit prohibition of talking about the past or the future. *Last Tango in Paris* was for both of us a favorite movie, and so we re-created our own version in my home country each time I departed for her hometown.

But the good-byes were rigged with all kinds of explosives. The moment I'd raise the prospect of seeing her again she'd pull up her drawbridge and dig a moat around herself, informing me we'd never see each other again. "We'd only make ourselves miserable anyway," she'd sneer. So I stopped asking permission and continued to lay over in Toronto for a few days every time I went to Havana with the express purpose of ambushing her. The more secure a setup she had with a man, the easier it was to entice betrayal.

Back in Havana Sofía finally smiled. "I know where I want you to take me," Sofía said. "Let's get off the truck and grab another car."

"Where do you wanna go?"

"Quinta Avenida. Let's go to Miramar and you can fuck this sadness out of me at Parque de los Ahogados. I'm tired of feeling grumpy. It's my favorite park and where I lost my virginity. While you fuck me I'll think about him." She smiled.

"Hold on, I'm still stuck on *ahogados*. Park of the *hanged*?"

"Yeah, from all the suicides who hung themselves off these incredibly haunting banyan trees there. The park looks like someone's nightmare."

"This is where you lost your virginity?"

"Mhmm," she said, waving at our driver in the rearview to stop the truck. "My old house isn't far. I'll take you to see where I grew up."

We stopped an old Plymouth that was huffing its way over to Quinta Avenida, the avenue where the Malecón ends and dips under a tunnel and climbs to blossom into a six-lane avenue, divided by a lush, tree-lined island for pedestrians to stroll in the shade or relax on stone benches straight out of Santa Monica, California. When you exit that tunnel Miramar isn't so much a different neighborhood of the city as a different world. The decay and despair of so many homes in Vedado give way to the abandoned, opulent mansions that run for miles, many converted into for-eign embassies. At night the most expensive *jineteras* across the city strut in their Lycra catsuits looking to lure diplomats and other rich visitors until someone accepts their price.

We turned off the avenue down a side street just before the spooky suicide park Sofía had mentioned. A man from a group playing dominoes over a table on the corner glared at Sofía in her summer dress and then over at me. He muttered something and they all stared at us.

"*¡Coño!* These tourists steal the best of *everything* in our coun-try," one of them moaned.

Our visit to her childhood neighborhood hadn't begun auspi-ciously.

Sofía turned and gave me a scolding look before smiling her satisfaction. "My people giving you shit definitely helps cheer me up."

"It's depressing as fuck," I said.

"People like you are all the same. The ugliest thing you can find traveling around damaged places is always another tourist. That's your biggest fear, isn't it?"

"I can't help where I'm from any more than they can help where they came from."

"Why should you be depressed? According to them you've sto-len the best *mujer* in all of Cuba. I bet they wouldn't have said the same thing about Fidel Castro's granddaughter. Who knows, maybe she'll see us around Havana."

This was an accurate forecast of my doomed last stretch in Ha-vana. And after this she walked away emphasizing her triumph with each voluptuous step and wrecking-ball swing of her hips while the domino table full of men hissed and shrieked their approval. I followed her over to the park until she reached behind herself to pull up her skirt. We unpacked some much needed cheer and goodwill at the Park of the Hanged under one of the nightmarish banyan trees while Sofía sarcastically called out the name of the guy she lost her virginity to as a means of encouraging me to pick up the tempo before we got arrested.

Afterward, we wandered a few blocks off the avenue and turned up at a residential street littered with drowsy homes that wouldn't look out of place in any suburb across the United States. Most had the familiar Cuban sausage dogs behind fences yelping "Intruder! Intruder!" until they abandoned their posts once we went over to pet them and applaud their ferociousness.

"The next house was ours," Sofía said softly. "They painted it yellow. It was nicer pink. I wonder if the man my father sold it to still lives there now. Probably. I've heard he's had a terrible time since he bought it ten years ago."

"Who was he?"

"A Spanish businessman. Supplies the hotels in Miramar with various things. I don't know him well. I don't really know why I'm taking you here actually."

Sofía opened the gate and I followed behind her into the front yard of her former home. As she walked she looked a little shaken glancing over at her neighbors' properties. When we got to the front door we could hear what sounded like a sledgehammer coming from the backyard. We went around the side of the house and saw construction workers being overseen by an older, debonair gentleman who'd brought out a pitcher of mojitos and was pouring glasses.

"*¡Oye, Mario!*" Sofía cried out.

Mario turned around and smiled wide with his lips slowly parting.

"Still here?" Sofía laughed.

"I've been stranded ever since I bought the place. Look at you. You're as beautiful as your mother. Come closer so I can give you a kiss."

They talked for twenty minutes while Mario showed Sofía the changes he'd made to the house in an attempt to improve its value for a sale. In between Mario pointing out his changes and Sofía updating him on her family on the island and in Canada, she showed me where she'd taken her first steps, where she'd slept with her brother and aunt, and the room where she'd kissed a boy for the first time. It was as if we were viewing her past and the forgotten dreams she'd long since abandoned behind the glass of a pawnshop window. In every room we entered she made a face like her heart caved in.

"It's a beautiful home," I said to both of them. I turned to Mario. "Why are you trying to sell it?"

He sighed as Sofía shook her head.

"My friend." Mario put his hand on my shoulder. "As I'm sure you know, to *visit* Havana is paradise. But to *live* in Havana is hell. And that's before I could even begin to explain what doing *business* is like in this fucking country. Over the years they've come here and seized my car, my motorcycle. I'm harassed constantly. They've seized all kinds of things. You can't do business here without dealing with the black market. Of course the government knows this. The illegal economy is bigger than the *official* economy. It's all institutionally corrupt and I was just too naïve to think I could ever navigate such a hideously broken system. I need to go back to Spain and start over. I give up. I've spent everything I've ever earned here just to improve this property to sell it off so I can finally leave. I'm dying faster than even this rotting-away city."

"Would you leave tomorrow if you could sell it?" I asked Mario.

"*Por favor.*" He laughed. "Would I leave tomorrow if I sold this place? I would leave *tonight.*"

"Brinicito is here trying to interview the family Guillermo Rigondeaux left behind."

"A very beautiful boxer. What a sad face he had even before Fidel called him a traitor. A true Cuban champion for his time."

"How dangerous is it to try to talk with them?" I asked Mario.

"Two government cameras are focused on his house twenty-four hours a day, seven days a week. Easily the most politically radioactive home in Havana. If you go, be prepared for a knock on the door any second and to be escorted to the airport by security. I wouldn't go if I were you."

"I don't even know where it is yet."

"*Qué va.*" Mario snickered. "We all know where it is. Boyeros. Near the airport. Everybody knows the little green house. His house was on the news here for weeks after he tried to defect. Stay here, I'll go inside and get a pencil and paper and draw you a map."

After he'd finished sketching the street and government buildings next to Rigondeaux's home, I asked how he knew the directions were accurate.

Mario smiled and asked me to stop any taxi on the street, secure a ride, and then ask them to take me to the address he'd written down. After we'd left her old home, Sofía and I tried this twice back on Quinta Avenida. Both times drivers gave us an incredulous look before driving off. It was pretty evident this was a real danger in a land where, if there was a suggestion you were sympathetic to one of the most famous living traitors in any way, your whole life was in peril. Maybe not just *your* life, either; anyone close to you, also. While you aren't likely to meet a people more generous, *nobody* can hold a grudge like Cubans.

JUDAS

A revolution is not a bed of roses. —Fidel Castro

"*LISTEN*, BRINICITO," SOFÍA WAS SAYING in bed at our apartment, late on the night before we went to the house Fidel had given Rigondeaux as a reward for his first Olympic medal. "We don't have long in Havana together. It's only because of Rigondeaux winning his fight that we have this time together, so I'll go with you to this house. I'd like to meet his family. Keep in mind, if we visit that house you're never going to be let back into this country again. So if you're comfortable with that, you better get everything you want to film in Havana before they take you away."

The phone rang.

"*Oye, campeón,*" a voice slurred. I knew from the word *campeón* that it was a boxer, all right, but whoever it was, he was drunk out of his mind and I couldn't make out much. "*Lo siento, campeón.*

Lo siento. Emergencia. Por favor. Lo siento. Mi familia. Emergencia. I must see you right away. *Lo siento.*"

The only boxer I'd ever spoken with on the phone who was drunk was Teófilo Stevenson. He'd declined or indefinitely postponed every request I'd ever made to meet with him and usually ended each phone call with the same tragic question, "*Campeón,* what *time* is it anyway?" I'd answer with the time and he'd follow up, "*Bueno.* Which *day* is it?" After I'd tell him the day he'd break my heart again asking what month it was. It made no difference what hour I called him. No matter how early it was that I called him on his cell phone, Stevenson was to some extent intoxicated.

But after a dozen of these horribly awkward phone calls, I was very familiar with his nasal voice that enjoyed toying with me, using Russian and English sprinkled into the conversation. This wasn't him or any voice that I recognized. Then it dawned on me. . . .

"*Héctor?*"

"*Sí,*" he groaned, clearing his throat. "*Lo siento, campeón.* But I must come over."

"What's wrong?" I asked.

Sofía was glaring at me.

"*Con permiso,*" I told Héctor. I turned to Sofía and covered the phone: "He says there's some kind of family emergency and he has to come over."

"He's drunk?" she asked.

"He's drunk or he's badly injured. He sounds *awful.*"

"He knows where we are?"

"Yeah."

"*Madre mía,* Brinicito. There's no *family emergency.* He needs

money! Don't let him come over here. Give me the fucking phone,"
she demanded, reaching over to grab it.

"This has never happened before! Héctor's a friend. What if
there *is* an emergency?"

"*Right*," Sofía lamented. "Decide now how much you want to
lose when he's in our apartment begging and refusing to leave unless you pay him. And keep in mind how it looks having a drunken
two-time Olympic champion puking and stumbling his way to
our apartment at this hour of the night."

I took my hand off the phone. "This is a family emergency?"

"Please. I must see you. Please. Please, please, please . . ."

"I can go to you."

"*No*," Héctor insisted. "I will be there in thirty minutes. Stay,
where you are. *Please*."

"Okay."

He hung up the phone.

"You think you're being a friend right now," Sofía groaned.
"All you've done is made yourself a target."

I got dressed and left our apartment and went out onto the
roof to keep a look out for Héctor's arrival. Even as late as it was,
broken-down American gypsy cabs haunted Calle Neptuno like
meandering spirits climbing toward the magnificent front steps
of the University of Havana and the bizarre Napoleon museum
nearby, only to swing off along the bend toward the Coppelia ice
cream stand and under the looming bulk of the Habana Libre,
where the city's increasingly visible homosexual cruising community roamed at night. Fidel used to send them off to gruesome
labor camps enclosed in barbwire, but things had slowly improved. Looking out toward Miami, a blackout extended down
every street leading down to the Malecón, interrupted in distant

pinpricks of light from the ends of cigars smoked by unseen figures. I sat on the edge of my roof dreading Héctor's arrival while
I watched the procession of Fords, Oldsmobiles, and Cadillacs,
all with their ghostly, lonesome headlights drifting over the shattered terrain of broken streets toward my apartment until they
passed and receded on their way to complete their city-wide circuit. One car honked the theme of *The Godfather* to warn stray
animals of their approach or maybe gently interrupt a couple arguing in the shadows, seeing if they wanted to be picked up. The
Hotel Nacional was only a mile or so away, where Michael Cor-
leone met the rest of America's most powerful fictional gangsters
on the rooftop and sliced off pieces of Cuba, frosted over a cake,
dividing up ownership until Castro ruined everything. When
the car honked the opening bars of the theme again, dogs on a
neighbor's rooftop howled their attempts at harmony as several
couples leaned against their wrought iron balconies, under their
laundry lines swaying limply in the warm air, and turned in our
direction. I noticed a hand-painted portrait of Camilo on the roof
of a Buick. One of the most beautiful surprises I'd ever seen was
witnessing children across the country observing the anniversary
of Camilo's death from a plane crash shortly after the triumph of
the revolution by bringing flowers to the ocean and rivers. Many
rumors claimed Fidel was responsible for the crash.

When you wake up from a bad dream in Havana, it always
takes longer than you've ever experienced in your life to make sure
that you're really awake. I kept wanting to go back inside my room
to ask Sofía if Héctor had really called and was really on the way
over. It was only after Héctor finally arrived and spilled out of the
cab and fell into the gutter that I knew it was real. A group of
men playing dominoes on the corner came over to help him up.

Suddenly the streetlight burned out and there was nothing but darkness and urgent voices.

I ran down several flights of stairs and found Héctor crawling up the fifth stair, having thrown up on the landing. The stench from the vomit and the alcohol wafting off him was overwhelming. He was wearing a bright red Cuban national team volleyball jersey that was soaked around his belly from the puke.

"Do you need an ambulance?" I asked, taking his arm and flinging it over my shoulder.

"*Todo bien,*" Héctor grunted. "Your stairs are an abomination against humanity."

"You need a doctor?"

"*No,*" Héctor shouted. But he was out of breath. "My daughter . . . She needs my help. I need your help. . . . I didn't know who else to ask. I know how this looks. If you can give me a hundred CUC it could save her life. *Please.*"

What the fuck was there to say?

"Stay here," I said. "I'll go up and get it."

Héctor retched and his cheeks blew up like Dizzy Gillespie's for a second before I hoisted him up so he could puke over the side of the stairwell. Dogs inside the apartments just above us sounded their alarms as Sofía's footsteps cascaded down the stairs toward us.

A neighbor who opened his door hissed at us behind his barred gate. "*Ay* . . . who is this person? You need *security?*"

"No," I said. "This is a friend. Everything is okay."

Sofía walked past the neighbor and stopped a couple of stairs above us.

"Listen," I told her. "This is a really fucked-up situation that's going to get a lot worse in a hurry."

Sofía ignored me and cast a steely glare at Héctor. "¿*Cuánto?*" was all she asked.

I took a cab with Héctor to make sure he got home okay, but everything was pointing to the fact I didn't have much time left in Cuba. Sofía and I left the next morning for Boyeros with Mario's map. We got dropped off a few blocks from where Rigondeaux's family lived in their half of a little green duplex. Sofía knocked on the door and Rigondeaux's wife, Farah Colina Rigondeaux, answered the door. I could see the outline of their two children, Guillermo Jr. and César, now eight and seventeen respectively, behind her in the living room.

I explained who I was, unsure of how she'd react. I'd spent a lot of time with her husband after his escape and gained a measured respect for him in the process. After a pause she invited me in with a warm smile, as if I were a neighbor. She had spent fourteen years with Rigondeaux before he escaped. The living room looked exactly the same as when the international news crews had covered his famous defection. Small TV in the corner, a red couch, a few pictures on the wall of the family together, some medals and trophies from Rigondeaux's career, blinds that looked perpetually drawn.

She broke the ice by telling me she'd originally met him at one of his fights. He noticed her in the crowd while he was sitting on his stool between rounds. She laughed until it was clear she was about to cry.

Suddenly Farah's expression changed as she assured me the police were tracking me and asked that I be very careful for the rest of my time in Havana. "Your phone, e-mail, movements, *every-thing*. Beeg Brother knows everything."

A camerawoman I'd hired had visited a friend who had taken a trip to a central police station and told me that for every two cameras in Havana (which in many areas was nearly every block) there was one policeman assigned to monitor all movements.

I told Farah that the reason I'd come was to bring footage of her husband to her family and to bring back footage of their family to Rigondeaux. I owed him that much for giving me such access to his life.

With her children beside her, we looked over the photos and video of her husband I'd brought. Guillermo Jr. brought photos of his father over from the back of the apartment for me to look at. In the back of my mind I was wondering how much time we had before there might be an ominous knock at the door.

"He looks very sad, doesn't he?" Farah said to Sofía. "Obviously what affects us most here is his absence. More than anything, we miss his presence, especially our smallest child, who needs him a lot. Above all, he's a good father and husband. Regardless of what happens, I have confidence in him. And he will never abandon us for anything. The last time he sent some things to our son, my mother told him, 'Now you should be happy because your dad sent some stuff.' He told her, 'I will only be happy when my dad comes to see me.' Those were his exact words."

Farah told us how on the last day she saw her husband in Cuba, he had stayed home from working some menial job he'd found so that he could play with his small son. He told her he was going east to Santiago, his hometown, but in fact he'd gone west to leave some days later. She told me that he called her the moment he arrived safely in Miami and that the journey—through a horrible storm—had been the most frightening experience of his life. She cried talking about how much Rigondeaux's mother's death had affected him shortly after he made it to Miami. Not long after, his son had gotten sick just before Rigondeaux fought for a world championship. Guilt-ridden, he braced himself for losing another family member he was helpless to be with. The trauma outside the ring had nearly derailed his professional career in America on the ironic basis of him *not risking enough* in front of a paying audience. Farah assured me he called regularly and sent money. She emphasized that he was a decent human being and the love of her life. She assured me again—and also her children at the same time—that he would never abandon them. Farah said Rigondeaux had never discussed the specifics or anything else about leaving, but she insisted the government had left him with no choice.

I asked Guillermo's eight-year-old son what he thought of the father he hadn't seen in more than two years. He gave me a hard look for a second and ran into his room. Before I could apologize to his mother, he ran back out to the living room with a poster of his dad and opened it up for me to see. The poster was bigger than he was. He brushed his cheek against his father's and looked up at me. "I miss him. I miss watching him fight. My father is my hero."

Rigondeaux's wife rubbed her eyes and turned away from her son to me. "He's a hero to *both* of us."

"Can I come back to speak with you once more tomorrow?" I asked.

"Of course. Just be careful."

Harvey Milk said that although you can't live on hope alone, without hope life isn't worth living. I still believed that when I first met Rigondeaux in 2007. Catching up with him in the United States made it harder. No matter what the restrictions were regarding baggage limits on that smuggler's boat, none were traveling light. Rigondeaux and the rest of the people on that vessel had left everything they'd ever known behind, perhaps forever. Maybe the weight of their hope was their greatest vulnerability. Where could you hide it?

The following afternoon, on Sofía's last day in Havana, I hired a cinematographer from Cuban television under the table to come along for our return to Farah Colina's house. Farah wasn't answering her phone as we drove over.

Both Sofía and the cinematographer were dead certain "security" had gotten to her and was closing in on us.

"If she has not answered the phone, we should not be doing this," Sofía warned. "We will get arrested. This is a very vindictive system."

The cinematographer nodded solemnly. "This is a very dangerous place to go right now."

We arrived at Farah's house and climbed the stairs. Her seventeen-year-old son peeked out the window and told me his mother had left Havana for La Lisa to visit a dying relative. He was a very bad liar. He immediately tried to shut the window before saying anything else. I managed to keep him for long enough to ask him if he'd like to talk for a minute. He subtly gestured in the direction of the camera trained on their house across the street. "You should leave now," he said. "I'm sorry."

We drove back down the hill and dropped the cinematographer off along the way before the driver let us out near the Prado.

I went over to a pay phone and made some calls to Teófilo Stevenson and Cristian Martínez's coach. Stevenson was pretty clearheaded and actually remembered that I'd asked him for an interview a dozen times before. I told him this was the last time I'd have a chance to meet with him if he was at all willing. "Call me in an hour, *campeón*. I'll look at my schedule." I called a friend of his who worked as a translator for diplomats and asked if he could come over to his house to make a case for the interview. If it was going to happen it had to happen in the next forty-eight hours. Martínez's coach agreed to bring Cristian over to my apartment that night. I was going to give both Martínez and Stevenson the best shot I could for an interview, and if they panned out take off for the airport with the footage immediately after.

I was getting horribly paranoid at that point and snagged another car off the street to take us to the Yara movie theater next to the Habana Libre so that I could lay low inside for a couple hours with Sofía. Along with a packed house, we sat in the back of a roasting-hot theater as the curtain rose on a local film called *Ticket to Paradise*. Five minutes into the matinee it was clear we were watching the most excruciatingly depressing Cuban film ever made. The "ticket to paradise" for the Cuban teenagers struggling to survive during the Special Period in the film was fucking their brains out in every orgy they could find so they could contract HIV and be quarantined along with everyone else infected with the virus and receive three square meals. Once they succeeded in their heartbreaking quest they screamed for joy while what seemed like a third of the theater broke down in tears remembering the era.

"Let's get the fuck out of here," Sofía demanded. "I already lived through the Special Period once, I don't need to revisit it."

Whatever path we took across the city where Sofía was born, her whole life seemed to be pressing against her, not just behind and in front of her, but from all directions at once.

25

WHISTLING PAST THE GRAVEYARD

A revolution is a struggle to the death between the future and the past. —Fidel Castro

EARLY THE NEXT MORNING I dragged Sofía's luggage over the potholes of Calle Neptuno to her grandmother's house to say good-bye. We didn't look at each other walking down street after street, but we held hands until she'd complain I was squeezing too tightly. Her head was high, while my chin was down against my chest. I saw a dead chick in the gutter that a stray cat was toying with. I don't remember much else about that walk.

We stopped outside her grandmother's apartment and I let go of her hand and told her I couldn't wait with her for the taxi to take her to the airport. We heard Nat King Cole singing "Nature Boy" out someone's barred window, "The greatest thing . . . you'll ever learn . . . is just to love . . . and be loved . . . in return."

She smiled at me when she saw that my eyes were wet.

"Oh *pleeeease*. You acting like you never see me again."

But I hadn't thought that far ahead.

"I think it's a little worse."

"Why is that, Brinicito?"

"I'm crying because I won't see you *tonight*."

"See? What did I tell you the first time I saw you? No chemistry between us."

I kissed her and she bit my lip hard enough to draw blood. With her teeth inside my upper lip, I smiled without being able to look at her and ran my hand through her hair. She let go and I told her that I loved her before stepping away and turning the corner. I caught the first taxi that stopped and told them to drop me off at Colón cemetery in Vedado.

I've always loved cemeteries. When my father took me to new places as a kid, for our first stop we'd always stop at the local cemeteries and make a game of tracking down the first person laid to rest. Colón was the most beautiful cemetery I'd ever seen, filled with all the marvelous people who added their weight, color, and melodies to Havana's Goya-like dreamscape. After being built in 1876, over a million people had been buried in eight hundred thousand graves, with hundreds of impossibly detailed mausoleums, family vaults, and chapels so white under the sun they blind you when the tropical heat doesn't blur the air. The first man buried in Colón was the architect, Calixto Arellano de Loira y Cardoso, who never finished building it.

I've never met anyone from Havana—even those who left so young they can't remember it—who didn't seem to be sucking life from a bent straw living anywhere else. Part of Havana's twisted magic is how even visitors aren't immune to this disease, with some clumsy music inside your own heart playing an off-key karaoke version of the real symphony you observe behind the eyes of locals. The first time I ever visited Madrid and asked a stranger outside the Plaza de Toros who the greatest bullfighter in the world was, he listed off the names and held his hands apart to symbolize how close the matadors allowed the horns to their hearts. His hands got closer with each name until he smiled mischievously before concluding the list. "But José Tomás? He lets the horns come so close to his heart nobody can bear to watch. We all cover our eyes. His genius is so beautiful that nobody in Spain has ever dared to see it."

As the cab got closer and the 140-acre cemetery was in view, something besides Sofía or getting arrested gnawed at me. In the back of my mind, I had always yearned to be in Havana when Fidel would be laid to rest in Colón. Ever since I'd first seen *The Second of May 1808* in the Prado when I was eighteen, I'd been obsessed by Goya's take on Napoleon and the most powerful army in the world invading and meeting their downfall in Spain. With Fidel's passing, I wanted to witness that impossibly strange atmosphere firsthand and see what the air tasted like for Cubans the first day Castro stopped breathing it. "It's not my fault I haven't died yet," Castro once told Ann Louise Bardach, who'd flown over to interview him. She asked Fidel if he was the devil his enemies made him out to be. "If that is the case," Fidel replied, "then I am a devil who has been protected by the gods."

The world doesn't get to choose the destinations where its most colorful, important characters stain history's canvas. I've always played goofy games in my mind trying to imagine Shakespeare being born anywhere else, transplanting van Gogh to Detroit, or Napoleon to Mexico City, or allowing Hitler to fail at pastoral painting in a back alley in Shanghai. What impact could Fidel have had if he were born almost *anywhere* else but a small, impoverished island ninety miles off the shore of the most powerful civilization on earth? Even from such a meager stage, with such a humble role, he *still* managed to find a way of holding the world hostage and bringing it as close as it ever came to oblivion. What if he'd been born on third base? What would our world look like? What impact could he have had? Fidel didn't have a bust or a statue or so much as a plaque anywhere across the country, but his dent in history was undeniable. And unless Fidel died during my last twenty-four hours in his country, I'd be watching Havana on cable news the next day like everyone else. "All the glory in the world can fit into a kernel of corn," Fidel quoted José Martí, after Bardach asked him how he wished to be remembered.

I was meeting a cinematographer named Ana María at La Milagrosa's grave, Colón's most popular. Ana María was a young girl fresh out of film school who worked for Cuban television. Ría had helped me find her. La Milagrosa's grave belonged to a girl named Amelia Goyri de la Hoz. Amelia was buried, along with her child, in 1903. They had both died as Amelia tried to bring the child into the world when she was only twenty-three years old. Inside their tomb, Amelia's infant son was placed at his mother's feet. When both bodies were exhumed, according to legend, the child was discovered in his mother's arms. Amelia's inconsolable widower returned to his bride and child's grave each day for the last seventeen years of his life. It was said that her widower never accepted their deaths and instead believed they were asleep beneath the ground. He installed a brass knocker over the grave and each day he brought flowers and knocked on the grave three times as a secret signal. After the knocks, he would cry out, "Wake up, Amelia! Wake up!" Since I'd first started coming to Havana and visiting Colón, the grave was guarded every hour of every day by a cult devoted to La Milagrosa. A sculptor had built a statue of Amelia clutching her child over the grave and I never once saw all the white marble of her tomb unadorned in fresh flowers and troves of offerings from people praying to her to look after their kids or to allow for them to be blessed with children.

As I approached our meeting place, Ana María was talking with a few old women guarding the grave next to the statue of Amelia cradling her child. I noticed Ana María had a book under her arm and was smoking an unfiltered cigarette. She was tall and wiry, wearing a man's white undershirt and torn jeans, her hair fastened in two wild clumps behind her ears. She had an alluring mixture of soft femininity in her features and masculine grace in her posture and movements.

"So?" she said in perfect English. "Would you like to shoot the cemetery?"

"Yeah," I told her, handing over my camera. It wasn't a film camera since I'd been terrified they'd confiscate anything looking professional at customs. I had a shitty tripod with me also.

"This camera is *mierda, yuma.* Ría warned me about you. First she told me you had an affair with the granddaughter of Fidel."

"Why would she tell you that?" I asked.

"I have a boyfriend," Ana María declared.

"Because I slept with Fidel's granddaughter I'm a threat to the sanctity of all Cuban women in relationships?"

"Well." She smirked, changing the subject by holding up the camera as though it were rotting meat. "This tourist camera makes me even more uncomfortable. Ría also told me your work is sensitive. So I'm guessing you have *zero* clearance to do any of the work you're doing here?"

"If you can explain to me how I can *get* clearance in this country to work on anything sensitive—"

"Are we shooting something sensitive today?"

I shrugged.

"Dangerous?"

"You don't have to help me."

"*Ay*—"

"What?"

"We both know I need the money."

"And I'm fifty thousand dollars in debt back home and desperately need this footage."

"*Yuma*, will this put me in danger?"

I could see she was about five seconds from walking away, but I didn't know what to say.

From a pay phone the night before, I'd gotten as close to Teófilo Stevenson as I ever had, with him not *outright* rejecting an interview. "Call me tomorrow," he growled, before hanging up. Someone close to him had told me things had gotten so bad financially Stevenson didn't have enough money to put gas in the tank of his little car or replace a flat tire. But who knew how much money he expected to talk, let alone on camera. Who knew who was listening to our phone calls and might be closing in long before I ever had the chance to sit with him? Out of eleven million people in the country, three million were officially enrolled as CDRs spying on their neighbors.

Besides Stevenson, Cristian Martínez and his boxing coach, Yosvanni Bonachea, the stars of *Sons of Cuba*, a documentary that had won awards around the world on the film festival circuit, had agreed to come over to my apartment that afternoon to talk. Before I left Cuba for good, my Hail Mary was somehow managing to include Héctor Vinent, Félix Savón, *and* Teófilo Stevenson in my documentary defending their decision to remain in Cuba, the whole continuum of great Cuban heroes who rejected America's Faustian bargain. Then, with two years following Rigondeaux's journey toward a world championship and riches *in* America, I would offer Rigondeaux's life and reasons in defense of leaving. And then finally Cristian Martínez's role, just before his sixteenth birthday, staring down his first Olympic Games, seemed to offer a unique view on where Cuba's next generation on the horizon wanted to go.

Cristian had come of age just as Fidel had stepped down from power. "If the U.S.A. dares to attack us at this sad moment," Cristian said the day after Fidel announced his state secret illness, "we'll run out to defend our country." Fidel had rewarded Cristian's father with a car and an apartment for his contributions to the revolution. But that home was in shambles and the car had long since broken down and there was no money to repair any of the damage. Cristian, like the others, would have to weigh the life of his father, and the lives of all the great boxers who came before him, in order to determine the right path to take. Perhaps where he went, and his reasons for doing so, would point the way where all Cubans of his generation might easily follow.

There was some additional pressure on me talking to Cristian Martínez, as the manager who'd gotten Rigondeaux off the island was interested in doing the same thing with this boy. I'd been asked to feel the teenager out in terms of his receptivity to making the jump. To broach the topic of Cristian's defection meant prison time for me, and the certain death of Cristian's boxing career before it ever got started. Even creating the perception I was trying to help facilitate Cristian's escape was a serious offense against the revolution. "Cuban boxers fight for a better future," Cristian had told the cameras as a child of twelve. "We Cubans are fighting from the moment we are born."

"I think the next twenty-four hours are going to be pretty dangerous, talking to who I want to talk to," I explained to Ana María. "There are risks. It's up to you if you want to help me or not."

We looked at each other for a tense moment until we both smiled.

"I was expecting a womanizer from how Ría described you. A *romantic* is even worse. *Joder*. No more talking. If you like, we could shoot one of the funerals taking place here. Ría told me you play a lot of chess. We could shoot some of the famous graves and start with Capablanca, with his giant queen over the grave. I love that grave. Alejo Carpentier is buried here, if you are partial to writers. Dulce María Loynaz, if you like poets. Máximo Gómez, if you prefer military men. Chano Pozo, if you want a musician. Tell me where we should start."

"Today I'd like you to shoot anything you want. We can go anywhere you think is special. Take me to your favorite places. Today let's just film *your* Havana."

"Shouldn't we be filming *your* Havana?"

"I don't have the stomach for it today."

"This is the weirdest assignment I've ever been given."

"Later this afternoon," I said, "I'd like you to shoot an interview with a young boxer at my apartment and also film him exercising with his coach on my roof. I'd like you to film him with all of Centro Habana and the skyline behind him while he shadowboxes and trains with his coach. Until then I just want to get my mind off of a few things."

"Why do you seem so sad?" she asked.

"I don't have much time left in Havana," I told her. *Maybe even less time than you think*, I reminded myself. "What's the book under your arm?"

"My *favorite* book." She smiled. "*The Unbearable Lightness of Being.*"

"Let's shoot for several hours, and then we can go somewhere before the interview at my apartment and maybe you can read some of it to me?"

"I told you that I have a boyfriend."

"I'm not asking you to be my whore. You have a beautiful accent and I'd like to hear you read. Reading isn't cheating."

"Reading *Kundera* to a stranger isn't *far* from cheating."

"You don't have to read anything to me. You can think it over while we shoot your city."

"You're just going to use me to get over someone else." Ana María smiled.

"Not really," I disagreed. "I'm just trying to use you."

"That's sad, but I like that a little better."

We spent the rest of the morning and afternoon filming all over Havana. After filming some famous graves around the cemetery, we captured kids enjoying rides inside Jalisco Park, communism's clumsy answer to Disneyland. Nearby, Ana María leaned over our old Ford Thunderbird's window to shoot a long line of teenage students eagerly waiting to be let into the Charlie Chaplin Cinema to watch a matinee·of *City Lights*. I watched her lie

back on the ground and film some Orson Welles angles of little
boys picking off beer cans inside a corner shooting gallery. She
filmed gasoline rainbows swirling over the puddles that glazed
the gutters of Centro Habana. She caught a stickball homerun
smashing a window from an intersection in Centro Habana while
bootleg DVDs of *Annie Hall* and *Manhattan* were peddled behind
an outfielder punching his ratty glove. Down the street from the
Karl Marx Theater, some lunatic was high above us on his balcony, screaming obscenities about Fidel while collecting laundry
from a line. "If the revolution had worked out, I ask you why are
none of Fidel or Raúl's children in politics? How many of them
have left? Answer me that!" Three teenagers laughed from a balcony across the street, passing around a joint they smoked in the
peculiar Cuban style, through a nostril.

We went back to my old gym in Old Havana and filmed children following instructions from Héctor, who remembered nothing from his drunken visit to my apartment. Ana María wandered
with her camera around seniors assuming poses with yoga classes
in the park, construction workers wiping the icy froth from their
mouths at *guarapo* stands, fathers and sons window shopping at
the Adidas store, tourists and whores leaving or entering hotels,
Che look-alikes. Outside the Capitolio we filmed a man with a
hundred piercings in his face sticking his tongue out at us while
he posed with tourists being photographed by the portrait artists
with their century-old cameras.

We got in the back of a Chinese taxi and peddled around the
most desolate slums of Old Havana until we arrived ten minutes
later in the most beautifully restored area of Plaza Vieja and her
pristine fountains. Ana María filmed kids lounging in the courtyard of the university surrounded by palm trees and tanks. We

rode past the statue of El Caballero de París, maybe the world's most beloved homeless man who ever lived. Long before the revolution, when they installed the Caballero in Mazora, Havana's mental institution, there was such a protest across Havana that he was released by presidential order. He was invited to meet the president and his cape and mysterious belongings were returned to him. After the triumph of the revolution, he told the press that Castro and the other rebels had stolen his personal sense of style with their beards and grungy fashion. El Caballero died in 1985, and almost anyone I'd ever met who lived in Havana before that time, if you mentioned his name, produced such an incredibly thrilled smile recounting their interactions with him that it was impossible not to fall in love with him yourself.

Schoolchildren marched across the Malecón in their uniforms. For the first time, I noticed some of them wore headphones. Cell phones were in the hands of teenagers rumbling by on skateboards. Many didn't have enough money to pay for texting, let alone phone calls, but they clasped their phones everywhere they went as status symbols. Conspicuous consumption, too: the house band at El Floridita played "Guantanamera" and all the other deflated standards for tourists in Hemingway T-shirts, smoking Montecristos lit from red-uniformed bartenders waiting on blenders churning daiquiris.

Even after a little more than a decade of returning again and again to this city, it had changed completely on me, and was changing even faster now than I'd ever seen before.

"Of course it's coming," Gary Indiana, an American writer and filmmaker who had spent many years returning to Cuba, wrote of one visit to Havana. "Coming here, coming soon, the gathering tsunami of Our Kind of Capitalism. iPad, iPod, YouTube, Buy

It, Love It, Fuck It, Dump It, Buy Another One. The people who sell all this shit say it's what the people want, and they're not wrong. But if the people knew what they were in for their heads would explode."

Yoani Sánchez, Havana's world-famous blogger, once described the Cuban people as birds in a cage, birds reduced to servility, living a life of limited liberties in exchange for the seed and water of the education and health care systems. "Cubans wish to fly," she said. "Yet the cage is well made and the bars are thick. And, by the way, neither the birdseed nor the water is all that great." The analogy had always echoed what Guillermo Rigondeaux's experience had been of Cuba and why he left. Yet as it turns out, he'd chosen, despite an offer to smuggle his family out with him to America, to leave his family behind in the "cage" of Cuban life. During my first interview with him after his escape from Cuba in 2009, I asked him why. He explained that, unlike Cuba, if he failed to succeed in the American system he would be left to die. He was bankrupt if anyone in his family got sick. He was thrown out of his home if he couldn't pay the rent. He would be hopelessly unable to support his children to pursue an education to give them a better life than he could have ever hoped for if boxing hadn't been his calling. He was more afraid to subject his family to the risks of America's system than to allow his family to live the rest of their lives without him, suffering the cost of his choice in Cuba.

"If I didn't think the water surrounded me like a cancer," Virgilio Piñera wrote in his poem "The Island Burdened," "I could have slept easy . . . the weight of an island in the love of its people." I'd heard so many people dismiss anything they saw sent back to them from Cuba that looked remotely positive as merely evidence of a Potemkin village. On the other side, three years in, the voters who'd put President Obama in office were suffering the effects of a hangover with what amounted to their Potemkin president.

We got dropped off at my apartment in Centro Habana and went up on my roof waiting for Cristian and his coach to arrive. Ana María lit a cigarette and took in the views across her city— the Malecón, the dome of the Capitolio, the decaying rooftops and azoteas—then she turned inward with her chin resting against her palm.

"Can I make you some coffee?"

"Do you have any rum to go with it?"

"I'll bring the bottle," I said.

"Will you drink with me?"

"I don't drink."

"You are a very *strange* person."

While I made coffee over the stove and pulled the Havana Club from the icebox, I was sizing up the situation with this kid and the coach who loved him. Turning over all my preconceptions and what I'd learned about these Cuban boxers I'd met, I felt more uncertain than ever about what to really ask someone like Cristian, with so much of his life in front of him. Could his answers ever have a hope of revealing more about him than my questions revealed about me? I wasn't sure if I was doing him any favors letting him know that people internationally were already keen to bankroll his escape and start the same money drip they'd offered many of the fighters who'd left. Maybe the only reason he'd agreed to come to my apartment was to hear the offer. Did Guillermo Rigondeaux's fate in America, never seeing his family again, look more appealing than Héctor Vinent's complete inability to support his own family after staying? And between them, who had the moral high ground? Or was life so hard for Cristian already that it didn't really matter anyway?

I came back outside with the coffee and rum and found Ana María crumpled up on the corner of the roof, with her back to Miami, holding her favorite book.

"*Yuma,*" Ana María said. "Would you still like me to read to you from Kundera?"

"Very much."

"Today wasn't what I expected," she said. "At first I thought it would be a *feo* day with you, but now all I have is this strangeness."

"Why is that?"

"You're so obsessed with us as a people being torn between two horrible choices, but I have no desire to leave. And I don't know why we look so exotic to people like you in the first place."

"You've never wanted to know what the rest of the world was like?"

"Everything about you tells me what the rest of the world is like." She laughed. "Do you think that someone who sleeps with a thousand women understands more about a woman's nature than a man who only stays with one?"

"Depends on the guy, doesn't it? Both could be cowardly choices."

"Yes, they could."

"Why wouldn't you want to see other places?"

"Why?" she asked.

"Why *not*?"

"You are free to travel anywhere else and yet you keep coming back here. You think it's tragic I've never been on a plane in my life? You think I'm sad because I've never left this island?"

"I've met a lot of people who consider this island a prison."

"Maybe it is for them. But wouldn't Miami be another kind of prison for them, too? From all the people who visit here from cities all around the world, all I learn is how much these other cities wish to be like one another. People do the same things. They have the same struggles. They have the same fears. I see how afraid these people and their cities are to be anything different, let alone unique. Isn't that why all these boxers who turn down all their money are so threatening to their values? Don't they seem scared to question any of their own values for even a second? These cities and their people aren't even stereotypes, they *aspire* to be stereotypes. El Norte has never wanted anything from us beyond reopening the casinos, fucking our women, having our men serve them mojitos with a smile, turning us back into their tropical resort. They tell us how fascinating Havana is with time standing still, but all I see is how everywhere else people rush to the point without spending any time wondering what the point *is* in the first place."

"You don't want anything to change?" I asked.

"Havana couldn't be anywhere else if it tried!" She took a swig from the bottle. "I could have been born in any city in the world and made life *bearable*. This is the only city in the world where my heart is always in flower. Every day of my life something makes me laugh until I cry, whether from something sad or something beautiful. No one I've ever met or anything they've shown me inside their silly gadgets has ever convinced me I'd be in bloom anywhere else."

"How do you think this boy coming over will view his future?"

"Like any other sixteen-year-old. He dreams of his chance to be in America like Dorothy on the Yellow Brick Road headed for Oz."

Right then Cristian and his coach, Yosvanni, stepped out into the glare of the sun on my roof, both panting from the climb up the stairs. Cristian was wearing a Yankees cap that shielded his eyes, a buttoned-up jean jacket with the collar flared, and jeans. Yosvanni was wearing a Cuban national team sweater and red track pants. Both had a gym bag slung over their shoulders.

In *Sons of Cuba*, Cristian had been shown as a sensitive boy devoted to his parents and his country. Now he had grown, just before the brink of manhood. He had an air of independence and detachment to his gaze that was absent from him during his years participating in the film. Yosvanni remained ever watchful of his star pupil, but had the easeful confidence and grace of someone who'd managed to walk between the raindrops of Cuban society.

Cristian came over and tapped my shoulder. "After you film us for a little while up here," he said, smiling, his voice a couple octaves lower than I'd last heard it, "maybe you'd like to spar with me? I've sparred with heavyweights before. I'll go easy."

I looked over at Yosvanni removing some mitts from his gym bag. Without looking at us he was beaming approval.

"After we film this and the interview." Cristian tapped my shoulder again. "See how you feel."

Ana María tossed back another sip from the bottle of Havana Club and shook her head.

"How big is your apartment in New York?" Cristian asked me.

"The size of a closet."

"I would like to fight in Madison Square Garden one day. Cuba is changing."

Cristian changed into his gym clothes and his coach wrapped his hands, encircling his wrists and threading between his knuckles. As he stretched out his arms and legs and looked out over the rooftops toward the Capitolio, I saw bits of Stevenson, Savón, Vinent, and Rigondeaux in his pride and casual elegance. They'd all been in his place once. Cristian turned around and located his shadow and began throwing combinations in the air.

When several of Cuba's finest boxers had left the island, Yosvanni had asked Cristian and all his pupils the question he had been forced by the government to ask: "Would any of you betray your coaches and comrades?"

"NO!" the children cried in unison.

"So you're not traitors?" Yosvanni asked with emotion in his voice. "You're *not* going to betray the fatherland or your team?"

All the children before him shook their heads vehemently.

Now Yosvanni approached me as we watched his star.

"How are things going for Cristian?" I asked him.

"He's extraordinarily special. But politics are getting the better of him."

"Why?"

"Because of the film there are many jealousies. There are many jealousies with teammates and with coaches. They assume that we were paid for our participation in that film."

"Were you paid?"

"No," Yosvanni stated flatly. "But the *perception* remains. And he's being punished for it. He's not where he should be in terms of his talent and ability. His performance is flawless, but that doesn't mean he'll be given the opportunities he deserves here. I see this with so many of the great boxers—the safest place on earth for them is inside the ring. I love this boy as much as my own children."

Ana María filmed Cristian skipping rope and working relentlessly with his coach, round after round, for thirty minutes under the sun, hardly breaking a sweat. I sat on the edge of the roof and watched them together, imagining where both would be a few years on. I went back inside the apartment and brought everyone a pitcher of ice water and we retreated to my living room, where I set up a couple chairs for Yosvanni and Cristian in preparation for the interview.

"Cristian is the first boxer I've spoken to who has his career in front of him." I sighed. "If Cristian has any questions for me about where Rigondeaux's career and life have gone in Miami, I'll tell you whatever I can about what I've learned. I think it's important. People internationally are already looking at you. The people who were interested in Guillermo are interested in you and I'm worried about you for that reason. If your life changes and things get more difficult, this is a very tempting reality."

Cristian said nothing, only glared vaguely in my direction.

"When I saw you in the film, one of things that stuck out for me and many other people was the way you responded to the boxers who left—"

This brought Cristian to life. "Everyone is entitled to their opinions and to do with their life as they please. It was their careers and their own choices."

"You didn't feel that way as a boy in the film," I said.

"I was a kid back then."

"So why the change?"

Cristian smiled and brought his elbow up onto the armrest of the chair and rested his chin on the palm of his hand. He gazed up at the ceiling fan.

"I can speak to you about that," Yosvanni interjected. "It's not the same for a boxer or anyone else to receive for an interview a bit of money to resolve a problem you have at home. But at the same time, staying with your family—that is *very* different from receiving money and immigrating to another country where you are going to be away from your family. Your friends and the people are not going to love you the same way. Because after your glory days in that place are over, you won't be looked up to as Teófilo Stevenson or Félix Savón are here. There is no higher gift than kids wanting to become what you are."

Cristian turned to his coach and they looked at one another in silence. Suddenly Yosvanni reached over and put his arm around Cristian: "Here is the *next* Teófilo Stevenson or Savón."

And in my mind I went thousands of miles away to Rigondeaux defending his decision to turn down becoming the next Stevenson or Savón. "Everyone is entitled to their own opinion." Rigondeaux, too, had shrugged, flashing his gold grill. "I don't think for them, they shouldn't think for me. Those guys are history. Their time is long gone. Those guys had a chance, they didn't take it, and they got screwed." He laughed. "Those opportunities don't repeat themselves. They laid that opportunity on the table and I took advantage of it and now I'm here in Miami. If not, I would still be there in Cuba, just like they are, struggling. I would be in Cuba living off of photos and memories. Telling people what I did, that's all you are left with."

Héctor Vinent had made an almost identical confession about what his life was left with, leaving the temptation of America behind.

Cristian cleared his throat and brushed some dirt off his knee. "In every decision I've ever made my mom has been very supportive. And our ambition is for me to be *greater* than both Stevenson and Savón."

"Greater?" I asked.

"Yes." Cristian laughed. "Things could change and professional boxing could return to Cuba."

"Fidel has banned professional sports for the last forty-nine years on the island. If professional boxing *doesn't* happen on the island, how does that make you feel?"

Yosvanni turned and stared intently at his pupil just as Cristian shrugged his and maybe all of his generation's answer to what came next.

26

HEROES FOR SALE

Teófilo Stevenson deserves the recognition of the Cuban people. . . . We believe this man set a very valuable example. This young man, the humble son of a humble family . . . said he would not exchange his people for all the dollars in the world.

—Fidel Castro's tribute,
after Stevenson's death on June 11, 2012

TEÓFILO STEVENSON WAS PERHAPS the only man on the planet who was not only Muhammad Ali's equal in the ring, but could surpass him in what the poet Federico García Lorca referred to as *duende*, that ephemeral quality that separates the immortals from the rest of us. Stevenson was someone authentic, a man whose pride and principle bowed to no one.

A generation after Stevenson turned down all the millions America was offering, when Orlando "El Duque" Hernández would have had to literally work a million years in Cuba to earn the 105 million the Dodgers gave an inferior pitcher, Kevin Brown,

El Duque calmly explained to journalist Steve Fainaru: "I know the prettiest word in the world is 'money.' But I believe that words like 'loyalty' and 'patriotism' are very beautiful as well." Even more telling is that after El Duque helped the Yankees win the World Series only months after his escape, he *still* maintained he never would have left his home had his hand not been forced. According to statistics I've read, during my time traveling to Cuba between 2000 and 2012, just under a million Cubans—941,953—legally traveled abroad, with 12 percent never coming back.

"Cuba's best athletes don't stay there because of love of country," the Miami-based journalist Dan Le Batard wrote in the February 17, 2014, "Cuba Issue" of *ESPN The Magazine,* to which I also contributed. "If the government were to collapse, if the rules were to change, those athletes would end up lapping onto our shores like so many waves, families in tow." Le Batard, born in New Jersey to Cuban parents, then zeroed in on Stevenson's famous words and explained, "This is one of the propaganda machine's greatest quotes, but it is also the largest kind of lie, the one that has to be told when the truth is not allowed. First of all, Stevenson didn't have any understanding of what those dollars meant."

So who does understand? A man with nothing or a man with everything? Stevenson seemed to encompass both extremes. In May of 2011, when I sat down with Teófilo Stevenson in his modest home in the comfortable Havana neighborhood of Náutico, his precarious physical state gave every indication, contrary to Le Batard's estimation, that Fidel's "favorite athlete" bore all the scars of turning down the life he might have lived away from his beloved island. By now Stevenson was a full-blown alcoholic, without enough money to replace a flat tire on his car. Yet while his life remained an open wound, I saw no evidence of regret or deceit as he offered the reasons behind an impossible decision. On the other side of the Florida Straits, it wasn't as if Mike Tyson, having earned nearly half a billion dollars in the ring, was less damaged.

When Stevenson agreed to talk about all the millions he turned down, he asked me for money, about a hundred dollars. I suppose you could choose one of those sums as a symbol to define the man and neatly illuminate who he was and what he stood for. Then again, if you just chose one, I'm more inclined to think your choice illuminates a lot more about who *you* are.

Two years after Stevenson's death on June 11, 2012, I arranged to meet with his daughter, Helmys, on the tiny Mexican island of Isla Mujeres just off the Cancún coast, where she's lived and worked for over half of her thirty years. Isla Mujeres had just been splashed all over the news, revealed as the place where, in 2012, Yasiel Puig, the latest Cuban defector superstar athlete, and now an outfielder for the Dodgers, had been held hostage at machete point in a dingy hotel room until a ransom for his freedom was paid.

Late one warm night, I picked Helmys Stevenson up at the island's ferry terminal. She was easy to spot in the crowd, as striking in her own way as her father. Aside from her beauty, even without her heels she was a head taller than most of the men around her. I looked at her a few moments before she saw me and waved a hand high above her head like Venus Williams in mid-serve. She was another of these girls Cuba has in abundance, women who seem as if they entered the world peeled off a cigar box, all curves and color.

The last time I had been on her island speaking with her father, after Sofía left, I'd resumed my fling with one of Fidel's granddaughters for one last night. This hadn't led to an especially pleasant departure from Havana's airport. I smiled at Helmys and waved back and took one last deep breath before I crossed the street to meet her.

"There may be no entrapped pool of human talent left on earth with the dollar value of Cuban baseball players."
—Michael Lewis

"In a no-tell motel on Isla Mujeres, eight miles off the coast of Cancún, Yasiel Puig's escape had come to a halt," Jesse Katz's April 13, 2014, *Los Angeles Times Magazine* profile of Puig's escape began. "Confined to a corner room at the end of a shabby horseshoe-shaped courtyard, he could only wait and hope, for his value to be appraised, his freedom to be bought."

A day later, Katz's account of Puig's pursuit of the American Dream from a smuggler's boat was the biggest sports story in the country, if not the world. Puig had risked everything to abandon a life in Cuba and be marooned in Mexico, a way station of sorts, where he was incarcerated by the difference between the $17 a month he earned in Cuba and the $42 million he would sign for in Los Angeles. Katz, while still in the eye of the media hurricane, wrote me, and described the ensuing days after the article broke as "pretty much the craziest week of my life—thirty-three TV and radio show appearances and counting." A Hollywood bidding war erupted and a movie deal followed within a week, the myth already shaping reality.

With some clues from Katz, I spent a couple weeks sniffing around Isla Mujeres. I was looking for the motel where Puig was held after he'd swum ashore in darkness against riptides and blindly negotiated razor-sharp coral after being dumped from a smuggler's boat.

"There's a titty bar called the Casablanca, on the western side of the island," Katz pointed out as a reference. He then explained, "I was trying to speculate where you might take a girl if you happened to be leaving that joint in search of temporary lodging."

Before the hat is passed around, Isla Mujeres—Island of Women—is only three dreadfully guitar-strummed songs on the tourist ferry from Cancún's bloated coast. My aunt has had a little hotel there for five years and has been visiting for the last thirty, but I hadn't seen Isla Mujeres' name in print before the Puig story. As she cast a finger over the waters toward the place where Puig most likely arrived, she told me the government plans to build a smuggler's museum on the Caribbean coast of the island. Officials want to showcase all the vessels the Mexican navy has captured from various drug and human traffickers.

She then pointed out the beach where the most recent smuggler's boat arrived and where three people drowned before reaching shore. A handful of refugees were arrested, but the rest scattered and disappeared on the island. A long-abandoned, half-built timeshare condominium complex stood watch over the desolate shore. A flapping red flag warned tourists not to enter the water due to deadly currents. A mile away, a dozen cigarette boats were docked next to the heavily guarded Mexican naval base. Soldiers patrolled the nearby tourist beaches armed with M-16s as locals sauntered around the sand peddling jewelry.

Enough Cubans have passed through this place that the once sleepy fishing village now has a strange Havana aftertaste immediately discernible as soon as you get off the boat. Cuban music wafts out of restaurants·as whispers peddle cigars on darkened back streets. The island is overrun with golf carts sending iguanas scampering off the roads, many carts decked out to look like the 1950s American cars left behind and still on the roads in Cuba. Although Isla Mujeres mirrors Cuba's crocodile shape on a map, in the daylight the tourist coast on the western side of the island feels like a miniature, dressed down, ersatz Miami Beach. But after the sunset stains the sky, the rusty electric streetlights hum and smear their old-penny glow against narrow streets. Then everything on Isla Mujeres opens up like a chocolate Christmas advent calendar, just as Havana does.

As far as cities go, Havana is a festering treasure chest, a primary color. Isla Mujeres' palette is fresher, but still, somehow, not as bright. There are a lot of cities in this world that can break your balls, but nowhere I've ever been can break your heart and leave it bleeding like Havana. When you leave the scab comes off and the wound never heals. And after you first arrive, you're told by many that *everyone* deserves to have Havana as a *ciudad natal*, a hometown. This is an ugly condition I'll confess very uneasily: I'm homesick for a place I wasn't born to.

It always amazed me how people with so little are willing to share so many precious things with strangers. But they do. That's why I spent twelve years doing anything I could think of to spend as much time in Havana as I could, mostly exploring the other side of Puig's story's coin. One of the reasons I came up with to go back ended up being to film a documentary. And filming that documentary, paradoxically, has cost me the chance of ever being able to return. Small potatoes compared to anyone else missing Havana with any skin in the game, I know. But forty-two million dollars, the amount of the contract Puig signed, seems enough incentive to me for *anyone* to risk their life, even abandon their family and country forever, to cash in. People sell their souls every day for a lot less in New York, where I live now, and it doesn't raise eyebrows or turn heads. And *those* people have all the options in the world living in the greatest country on earth, don't they?

No, I understood why Cubans left within five minutes of arriving. Who didn't? What I wanted to know was why so many Cubans *stayed*. And I wanted to know the cost of that decision, too, and the price of leaving, to know why so many lives of refugees like Puig, despite hitting the American Dream jackpot, somehow remain so unbearably incomplete without home. In 1956, as Russian tanks rolled outside her apartment, my mother abandoned most of her family and left Budapest as a refugee from communist Hungary. She was happy with the new life she found and was never nostalgic for what she left behind. For many reasons, it's entirely different for Cubans.

I have a dirty little habit of distilling every city I've ever visited into the historical person I'd have most wanted to meet and share a cigarette with. From the first moment I set foot in Havana my dream was to speak with Teófilo Stevenson, Cuba's twisted answer to Vincent van Gogh. If van Gogh, in part, captured the world's imagination by not being able to sell masterpieces, Stevenson did so by *turning down* every offer. The world knew he was good, but they weren't sure how good. Shortly after Stevenson's death, George Foreman told me Stevenson was far and away the best heavyweight fighter of his era. He was sure that if Stevenson had left Cuba and become a professional he could have been the dominant heavyweight of his time. And of course, Stevenson had that shot at Muhammad Ali, not just to

defect, but to conquer. But it was a lot more than that, too. Forget the question of whether or not he could have beaten Ali.
Stevenson could have *been* Ali. How much was that worth? What
was the cost of saying no to *that*? Could there be a principled
position to justify such a refusal? The answer depends on who
you ask.

I tried for years to ask that of Stevenson, but when I finally
heard his voice over the phone agree to sit down on camera, I assumed my days in Cuba were numbered. I knew that showing the
condition Stevenson was in to the world would go over on the island about as well as releasing a sex tape of Michelle Obama in
the States. If, at his height, Stevenson was an emblematic hero of
everything that succeeded for the revolution, his deterioration remained just as potent for what had failed.

I wasn't happy about that. Exploring Castro's pawns in Cuba
and exposing anything negative also makes you a pawn to all his
enemies ninety miles away. Both sides don't have much of a track
record for nuance of opinion.

Of course, there was nothing unique about the circumstances of
Puig's story any more than there was with Stevenson's. *Se fue* (he
left) and *se quedó* (he stayed) are decisions that have scarred and
defined the identity of every Cuban family and have been around
since Fidel Castro and the revolution split in half nearly every family on the island.

It's estimated as many as ten thousand Cubans—men, women,
and children—are smuggled off the island to Mexico each year.
The drug boats the navy catches are mostly from Colombia, but
nearly all of the speedboats trafficking human beings that have

been impounded in Isla Mujeres have Florida plates and are owned by Cuban ex-pats. With Cuban smugglers, it's always about people, that fragile contraband that breathes and weeps—their own people are driving this industry. One smuggler I'd been exploring in my documentary, the Caribbean Queen, earned that nickname because he always dressed in drag while smuggling people, a tactic he adopted because Cuban authorities were forbidden from shooting at women. Castro had warned if he ever caught him, he'd cut off his balls.

The Queen made untold millions profiting from Cubans' egregious desperation. "Venture humanitarianism," Steve Fainaru called it when he wrote of El Duque's escape.

Isla Mujeres, only four miles long, has become an even more desirable destination for smugglers than the Cancún mainland three miles away. From Isla Mujeres' seawall *malecón* to Havana's is a distance of 308 miles; to the western edge of Cuba, only 96—about as far as from Cuba to Miami. Some vessels, I was told, took as long as eighteen days to make the journey. On the way, boats capsize, people drown, children starve and get dehydrated—people are sometimes tossed into the water if the boats are given chase. I've reviewed grainy U.S. Coast Guard footage of some of these human atrocities and it looks like something from the foul corners of Goya's imagination. One of the first jokes I heard upon visiting Cuba asked, "What is the primary source of food for sharks in the Florida Straits?" The answer? *Cubanos. Ja, ja, ja . . .*

The drug cartels in Mexico who back the trade see human smuggling as little more than a way to diversify their portfolios. At ten thousand dollars a head, the going rate to Mexico is one-tenth the asking price for direct passage to Florida, so they make up the difference in profit through pure volume. With an average of thirty Cubans smuggled per trip, this is big business for everyone involved: a hundred million dollars a year at least, in a place where that amount of money feels more like one billion. "COD" doesn't mean "cash on delivery" in this transaction; it means "cash or death." The real "winners" of this sordid enterprise, the cargo, like Puig, are shackled and held for days and sometimes die awaiting payment to be made while bankrupt policies on both sides of the ninety miles only encourage this perversely thriving industry to grow and become ever more profitable. As Joe Kehoskie, a friend and baseball agent who has dealt with Cuban refugees for many years, put it, "As it gets more lucrative it'll only draw in more of a criminal element than exists and get worse."

Cuba's athletes are worth billions *anywhere* else but their home. While less than 1 percent of all of Cuba's athletic talent have abandoned Cuba since the "triumph" of the revolution, over the last few years more Cuban ballplayers and boxers than ever have entered these smugglers' boats and perversely transformed into the most expensive human export on earth. Even after the athlete's fee or ransom for transit is paid, a sizable backend chunk from the contracts these athletes make in the United States must still be coughed up under threat of murder or harm to families back on the island. And while the press debates whether financing these athletes amounts to human trafficking, it's puzzling what exactly is required for it to be recognized as something even more malevolent: a modern slave trade. Athletes like Puig, despite their multimillion-dollar contracts in the United States, remain indentured servants who have to work off their debt.

Despite this, the incentive to leave is only going to grow as the offers continue to get bigger and bigger. Kehoskie estimates there are at least a half dozen other Puig-sized contacts awaiting players who thus far have proved to be, in the language of the trade, "true believers."

It has long been this way. Back in 1492, encountering Cuba for the first time, Columbus described it as "the most beautiful land that eyes ever beheld." Of course, this was just an unexpected detour from the real objective of his voyage. Fortunately, the Taino natives quickly brought everything back into focus when they greeted their visitors with offerings of gold (which held no value in their society) and happily disclosed other places where more could be found. Columbus and those who followed promptly enslaved the natives and enlisted them to mine for any and all gold that could be seized and returned to Europe.

Columbus and his men also rounded up the Taino wives and female children and after endless gang rapes sold them into sex slavery back in Spain. Once the remaining natives of Cuba fully understood that insatiable lust for the island's natural resources was the reason behind Columbus and his men's continued presence, they dispensed of whatever gold they still had into the sea in hopes of ridding the island of its intruders. Farther inland, the Tainos dumped their gold into rivers. By the 1530s, nearly all the Tainos were wiped out by a combination of genocide, slavery, starvation, suicide, and disease. Nearly five hundred years later, athletes like Puig have replaced gold as Cuba's most lucrative treasure.

Today history repeats itself as Cuba's loot once again enters the sea in protest, but this time the protest is in opposition to the original Taino values—the ones that saw gold as no more valuable than anything or any*one* else—now advanced by Castro's government. Now Cuba's treasure willingly throws itself into the sea for top dollar.

"America . . . just a nation of two hundred million used car salesmen with all the money we need to buy guns and no qualms about killing anybody else in the world who tries to make us uncomfortable." —Hunter S. Thompson

I interviewed Teófilo Stevenson in his home in May of 2011, the same week Osama bin Laden, the CIA's "most dangerous man in the world," was killed. On the way over to Stevenson's house I drove past a dozen billboards of Che Guevara, Cuba's most revered revolutionary hero. Today, most Americans know him from a popular tourist T-shirt, even worn by one New Yorker I saw celebrating bin Laden's death by lighting a Cohiba cigar. But Che was *also* executed by CIA order back when he was listed as the "most dangerous man in the world." I wondered if kitsch could do for bin Laden one day what it did for Che's legacy.

I'd already taken one too many chances interviewing famous boxers under surveillance by the government. Coupled with that fling with Fidel's granddaughter, things were getting edgy for me in Havana. There are moments in Cuba when you never know whether you've arrived at the wrong place at the right time, the right place at the wrong time, or—the most sinister of all—simply the *last* time. Cars full of strangers would pass by gleefully pointing up at security cameras. I figured if the police were coming, they were coming. I called Stevenson again from a pay phone and he reluctantly agreed to meet.

Okay then, *fuck it*. One way or another, I would never have another chance. Hold on tightly, let go lightly. I stopped a gypsy cab and offered him a day's fare for a round trip to take me and my translator across town to Stevenson's home in Náutico, near the Marina Hemingway.

The translator told me that the best chance we had to coax Stevenson into talking on camera was to bring him some suitably "respectful" vodka as a present. Stevenson was known to trick a lot of journalists into throwing him a party for everyone he could find on the street and then, when the time came to film, curtly call the evening to a close. My friend Bobby Cassidy, a writer in New York, had been duped in the same manner.

When we arrived in Náutico, we grabbed a bottle from a kiosk and walked the rest of the way to Stevenson's house. The neighborhood was green and lush, far more cheerful than Félix Savón's place, but reports of Fidel giving Stevenson a "mansion" were nothing more than propaganda. What passes for a luxurious neighborhood in Cuba is, by American standards, sad and drab. Fresh coats of paint and old Russian cars—Ladas locked behind fenced-in driveways—are the only signs of relative affluence. Most Cubans elsewhere, of course, have no money for cars or paint in the first place.

My translator grew quieter the closer we got to Stevenson's home. It was clear that he was having second thoughts about being involved with this. He'd spent time with Stevenson before, translating for diplomats who wanted to meet him. He had not enjoyed the experience.

"How bad is he?" I asked him.

"Have you ever spoken to him on the phone when he isn't drunk?"

"I don't *think* so," I said.

"Exactly." He shook his head.

In conversation, he often didn't know what day or month it was. I was never sure if he was joking. He'd switch from English to Spanish to Russian. If Muhammad Ali was locked in his body as the physical cost for his career, what was the price Stevenson paid locked in the vise of this body politic?

"I think it's fairly obvious how bad he is, isn't it?" my translator lamented. "He's not meeting you for the pleasure of speaking with a foreign journalist. He needs the money. So do I. So does everybody in this fucking country. This man is a great hero of mine and to many around the world, and having him reduced to this makes me feel ashamed."

"Do you even think he'll talk with us?" I asked.

"I doubt on camera. He's not well. There's his car up ahead. There." He pointed to a rusting green early-1990s Toyota behind a fence. "That's his. He turned down five million dollars and he drives *that*. Do you think I'm proud of my country for that? That's the house of Teo. By Cuban standards it's nice, but in Miami he would have lived in a palace. You want to know how hard things have gotten? He doesn't even have enough money to put gasoline in his car."

In 1987, Stevenson had been involved in what many assumed was an alcohol-related car accident that took a motorcyclist's life. The crime, if indeed it *was* one, was swept under the rug to preserve Stevenson's iconic status. He was never charged or convicted of any wrongdoing, and although he slowly receded from public view, symbolically he remained a lodestar for Cuba's moral compass. Many Cubans still set their moral watches to Stevenson's clock, and even some of those opposed to his socialist principles admire the man's courage and conviction.

I wasn't looking forward to undermining that. Galileo wasn't put in prison because he was wrong about anything he discovered looking through his telescope; rather, he was incarcerated simply because he saw what others didn't wish to see.

When we arrived at Stevenson's driveway we could see through the padlocked fence that his front door was open. My translator hollered out and a few tense moments later Stevenson, shirtless and in blue track pants, a cigarette dangling from his lips, wound his stiff six-foot-five frame into the entryway with care, bracing himself against the doorjamb. I wasn't sure if the fragility in Stevenson's movements owed more to his boxing career or the booze. Nonetheless, he'd recently celebrated his fifty-ninth birthday and still looked lean and handsome.

Stevenson approached us, holding out the key to his gate while my translator turned to me with a look of dread.

Teófilo Stevenson won his first Olympic gold medal in 1972 and his last world amateur championship in 1986. He won 302 fights and once went eleven years without a single loss. The offer to fight Muhammad Ali came after Stevenson won his second Olympic gold medal in Montreal in 1976.

Ali was a man adept at finding weakness in his opponents and cruelly exploiting it to his own advantage, yet he never saw weakness in Stevenson, not even in his refusal to turn professional and face him in the ring. He admired a man standing up for what he believed in, as Ali had done when he refused to compromise his spiritual beliefs to fight in Vietnam. In 1996 and 1998, Ali donated a total of $1.7 million worth of medical aid to Cuba as a way of opposing the economic embargo against the island nation, which had contributed so much to the brutal economic crisis of the previous decade. Stevenson greeted Ali at Havana's international airport and they were inseparable during both of Ali's visits, equals.

Stevenson pried open his lock and pulled back the gate until we had entered and then proceeded to lock us in. There were rumors that he kept a pistol Fidel had given him personally for protection. He offered a warm handshake and smiled, yet his eyes were bloodshot and turned sad the moment he noticed my camera.

"Please come inside," he said in English.

"You like speaking English?" I asked.

"As long as he doesn't start the Russian. . . ." My translator smiled in Stevenson's direction.

Once we got inside his home—surrounded by photographs, mementos, and trophies—Stevenson pointed to a chair for me to sit in while he sat across from me, the street visible to him out the open front door. I quickly realized why this was: every last person who walked by, spotting Stevenson, sang his name in joy, raising a hand of praise, and it lifted his spirits. I handed the bottle of vodka to Stevenson and he tilted his head in thanks, asking the translator if he could go back into the kitchen and bring out some cups and orange juice for us.

Even though at the time I had no idea that this was going to be the last interview of Stevenson's life before his sudden death a year later in June 2012, I knew this wasn't going to be easy.

I turned and began attaching my camera to a small tripod. I was in the process of stretching out and unfolding it just as Stevenson lit another cigarette, turned to our translator, and said in Spanish:

"Tell him he has to pay, or there is no interview. Make him come up with something."

"How much do we ask for?" my translator asked Stevenson.

"You tell me," Stevenson grunted. "You have experience in this. Give him a number."

"I say we ask for eighty or a hundred. I'm broke."

"Okay." Stevenson shrugged. "But I'm worse off than you. If I say there is no interview—"

Just then he noticed the camera pointed in his direction. "Don't film me now. No camera! Put the camera away."

I swung the camera away.

Stevenson was in an impossible situation. He not only rejected America's millions, but he also had to pretend there was no consequence. Stevenson had to be just as defiant in his choice as Puig was in pretending he'd reached salvation entering American life, with no lingering pain. Zero tolerance for dissent on this point cuts both ways. The emotional truth remains hidden.

"Is it off?" Stevenson growled.

I turned it off.

The translator spread out three cups before Stevenson and placed a large bottle of orange juice next to the vodka.

"We can talk but I don't want to be filmed."

"If you grant me an interview I have to film," I said. "That's why I'm here."

"For one hundred dollars you can film the pictures on my wall and have the audio of our interview."

"I'm sorry." I laughed. "On the phone I asked for a filmed interview. That's why I came here. That's my work."

Stevenson put out his cigarette on the floor and looked for another in an empty pack. I offered him one of mine.

"What is this?"

"American Spirit," I said.

"You want Teófilo Stevenson to smoke *American Spirit*?" He spat out the words. "Why did I ever let you in my house?"

With that, Stevenson went about preparing three drinks in the large paper cups. He filled all three cups to the brim, but two had nine parts orange juice to one part vodka, while the last had nine parts vodka to just a token splash of orange juice. Half the bottle of vodka was already gone.

"Okay." Stevenson laughed. "How long you want for our interview?"

"An hour?" I said.

Stevenson nodded thoughtfully, reached down for the suicide screwdriver, and hoisted it up toward me.

"Fuck that shit." I waved it off. "I don't even drink." I knew the drill. I had seen my own father try to drink himself to death, just as Stevenson was doing now.

"My friend"—Stevenson snickered—"my deal is this. If you pay a hundred and thirty dollars, you can have an hour with me on camera and film my trophy walls and pictures with Fidel and Ali."

"Done." I reached over to my camera.

"*Annnnnnnd,*" Stevenson added, "the time starts now, but you can only begin filming once you finish *this* drink. These are my terms."

"Those are your terms?"

"Yes." Stevenson smiled coyly. "Do you accept my terms?"

"Deal."

I took the cup of vodka, chugged it in five or six excruciating gulps, struggled not to vomit in Stevenson's living room for the next few moments, and once it had finally settled in my stomach, I reached over to turn the camera on to catch Stevenson's reaction.

"*Nooooo!*"

"Deal's a deal, *campeón*."

The translator shook his head. "You're *both* insane. What am I doing here?"

"Okay, one minute," Stevenson pleaded. "One minute." He staggered to his feet and wobbled his way into the dining room and found a shirt and cap after tossing aside some dominoes on his dinner table. He returned in a Che Guevara T-shirt and gray cap as armor and stared at me like an old lion.

I started filming. "Are you happy with your life in Cuba?" I asked him, my voice shaking. "Are you happy with the life you've had?"

"Happy? I'm happy. I'm *very* happy."

"No regrets?"

"*No.*"

"Why is that so hard for people to believe?"

"There are people who become immoral. I would never do that. I endure until the end."

"I've just come from Ireland, where Guillermo Rigondeaux had his last fight. He told me you defended him after he tried to defect."

"The Cuban system helped him. Where he grew up, in Santiago de Cuba? They did not have the conditions that the revolution has created today. He should have respected that."

"Félix Savón told me he felt Rigondeaux betrayed the Cuban people," I said.

"I rejected all that money. Because they wanted me to stay out there in the United States like Rigondeaux and the rest of them.

Rigondeaux decided to leave. He wasn't allowed to box anymore in Cuba. He betrayed the Cuban people. And . . . *he left.*"

"What does this decision feel like, to stay or to leave?" I asked Stevenson. "Is it a decision from the mind or the heart?"

"There are decisions that emerge from your heart and your soul and those decisions can't be betrayed. Now please stop the cameras for a moment. I don't want the children to see the champ smoking, please. It's a bad example."

On that warm night in Cancún, Helmys Stevenson wore a long white dress with her curly hair hanging over her shoulders. While she was built long and lithe like an Olympic swimmer, her arms were as large and sculpted as any middleweight boxer I'd ever seen.

"You lift trucks for a living in Cancún or what?" I asked her.

"I do no exercise." She blushed. "I'm fortunate with good genetics."

"You know, women box in the Olympics now."

"I heard."

"Maybe to settle the argument between your dad and Muhammad Ali I could promote a fight between you and one of Ali's daughters."

"Laila Ali was a world champion!"

"So was her dad when Teófilo got all those offers to fight him."

"I'll consider it."

Just as Ali and Stevenson bore an uncanny physical resemblance, Helmys could have easily passed as one of Ali's daughters. But I wondered how different her life would have been if she had enjoyed the benefits Ali's children enjoyed from his fame and fortune. Teófilo Stevenson was a national hero, but he could never offer his two children the comforts and security of the millions Ali would leave behind. Yet I saw no sign of this fact burdening this lovely woman in any way.

After I warned Helmys of the distance to where I had in mind for us to have dinner, she exchanged her heels for flip-flops.

I took her to the same hotel where Yasiel Puig was held captive under threat of having his arm chopped off by a machete until the ransom was paid. It was the only hotel that fit all the basic clues Katz had provided me: U-shaped, with a pool, looking out over the water at the massive Mexican flag on Cancún, and a drunken stumble away from that strip club. Katz had tried for weeks to identify it on Google images but failed. Since Puig had been held there, the hotel had undergone a *massive* renovation. I wonder where the money came from to finance that? My aunt was certain the previous incarnation of the hotel was the dive Katz wrote about in his piece.

We walked in the darkness along the shoulder of the road, a New York avenue worth of land dividing two seas. Helmys wasn't wearing perfume but the scent wafting off her hair, detonated by moonlight, was distracting.

"How did you leave Cuba?" I asked her.

"I studied international tourism in Mexico. I applied for a visa to stay and work in Mexico. I visit my home in Cuba as often as I can."

"Where did you grow up in Havana?" I asked.

"The house you visited, where my father eventually moved to, was in Náutico. We had the only swimming pool in that neighborhood, but he wouldn't use it for swimming. He liked turtles and ducks and let them use it. But before that home Fidel gave us a house near the Plaza de la Revolución, where he spoke to the Cuban people. Actually, our house was next door to Che Guevara's widow. Che's children were all my friends growing up."

"And was Fidel close with your father?"

"*Very* close." She slapped my arm for emphasis, as only the daughter of a three-time Olympic Champion might. "After I was born my father introduced me to Fidel and apparently I pulled his beard very hard while he cradled me in his arms."

"So you knew him while you grew up?"

"Of course. But I was . . . I was a little terrified of him. I could not speak to him *ever*. It was *Fidel*! But always I would ask my father if we were somewhere with Fidel in attendance. 'Please, can I speak to him?' And my father would ask Fidel to come over and he always would and I had no power of speech. It annoyed my father. But I just could never speak to him."

"Do you ever think about the kind of life you could have had if your father had taken all that money to leave?"

"Money is very nice." She smiled, caressing the shoulder she'd slapped before. "But I wasn't raised that way. I had a beautiful life in Cuba and I'm very happy with my life now."

"You don't think your father ever regretted his decision?"

"*No*. Was it an *easy* decision? No. Not for anyone. My father lived the life he always wanted to live on his terms. Maybe he lived it too much and it cost him an old age. But he had a beautiful life and gave me a beautiful life, also. He was exactly who he wanted to be."

Helmys and I passed by the Casablanca, the dingy strip club Katz had mentioned, cigarette butts and bottlecaps studded into their dirty driveway. We could hear Britney Spears singing inside, but no light was visible. The club was hidden from the little road by a hedge, a bit like a double chin hidden by a beard.

"Do you know about Yasiel Puig?" I asked her. "The baseball player who has become so famous in Los Angeles."

"Sure. Many Cubans come to this island or Cancún every year. Some, like him, are athletes who come for all that money waiting for them in the United States."

"You don't feel strongly one way or the other about his choice?"

"He has to live with his choice and whether it was right for him. I judge no one. It's none of my business."

"What about when people judge your father's choice? What about the people who don't believe anyone could do what he did, turning down all that money?"

She shrugged. "Just because someone does not agree with him or his reasons does not mean they have to accuse him of being a liar."

I only had the chance to meet Helmys's father once and I was sorry from the first minute that our exchange wounded a great man's pride, that for many it would reduce him. It took about the same amount of time with his daughter to realize he must have been as proud of his legacy, raising her, as he was of anything he accomplished inside or outside of a ring on behalf of the revolution.

"I brought some photos to show you of my father that I carry on my phone. I thought you would appreciate them. Some photos of my father and Fidel. My father and me. Many have never been published. Would you like to see them?"

She stood next to me, her hair in my face, and warmly flipped through the photos of her father's life. While there were no box-

ing photos in her collection, everything she showed me illumin-
tated all things I'd imagined he fought for. From his honeymoon
to intimate moments with his family, to being introduced to Nel-
son Mandela, to doing *the wave* with Fidel at the Pan Am Games—
all of it was bigger than life and handled with a coy smirk worthy
of any iconic Hollywood movie star.

"Jesus, your dad was a handsome guy," I said.

As she stared at her father's face on the screen she corrected
me, "He wasn't handsome. My father was *beautiful*."

Two years before, I had watched Helmys at her father's funeral
as nearly a thousand Cubans in attendance collectively broke down
in tears to mourn his loss. I watched her comfort her brother, a
little younger than her, as Stevenson's coffin was lowered into the
ground and every face in view grieved a beloved hero. I included
footage of this event in my documentary as a means of contrast-
ing how the prospective funerals of defector Cuban boxing champions might look in America, so far removed from friends and
family back home.

I wasn't looking to vilify or judge either decision; what I wanted
put on trial had always been the insidious choice itself, something
Puig and Stevenson and so many others know so well.

Trying to understand Stevenson's life and death, I asked my
father to watch my interview with him. It was a tense hour; he
saw a bit of himself in Stevenson, as did I.

When the film ended, my father referred me to a poem by
Rainer Maria Rilke. In 1905, Rilke was working as a secretary to
the sculptor Rodin and confessed he was no longer writing. The
artist sent him to the zoo and told him to look at an animal until he
saw it. Rilke imagined the view from captivity, from the inside out.

"The Panther" came as close as anything to help me bring Stevenson and Cuba's blur into focus:

His vision, from the constantly passing bars,
has grown so weary that it cannot hold anything else.
It seems to him there are a thousand bars;
and behind the bars, no world.

As he paces in cramped circles, over and over,
the movement of his powerful soft strides
is like a ritual dance around a center
in which a mighty will stands paralyzed.

Only at times, the curtain of the pupils lifts, quietly—.
An image enters in,
rushes down through the tensed, arrested muscles,
plunges into the heart and is gone.

ABOUT THE AUTHOR

BRIN-JONATHAN BUTLER is a writer and filmmaker. His work has appeared in *ESPN The Magazine, Vice, Deadspin, The Wall Street Journal, Salon,* and *The New York Times.* Butler's documentary, *Split Decision,* is an examination of Cuban-American relations and the economic and cultural paradoxes that have shaped them since Castro's revolution, through the lens of elite Cuban boxers forced to choose between remaining in Cuba or defecting to America. His e-original, *A Cuban Boxer's Journey,* is also published by Picador.